Fun with the Family™ Georgia

Praise for the *Fun with the Family*™ series

"Enables parents to turn family travel into an exploration."

—Alexandra Kennedy, Editor, *Family Fun*

"Bound to lead you and your kids to fun-filled days,
those times that help compose the
memories of childhood."

—Dorothy Jordon, *Family Travel Times*

Help Us Keep This Guide Up to Date

Every effort has been made by the author and editors to make this guide as accurate and useful as possible. However, many changes can occur after a guide is published—establishments close, phone numbers change, hiking trails are rerouted, facilities come under new management, etc.

We would love to hear from you concerning your experiences with this guide and how you feel it could be improved and be kept up to date. While we may not be able to respond to all comments and suggestions, we'll take them to heart, and we'll make certain to share them with the authors. Please send your comments and suggestions to the following address:

The Globe Pequot Press
Reader Response/Editorial Department
P.O. Box 480
Guilford, CT 06437
Or you may e-mail us at: editorial@GlobePequot.com

Thanks for your input, and happy travels!

INSIDERS' GUIDE®

FUN WITH THE FAMILY™ SERIES

fun WITH the Family™

GEORGIA

HUNDREDS OF IDEAS FOR DAY TRIPS WITH THE KIDS

CAROL AND DAN THALIMER

FIFTH EDITION

INSIDERS' GUIDE®

GUILFORD, CONNECTICUT
AN IMPRINT OF THE GLOBE PEQUOT PRESS

INSIDERS' GUIDE®

Text design by Nancy Freeborn and Linda R. Loiewski
Maps by Rusty Nelson © Morris Book Publishing, LLC
Spot photography throughout © Photodisc and © RubberBall Productions

ISSN 1540-8752
ISBN 978-0-7627-4546-3

Printed in the United States of America
10 9 8 7 6 5 4 3 2 1

To Chris and Tricia—*grand* traveling companions—
and Bailey, Michael, and Joseph
in hopes they will be too.

GEORGIA

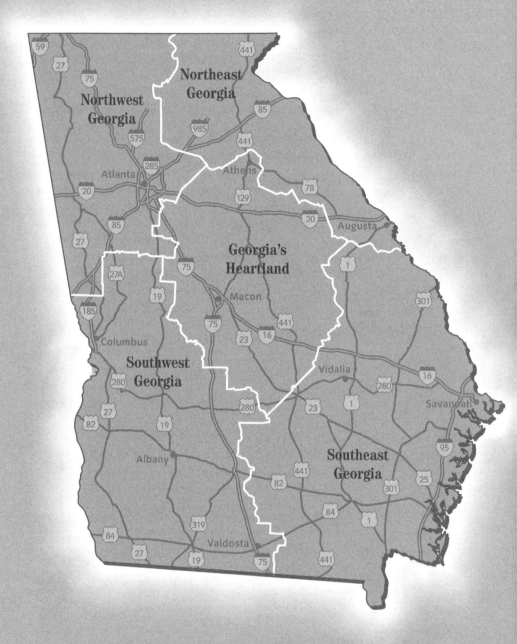

Contents

Acknowledgments

As always, a big thanks to our editors, Mike Urban and Jennifer Quint, for all of their assistance and especially their patience and encouragement. We'd also like to thank the following, who were of invaluable assistance as always: the regional representatives of the Georgia Department of Industry, Trade, and Tourism—Becky Basset, Director; Brittney Warnock, Metro Atlanta; Jeannie Buttrum, Classic South; Carey Ferrara, Colonial Coast; Fay Tripp, Historic Heartland; Janet Cochran, Historic High Country; Lindsey Hammock, Magnolia Midlands; Cheryl Smith, Northeast Georgia Mountains; Jeff Stubbs, Plantation Trace; and Maggie Potter, Presidential Pathways.

We'd also like to thank countless professionals and volunteers who work in local convention and visitor bureaus, chambers of commerce, tourism bureaus, and welcome centers. They're always the source of the most detailed and up-to-date information about attractions, festivals, lodgings, and restaurants. We couldn't keep this book up to date without them.

Introduction

When we moved to Georgia in 1979, our four children ranged in age from ten to sixteen. In between school, scouts, church, band, drill team, cheerleading, soccer, and horse camp, all of us managed to visit some of our adopted state's wonderful sights in the northeast Georgia mountains and on the beaches of the Golden Isles. Then we bought a travel agency, which rapidly expanded to three, and spent several years exploring exotic destinations elsewhere. It wasn't until we sold the agencies and began writing about travel for several local newspapers and magazines that we started a serious campaign to discover what else Georgia has to offer—especially in off-the-beaten-track locations. In our capacity as travel writers, we've combed Georgia to compile numerous other guides to traveling in the Peach State. Now our children are grown and on their own, married, and spread out all over the nation, so we're introducing the joys of traveling in Georgia to our grandchildren. We've investigated some of the state's marvelous family resort programs with Chris (now nineteen), Tricia (now sixteen), Bailey (three), and Michael (three). New baby Joseph will get his introduction to Tybee Island in the summer of 2008.

We've been to the vast majority of attractions listed in this guide, and the ones we haven't visited personally have been highly recommended by our friends at the state department of tourism, local chambers of commerce, or convention and visitor bureaus.

Although the state department of tourism divides the Peach State into nine tourism regions, we and our editors decided it would be simpler for readers to begin exploring Georgia if we divided the descriptions of family attractions in the state into only five areas: the Heartland, Northeast, Northwest, Southeast, and Southwest. The chapter for each region is introduced by a map that identifies the towns you will want to visit. Then the towns within each region are arranged from north to south and east to west so that you could actually start at the first town described and zigzag through the region, tracing a route all the way to the last town described. Some small hamlets have only one special family-oriented attraction, some have several, and others boast dozens.

Your family will be so enchanted with some of these places, you may never get to the next stop on the list. You'll want to return to others again and again. We hope you and your clan will enjoy exploring Georgia as much as we have with two generations of youngsters.

For Quick **Reference**

Throughout this guide you'll find some recommendations for family-friendly places to stay. We've tried to suggest a wide range of accommodations to appeal to almost any family preference or price range: resorts, hotels, motels, small inns, bed-and-breakfasts, and campgrounds. We haven't included national chain accommodations, assuming that you might prefer to try some properties with particular local flair. In case you're set in your ways, however, almost every town has one or more of the old standbys. Here's how to get in touch with some of the major chains found prevalently throughout the state. Otherwise, contact your favorite hotel chain or a travel Web site such as www.hotels.com; www.hotellocators.com; www.hotels-and-discounts.com; www.travelocity.com; www.orbitz.com; www.expedia.com; and the like.

- **Best Western,** (800) 780-7234; www.bestwestern.com
- **Comfort Inns and Suites,** (877) 424-6423; www.comfortsuites.com
- **Courtyard by Marriott,** (888) 236-2427; www.marriott.com
- **Days Inn,** (800) 329-7466; www.daysinn.com
- **EconoLodge,** (877) 424-6423; www.econolodge.com
- **Hampton Inns and Suites,** (800) 445-8667; www.hamptoninn.com
- **Holiday Inn,** (888) HOLIDAY; www.sixcontinentshotels.com/holiday-inn
- **Jameson Inn,** (800) JAMESON; www.jamesoninns.com
- **La Quinta Inns and Suites,** (800) 642-4271; www.laquinta.com
- **Quality Inns,** (877) 424-6423; www.qualityinn.com

Thalimer Tips for Traveling with Kids

Although there's never any guarantee that the backseat gang won't whine, "Are we there yet?" or fuss with their siblings, modern technology has made car travel much easier and more pleasant with built-in or portable DVD and CD players, handheld video games, MP3 players, iPods, and other techno distractions. If different people are listening to different things, then headphones are a must.

To keep the rug rats as entertained as possible, plan for frequent stops every hour or two whether it's to eat, take a rest room break, or visit an attraction. In the car, give each kidlet as much space as possible and keep them each occupied with age-appropriate toys and activities. Each munchkin should have a duffel bag, backpack, or tote with some of his or her personal favorite toys and books. A hard-sided plastic box in which to keep pencils and crayons can also serve as a desk or tabletop to hold food. Must-haves include a favorite blanket, pillow, stuffed animal, and/or other "security" item that makes the small fry feel more comfortable. Even with all the modern technology available, kids still enjoy singing silly songs, hearing or telling stories, and playing group games that require little or no equipment such as I Spy or identifying state license plates. Plan a surprise or two along the way such as a special tape or a new toy (or even an old toy that's been forgotten about). Rotate seats for variety. If things still get out of control, find a playground or some place to stop where they can let off some energy.

Bottled water, canned drinks, boxed juices, and individual-size portions of things like applesauce, fruit, and pudding (most of which don't even need to be kept cold) make carrying snacks a breeze. Just pack plenty of napkins, paper towels, and/or moist towelettes. In fact, bottled water is great for many things such as washing up or cleaning a scrape or cut. Be careful though. Often kids eat or drink out of boredom, and then you have to stop more often, they may get an upset stomach, or they may be so "wired," they're up all night. Give them too much sugar, and you'll have a vehicle full of hyperactive little darlings. To prevent too frequent bathroom stops, avoid caffeine drinks, which are a natural diuretic. Make sure to have everyone "go" before you depart from each stop and break up the ride every hour or so whether anyone's asking for a bathroom break or not. Avoid a lot of chips, candy bars, and other sweets. Carry "safe" snacks such as pretzels, animal crackers, all-natural fruit rolls, raisins, dried fruit, trail mix, crackers, Goldfish, rice cakes, cereal, granola bars, power bars, hard candies, gum, and cheese sticks or string cheese.

Kids love to act grown-up, and pint-sized suitcases and duffel bags with wheels fill the bill. Not only do the tykes feel like they have a new toy that turns a boring chore into a sure-to-please game, but it frees up Mom and Dad to handle other things (like a baby or very small child and their own luggage) and lowers the stress level for everyone.

Involve the munchkins in packing for the trip. They should choose loose, comfortable clothing. A safe bet is one outfit for every day of the vacation, but that doesn't mean each person has to bring seven shirts and seven pairs of shorts or slacks for a week-long trip. Mix and match to get a couple wearings from each item. We read about one enterprising mother who packs each day's outfit, including socks and underwear, in a separate plastic bag so that the tykes can dress themselves and don't have to worry about finding everything they need or things that go together. Choose bright colors and patterns that hide stains. Umbrellas, ponchos, and light jackets are a good idea too. Take our word for it, regardless of what the weatherman says, it will rain or be cold if you're not prepared. Of course, comfortable shoes are a must. Don't duplicate items, except maybe socks. If you run out of shampoo or need something else, you can always buy it. Bring several large plastic bags for dirty and/or wet clothing items, as well as for trash. Even if suitcases are stowed in the trunk of the car or in the cartop carrier, keep a change of clothes inside the car for quick changes after spills or accidental (or on-purpose) mishaps such as falling in a creek. Don't overpack—when in doubt, leave it out.

Buy or create a basic first aid kit with bandages, antiseptic, tissues, adult and child pain relievers, antihistamine, and diarrhea medication. You might want to carry your doctor's phone number. Don't forget items such as a hat or visor, sunglasses, sunscreen of at least 30 SPF, and insect repellant.

Miscellaneous tips:

- Carry an extra collapsible tote or duffel to bring home souvenirs picked up along the way, such as rocks, shells, postcards, stamps, charms, key chains, magnets, or holiday ornaments. Anything picked up along the way such as brochures, tickets, programs, maps, and other memorabilia, can be scrapbooked when you get home.

- A disposable diaper soaks up spills better than paper towels or napkins and has a plastic side to keep the liquid corralled until you can get to a trash can.

- Computer screen wipes are great for cleaning fingerprints and smears from inside car windows. A small vinyl tablecloth can be used for impromptu picnics, but in an emergency can serve as a temporary barrier between the car seat and a wet child.

- A Frisbee or a ball takes up very little room, but is invaluable for some quick exercise when making a stop.

- Likewise, a deck of cards takes up almost no room, but has innumerable possibilities for use while riding in the car (consult www.pagat.com for group and individual card game ideas).

- Decide in advance how much each child can spend each day for anything they want.

- Make time for free time.

- Come up with an emergency plan or meeting place in case family members become separated. Carry a photo of each child in case you become separated.

- Maintain a good sense of humor!

Check out these Web sites for more tips about packing for and traveling with children:

- www.activitiesforkids.com/travel/travel_hints.htm

- www.travelwithkids.about.com/cs/familytraveltips/a/packinglist.htm; www.onebag.com

- www.travelsense.org/tips/packing.asp; www.travelforkids.com

- www.piggyback.com/website/travel_tips

Keep in Mind

Most of the places we describe for fishing, including all the state and national parks, require a valid fishing license unless we note otherwise. Currently licenses are $9.00 for Georgia residents; out-of-state visitors pay $3.50 per day or $7.00 per week. A trout stamp is $5 for residents and $13 for nonresidents. Georgia has a reciprocity agreement with Alabama, Florida, and South Carolina, so residents of those states don't have to purchase a Georgia fishing license if they have a valid one from their home state. Residents of all other states must purchase a nonresident license. Call (800) ASK-FISH (800-275-3474) for detailed information about fishing in Georgia and other states. A weekly update on fishing conditions is given, as well as fishing and license information, freshwater and saltwater regulations, locations of boat ramps, common questions and answers, and more.

Georgia State Parks have a $3 ($4 at Tallulah Gorge) per day parking fee. It is good for all state parks visited the same day. You can, however, buy an annual ParkPass for $25. Join the Friends of Georgia State Parks and Historic Sites and get a ParkPass. Rates for camping at state parks range from $12 to $30. Call (800) 864-7275 for more information or consult www.gastateparks.org.

Please use the following guide to determine the cost of attractions, lodging, and restaurants:

Lodging

$	up to $50
$$	$51 to $75
$$$	$76 to $99
$$$$	$100 and up

Meals

$	most entrees under $10
$$	most $10 to $15
$$$	most $15 to $20
$$$$	most over $20

Attractions

$	up to $5 per person
$$	$6 to $10
$$$	$10 to $20
$$$$	more than $21

The prices, rates, and hours listed in this guidebook were confirmed at press time. We recommend, however, that you call establishments to obtain current information before traveling.

Attractions Key

The following is a key to the icons found throughout the text.

SWIMMING		**FOOD**	
BOATING / BOAT TOUR		**LODGING**	
HISTORIC SITE		**CAMPING**	
HIKING / WALKING		**MUSEUM**	
FISHING		**PERFORMING ARTS**	
BIKING		**SPORTS/ATHLETICS**	
AMUSEMENT PARK		**PICNICKING**	
HORSEBACK RIDING		**PLAYGROUND**	
SKIING/WINTER SPORTS		**SHOPPING**	
PARK		**PLANTS/GARDENS/NATURE TRAILS**	
ANIMAL VIEWING		**FARM**	

Georgia's Heartland

A sea of soft pinks and whites washes over the land in March when the peach and cherry trees blossom in profusion. But although the abundant production of peaches in the heartland has given the state of Georgia its nickname, the Peach State, the region may be better known for capturing the stereotypical

Thalimers'
TopPicks in the Heartland

1. Cheering for University of Georgia athletes at the Butts-Mehre Heritage Museum, Athens

2. Clattering through the Elder Mill Covered Bridge, Watkinsville

3. Going back to school at the Madison-Morgan Cultural Center, Madison

4. Indulging the kid in you at the Uncle Remus Museum and Park, Eatonton

5. Exploring the past at the Jarrell Plantation State Historic Site, Juliette

6. Swinging with Georgia's multitalented musicians at the Georgia Music Hall of Fame, Macon

7. Uncovering Native American lore at the Ocmulgee National Monument, Macon

8. Soaring at the Museum of Aviation/Georgia Aviation Hall of Fame, Warner Robins

9. Trotting along at the Lawrence Bennett Harness Horse Training Facility, Hawkinsville

GEORGIA'S HEARTLAND

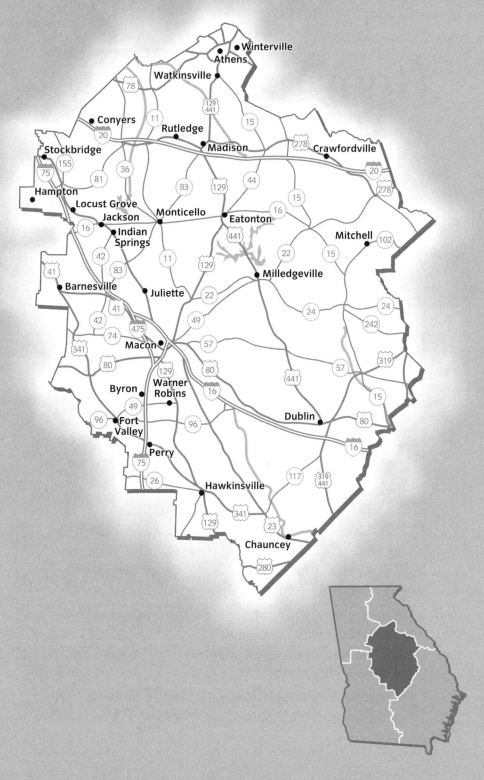

gracious, antebellum Southern way of life. In fact, so much of the area is suspended in the time prior to 1861 that the region is frequently used as a location for period movies and TV programs.

The scarcity of cities means lots of wide-open spaces where you can escape from the glare of city lights and appreciate the stars piercing the velvety black sky with pin-pricks of twinkling light, where emerald forests ring sparkling-diamond lakes dotted with the splashes of colorful sailboats, where miles of country roads made to meander are tailor-made for clans looking for the offbeat as well as the traditional. A great getaway hub, the Heartland is appealing to all sorts of travelers, from rough-it campers bent on outdoor pursuits to elegance-oriented silk-sheets-and-champagne types, fishing/boating addicts, museumgoers, shoppers, and families with children of all ages. An all-around adventure land, the alluring laid-back area boasts everything you need for a memorable vacation: seven state parks and historic sites, one national monument, five sizable lakes and numerous rivers, a state forest, several wildlife management areas, and the Oconee National Forest. The Heartland always offers more to do, and each visit turns into something new and exciting. And there's never a need to go hungry in the Heartland, which is noted for its famed down-home Southern cuisine.

Athens

U.S. Highways 78 and 441.

The Classic City, named for its counterpart in Greece, has been the home of the University of Georgia (UGA) since it was chartered in 1785. Generations of "Dawgs" have learned to "hunker down" here. Many a Georgia family can trace its roots to a relationship begun during college days at UGA. A center of culture and wealth spared during the Civil War, Athens boasts dozens of Federal, Greek Revival, and Victorian homes. Begin your visit at the Church-Waddel-Brumby House/Welcome Center, 280 East Dougherty Street; (706) 353-1820; www.visitathensga.com. You might also want to drop by the University of Georgia Visitor Center, Four Towers Building, College Station Road; (706) 542-0842.

Official Georgia

- **Fruit:** peach
- **Nickname:** the Peach State

Butts-Mehre Heritage Hall Sports Museum (ages 6 to 12)

1 Selig Circle; (706) 542-0842. Open year-round, Monday through Friday 8:00 a.m. to 5:00 p.m., as well as during home football games. Free.

On the occasional grumpy-weather day, sports fans of all ages cheer for the video displays, uniforms, playing equipment, trophies, photographs, and other memorabilia displayed at the museum to showcase the outstanding athletic accomplishments of the University of Georgia's male and female athletes, as well as those of Olympians who participated in the 1996 Summer Centennial Olympic Games, some of which were held in Athens. Challenge the kiddies to see who can be the first to spot the Heisman Trophies earned by Herschel Walker and Frankie Sinkwich.

Memorial Park and Bear Hollow Wildlife Trail (all ages)

293 Gran Ellen Drive; park (706) 613-3580, zoo (706) 613-3616; www.athensclark county.com/bearhollow. Open 8:00 a.m. to sunset weekdays, 9:00 a.m. to sunset weekends. Free.

Get your little explorers and go on a domestic safari to see more than 120 native animals, including black bears, bobcats, white-tailed deer, river owls, and otters that live at the 72-acre park's zoo. In addition the park features nature trails, a recreation building, a lake for fishing and paddle boating, picnic areas, and a playground.

Sandy Creek Nature Center/ENSAT Center (all ages)

205 Old Commerce Road; (706) 613-3615; www.sandycreeknaturecenter.com. Trails open daily daylight hours, center open Tuesday through Saturday 8:30 a.m. to 5:30 p.m., naturalists walks Saturdays at 10:00 a.m. Free.

Budding naturalists will enjoy the 225-acre park's trails through pristine woodlands, fields, and marshes as well as interactive exhibits and environmental education programs. Activities for energetic families range from salamander hunts to stargazing. The **ENSAT** (Environment, Natural Science, and Appropriate Technology) **Center** is a state-of-the-art learning laboratory with live animal exhibits as well as displays about energy-saving "green" technology, construction, and architecture.

Double-Barreled **Cannon**

This one-of-a-kind weapon, located in Cannon Park on the City Hall lawn on Hancock Street, was developed as a prototype "super weapon" in 1863 to protect the city from Sherman's army. Theoretically the artillery piece would fire simultaneously two balls connected by a chain. Unfortunately the device was spectacularly unsuccessful, so only one was ever built. It sits facing north—just in case.

State Botanical Garden of Georgia (all ages) 🚹 ⛄

2450 South Milledge Avenue; (706) 542-1244; www.uga.edu/botgarden. Open year-round, the grounds are open daily, 8:00 a.m. to 8:00 p.m. April through September and 8:00 a.m. to 6:00 p.m. October through March. The conservatory/visitor center is open Tuesday through Saturday 9:00 a.m. to 4:30 p.m. and Sunday 11:30 a.m. to 4:30 p.m. Free. The Tearoom is open Tuesday through Saturday 11:00 a.m. to 2:30 p.m. and Sunday 11:30 a.m. to 2:30 p.m. Closed Monday.

Families bloom when wandering along the 5 miles of wooded, flower-lined trails at this visual treasure to look at the rich flora of the area. Located on 313 acres on the Middle Oconee River, the grounds feature dramatic gorgelike ravines and spring-fed streams—providing plenty of open spaces for youngsters to go off on their own to run and whoop it up or to hone their senses and tune in to the delightful world of nature. Special collections include magnolias, shade and ornamental trees, flower gardens, and an international garden, but your little ghouls will probably be most fascinated by the poisonous and medicinal plants. The Dunson Native Flora Garden contains 300 species native to the Southeast. Tropical and semitropical plants as well as annuals of the season blossom in the large, modern conservatory/visitor center.

Sure to intrigue your little explorers is Clute's Kugel, located in the pavilion overlooking the international garden. A kugel (the German word for ball) is a perfectly balanced stone sphere that fits into a socket carved to the exact curvature of the ball. When water is pumped up from beneath the socket, it creates a thin film that lubricates the ball, causing it to revolve in all directions. Once the water is turned on, the ball will revolve until the water is shut off—and even a child can stop the ball or make it change direction. Your budding scientists will marvel at how an 816-pound ball of polished black granite could possibly float only $\frac{5}{1000}$ inch above the socket. A world map is engraved on the surface. This kugel was given and named Clute's Kugel in memory of young Clute Barrow Nelson, who died from a brain tumor. He had been fascinated by a kugel he saw in Houston.

For More Information

Athens Convention and Visitors Bureau, 300 North Thomas Street, Athens, GA 30601; (706) 357-4430 or (800) 653-0603; www.visitathensga.com.

A Tree That Owns Itself

"How can a tree own itself?" the small fry are sure to ask about the seemingly ordinary old tree at the corner of Dearing and Finley Streets. It seems that in the late 1800s, Professor W. H. Jackson enjoyed the shade of the tree so much that he deeded it 8 feet of ground on all sides.

Amazing
Georgia Facts

UGA was the first state-chartered, state-supported university in the country.

Winterville

East on Highway 72, then southeast on Voyles Road.

Carter-Coile Country Doctor's Museum (ages 6 to 12)
111 Marigold Lane; (706) 742-8600 or (706) 742-5891; www.cityofwinterville.com/html/doctor_s_museum.html. Open by appointment. Free.

Today's sophisticated kids who are used to pediatricians and specialists probably can't imagine a day when doctors were general practitioners, sometimes also did dentistry, and made house calls—at night even! Their parents and maybe even their grandparents may have never experienced this type of medical care. This museum, which is one of the few in the nation dedicated to the country doctor, is housed in the small clapboard building where Dr. Carter and Dr. Coile practiced before the turn of the twentieth century. Artifacts on display, including an original operating table, as well as antique surgical tools, parts of human anatomy, various medicine bottles, and dentists' utensils were donated by the families of several doctors who practiced in the area.

Watkinsville

South of Athens on US 441.

Watkinsville was once considered as the site for the University of Georgia, but it was decided that the existence of the Eagle Tavern made the town "too frivolous an atmosphere for studious young gentlemen," and the school was established in tiny,

Civil War Legend

A Confederate soldier remained concealed for weeks in a hiding place in the loft behind the enormous chimney of the Eagle Tavern, with food and buckets of hot coals handed up to him by slaves.

then-sedate Athens. The powers that be who made that decision must be spinning in their graves, because UGA has earned the reputation of a party school.

Eagle Tavern Museum (all ages) 🏛️ 🛍️
26 North Main Street; (706) 769-5197; www.visitoconee.com. Open year-round, Monday through Saturday 10:00 a.m. to 5:00 p.m. Free.

Let your little time travelers experience Georgia frontier life by exploring this restored tavern. During its colorful history the humble structure has served as a fort, a hotel, a stagecoach stop, and a store. One of the earliest surviving buildings in Oconee County, the tavern has been restored to its early Federal Plain–style appearance— "two-up, two-down." Using simple furnishings from the 1700s, the downstairs replicates the tavern where, for the price of a drink, travelers could spread their bedrolls; the upstairs depicts the rooms with real beds available to well-to-do stagecoach passengers. Other exhibits interpret the findings from several archaeological digs done on the property.

Elder Mill Covered Bridge (all ages) 🏛️
Georgia Highway 15 over Rose Creek. Always accessible. Free.

Take a trip into the past at this 1870 covered bridge before it becomes just a memory. Few of these nostalgic old spans remain in the state, and this is one of the last still in use on a public road. Not many of today's mod squad have ever seen a covered bridge, so this preserved and maintained span offers a pleasurable opportunity to appreciate the hollow sounds of the clattering floorboards made walking or driving through one. Shutterbugs will need a wide-angle lens to fit the bridge into the frame. A good bet for wannabe photographers are one-use panoramic cameras.

For More Information

Oconee County Visitors Bureau, 54 Nancy Drive, Watkinsville, GA 30677; (706) 769-5197; www.oconeecounty.com.

Stockbridge

US 441 South to Highway 186 West to Highway 83 West, then Highway 138 West to Stockbridge.

Panola Mountain State Park (all ages) 🏞️ 🏕️ 🌿

2600 Highway 155 Southwest; (770) 389-7801; www.gastateparks.org/info/panolamt/. Open year-round, this park has seasonal hours, so it's best to check ahead. Parking $3 except free on Wednesday.

A perfect place for an active outing, this park boasts hiking trails and wildlife specific to the Piedmont region. The most significant landmark is an awe-inspiring, gigantic, one-hundred-acre granite monadnock. Self-guided nature trails poke into the most secluded parts of the forest, and guided hikes also attract multigenerational tribes. Plenty of opportunities abound for your wild bunch to rip and race and yell to their hearts' content. Once the gang gets tired of hiking, they can get a second wind at the interpretive center, where there are animal exhibits and often nature programs. (*Note:* Pets and bicycles are not allowed on the trails.)

Conyers

East of Atlanta/Stockbridge on Interstate 20.

A self-guided tour of Olde Town Conyers features the Dinky, one of only three 1905 steam locomotives of its type in the world; the Old Jail Museum with a "hanging room"; a historic depot; and a botanical garden. Conyers is also the home of Nancy Fowler, who has been visited by more than one million people of all ages since 1990 to hear her messages from Jesus and the Virgin Mary. Her farm, which is open to the public, has walking trails, religious statuary, and a bookstore/gift shop, but Ms. Fowler no longer delivers regular messages.

Georgia International Horse Park (all ages) 🏕️ 🐎

1996 Centennial Olympic Parkway; (770) 860-4190 or (888) 860-4224; www.georgiahorsepark.com. Open for specific events; call for a schedule. Price varies by event.

All the pardners in your posse will enjoy horsing around at this equestrian center, which was built as the site of the 1996 Summer Olympic equestrian, mountain biking, and modern pentathlon events. Your little cowboys and cowgirls will love exciting competitions such as the Atlanta Spring, Summer, and Fall Meets; the rough-and-tumble National Barrel Horse Racing Super Show; dressage shows; and rodeos that occur periodically, as well as fairs, craft shows, and musical concerts that fill out the remainder of the yearly calendar. Part of the fun is wandering around the horse stables to see the equine stars and occasionally patting a velvety soft nose. During the events there are plenty of concession stands to assuage hungry munchkins. It's a must to bring a camera to these events; the pictures will be invaluable for show-and-tell.

For More Information

Conyers-Rockdale Chamber of Commerce, 1186 Scott Street, Conyers, GA 30012; (770) 483-7049; www.conyers-rockdale.com.

Conyers Welcome Center, 901 Railroad Street, Conyers, GA 30094; (770) 602-2606 or (800) CONYERS.

Rutledge

From Conyers take I-20 East to Highway 12 East to Rutledge.

"Small . . . But Special," Rutledge features shops of working artisans including glass workers, furniture makers, quilters, and others. Give the kids a chance to see how everyday items and works of art are created.

Hard Labor Creek State Park (all ages)

U.S. Highway 278/Fairplay Road; park (706) 557-3001 or (800) 864-7275; golf (706) 557-3006; www.gastateparks.org/info/hardlabor/. Open daily year-round, 7:00 a.m. to 10:00 p.m. Parking $3; cottages $$$; camping $; advance reservations for equestrian camping are required.

Whether your brood makes a day's outing or takes a week's vacation to visit this park, each of your little chickadees will find all the ingredients for a fun-filled vacation: golf, fishing, swimming beach, boating, horse stables, hiking trails, playground, and a trading post. For equestrians there are more than 22 miles of maintained bridle trails, providing up to five hours of riding, but the facility does not rent horses. If you can BYOH (bring your own horse), stalls and trailer parking are available, as are campsites for the humans. The park offers camping facilities, but if camping isn't your thing, you can tuck yourselves into a snug cottage in the woods.

Madison

East of Rutledge on Highway 12.

Madison, known as the city Sherman refused to burn, had a reputation before the Civil War as "the most cultured and aristocratic town on the stage route from Charleston to New Orleans." A large portion of Madison's outstanding architecture

was built between 1830 and 1860, but there are a significant number of Victorian structures from the late nineteenth century. Designated by the U.S. Department of the Interior in 1974, the Madison Historic District was one of the first such districts in Georgia to be recognized and is still one of the largest designated historic areas in the nation. In addition to several important sites open for tours year-round, some private homes are open for tours three times a year: May, October, and December.

Bruce Weiner Microcar Museum (ages 3 to 12)

2350 Eatonton Road; (706) 342-1799; www.microcarmuseum.com. Open Tuesday, Wednesday, and Thursday 1:00 to 4:00 p.m. (closed May through July and the week before and two weeks after Christmas). $ (proceeds go to the local humane society)

It really is a small world after all at Double Bubble Acres, the home of Bruce Weiner—owner of the Double Bubble Gum Company. Besides bubble gum, Weiner's next passion is microcars, and he owns and displays 150 of them at this museum. These tiny cars are not toys, but were actually used as transportation by Europeans after World War II. Called bubble cars, they resemble pregnant roller skates. In addition the museum showcases a collection of vintage 1950s kiddie rides (remember the horses, airplanes, or rocket ships often found at stores) and toy versions of the microcars.

Madison-Morgan Cultural Center (all ages)

434 South Main Street; (706) 342-4743; www.madisonmorgancultural.org. Open year-round, Tuesday through Saturday 10:00 a.m. to 5:00 p.m. and Sunday 2:00 to 5:00 p.m. $

Although your little scholars may tell you they don't want to be reminded of school while they're on vacation, they'll enjoy a stop at this old institution where the original bell still rings. Housed since 1895 in the imposing Romanesque Revival–style structure, the academy served as one of the first graded schools in the South. The edifice must have seemed like a castle to children who had never before seen anything but a one-room school, but even today's more sophisticated pupils are sure to be impressed by the majestic structure, which currently houses authentically restored and furnished century-old classrooms and a history museum filled with nineteenth-century decorative arts, artifacts, and interpretive information about the Piedmont region of Georgia, as well as permanent and traveling art exhibits. Performances of the **Madison Theater Festival** and other local, regional, national, and international groups are given in the apse-shaped auditorium, which still retains the original seats and chandelier.

Morgan County African-American Museum (ages 6 to 12) 🔠
156 Academy Street; (706) 342-9191. Open year-round, Tuesday through Friday 10:00 a.m. to 4:00 p.m., Saturday noon to 4:00 p.m., and Sunday by appointment. $

Your clan will be surrounded by history at this museum, which both preserves the African-American heritage and culture of the South and promotes an awareness of the contributions African Americans have made to the area. Just open yourselves up to their spirit—it's easy to sense the past when you remain open to its riches.

Lake Oconee (all ages) 🐟 🔠 🔺
Lake Oconee Tourism and Real Estate Council; (800) 886-5253; www.greeneccoc.org or www.visitlakeoconee.org. Open year-round; hours vary by park and season. Parking $2 at recreation areas.

Lake Oconee is a prime destination for creating vacation memories for your brood. It's all here: swimming, waterskiing, sailing, and fishing. Be sure to bring plenty of lures and bait. Several recreation areas provide campsites, beaches, docks, and/or restaurants. **Old Salem Park** (706-467-2850) and **Parks Ferry Park** (706-453-4308) have campsites as well as a beach and boating facilities. **Granite Shoals Marina** boasts even more: a boat ramp, covered boat storage, boat repair, a restaurant, lodging, gasoline, fishing supplies, and groceries. Call (706) 453-7639 to find out more.

For More Information
Madison-Morgan County Chamber of Commerce, 115 East Jefferson Street, Madison, GA 30650; (706) 342-4454 or (800) 709-7406; www.madisonga.org.

Crawfordville

From Madison take US 278 East to Crawfordville.

The small hamlet of Crawfordville is often used in movies; you may recognize it from *Home Fires Burning* and *Paris Trout*. It was also the home of nineteenth-century politician Alexander "Little Alex" Stephens—a man who was sickly and small in stature but a giant in heart and dedication to the cause of the Confederacy.

A. H. Stephens Historic Park (all ages) 🏛 🔠 🔠 🔺
456 Alexander Street; (706) 456-2602; www.gastateparks.org/info/ahsteph. Park open daily 7:00 a.m. to 10:00 p.m.; historic site museum open Tuesday through Saturday 9:00 a.m. to 5:00 p.m., Sunday 2:00 to 5:00 p.m. Closed Thanksgiving, Christmas, and New Year's Days. Parking $3; historic site admission $.

Active families appreciate that they get two-for-one attractions at this park, which combines recreational fun with the educational resources of a historic site. The park occupies the property of Alexander H. Stephens, known as the Little Giant, who served as a U.S. senator, the vice president of the Confederacy, and governor of Georgia.

A pleasant place to spend a day or a week, the recreational side of the park boasts an all-around package: two lakes, fishing, boat rentals, 3 miles of nature and hiking trails and even 12 miles of equestrian trails (BYOH—bring your own horse). Even the smallest tot can learn to skip stones into the lake or angle for a finny creature. If your brood is into roughing it or semi roughing it, why not call it a day without moving on? The park offers campsites and cabins.

Curious kidlets can take a trip into the past and learn more about the Civil War and the famous Georgia statesman at his home, Liberty Hall. Original furnishings and Stephen's personal memorabilia give an authentic glimpse into the man and his times. Surrounding the house are Stephens's grave and several outbuildings including a detached kitchen and servants' quarters.

If any of the tiny tots' attentions wander while touring the house, they'll perk up at the adjacent Civil War Museum, which displays one of the state's best collections of uniforms, weapons, medical equipment, documents, letters, and Civil War reunion souvenirs. If your progeny are like ours, they'll be particularly fascinated by the reality of the life-size dioramas depicting scenes from the Civil War: a family sending its sons off to war, soldiers in camp, and women at home supporting the war effort. **Victorian Christmas at Liberty Hall** is a re-creation of the holiday in Stephens's time. The little ones' eyes will pop out at the glittering fairyland of sparkling lights, displays, and Christmas trees.

Why **Liberty Hall?**

First, Stephens felt that he was at liberty to do anything he pleased there. Second, any friend or even complete stranger could feel at liberty to spend the night at his home. In fact, he had a special room, called the Tramp's Room, built to house travelers who needed a place to stay.

Eatonton

From Crawfordville take Highway 20 South to I-20 West to Highway 44 South.

"You can do anything you want to me, Br'er Fox, but whatever you do, please, please, don't throw me in that briar patch." The Uncle Remus/Br'er Rabbit stories have been charming the small fry for almost one hundred years. Eatonton was the childhood home of journalist and author Joel Chandler Harris, who re-created the slave tales he had been told as a child. Stop by the courthouse for a photo of your little critters with a statue of a brightly dressed Br'er Rabbit cavorting on the lawn. The town's literary connections extend to the present day: Eatonton is also the birthplace of Alice Walker, Pulitzer Prize–winning author of *The Color Purple*. In addition, the town is another gateway to Lakes Oconee and Sinclair.

Uncle Remus Museum and Park (all ages)

US 441; (706) 485-6856; www.uncleremus.com/museum.html. Open year-round, Monday through Saturday 10:00 a.m. to noon and 1:00 to 5:00 p.m., as well as Sunday 2:00 to 5:00 p.m.; closed Tuesday November through March. $

Youngsters and the young-at-heart love the exhibits about Br'er Rabbit, his pals, and foes that are found at the museum. A must-stop and perennial favorite, the museum is housed in two log cabins reminiscent of the slave cottages where Uncle Remus spun the yarns about the amusing, lovable creatures for the Little Boy. In addition to displays about plantation life, the collection includes Harris's personal memorabilia, shadow box scenes, and carvings of "de critters." The rug rats can find out even more about plantation life in the surrounding park that contains historic outbuildings and old-fashioned farm tools.

Rock Eagle Effigy (ages 4 to 12)

Rock Eagle 4-H Center, 350 Rock Eagle Road Northwest (off US 129/441); office (706) 484-2899; www.rockeagle4H.org. Open year-round during daylight hours. Free.

It isn't just the small fry who are astonished by one of the most ancient and unusual attractions in Georgia. The whole gang (even pseudo-sophisticated teenagers) are awed by the gigantic figure of a prone bird measuring 102 feet from head to tail, 120 feet across the wingspan, and rising 10 feet above the ground. The bird form is believed to have been built by Native Americans of the Woodland period, more than 2,000 years ago and was probably used for religious or ceremonial purposes. Constructed entirely from milky quartz, the rocks, which range in size from baseballs to boulders, were brought from a quarry nearby or from as far as 100 miles away without the benefit of horses or wheeled vehicles. Curious kidlets are eager to scramble up the staircase to the top of the tower that was constructed in the 1930s so that the tumulus can be viewed from above. (You can only get good photos from the tower.)

At the center, other opportunities abound for outdoor fun: A 110-acre lake for boating and fishing activities and shady picnic areas make for a day of family fun. The only drawback is that swimming isn't permitted.

For More Information

Eatonton-Putnam Chamber of Commerce, 105 South Washington Street, Eatonton, GA 31024; (706) 485-7701; www.eatonton.com.

Monticello

West of Eatonton on Highway 16.

This gracious, small Southern town, where the past is preserved for you to see, was the home of country music star Trisha Yearwood and is also known as the Deer Capital of Georgia. The entire town is listed on the National Register of Historic Places.

Charlie Elliott Wildlife Center (ages 4 to 12)

543 Elliott Trail, Mansfield; (770) 784-3059. Open year-round; grounds always accessible, center open Tuesday through Saturday 9:00 a.m. to 4:30 p.m.; Sunday (April through October) 1:00 to 4:30 p.m. Free.

More than 6,400 acres, including twenty-nine ponds, a five-acre rock outcropping, 5 miles of trails, a multiuse trail open for hiking, biking, bird-watching, and horseback riding (BYOH), and an educational center, provide a delightful menu of activities. Programs geared for the little ones are offered in summer. The museum at the center, which was named for native son Charlie Elliott, writer and former southern field editor for *Outdoor Life Magazine,* showcases books, photographs, and hunting and fishing memorabilia donated by Elliott as well as a replica of his den. Other exhibits include interactive wildlife displays, a freshwater aquarium, and a bird-watching alcove overlooking ponds and a native plant garden. Youngsters enjoy the scavenger hunt worksheet.

Oconee National Forest (all ages)

(770) 297–3000; www.fs.fed.us/conf. Free.

The junior set can enjoy any number of escapades in the vast acreage of the national forest—a fantastic all-in-one spot for clans seeking adventure and variety. Encompassing 11,500 acres, the forest includes the **Sinclair Recreational Area** on Lake Sinclair, two boat access recreational areas on Lake Oconee, and two wildlife management areas. For little squirts who love to trek and would get a kick out of a real ghost town, visiting the **Scull Shoals Historical Area** is a great way for them to learn about Georgia's past. Reached by gravel road or a 1-mile hiking trail, the remains of a once-prosperous town include ruins of Georgia's first paper mill, a cotton gin, and a textile factory. From there the **Boarding House Trail** leads to the vestiges of an old boardinghouse, while the **Indian Mounds Trail** traverses the Oconee River floodplain to two prehistoric Native American mounds. A truly fabulous place for your tribe to spend a day, the forest contains numerous hiking trails, and five horseback-riding trails meander through the timberlands. Camping is permitted forestwide. For more information, including *A Guide to the Chattahoochee-Oconee National Forests,* call (706) 485-7110 or write to Oconee Ranger District, 1199 Madison Road, Eatonton, GA 31024.

For More Information

Monticello-Jasper County Chamber of Commerce and Welcome Center, 119 West Washington Street, Monticello, GA 31064; (706) 468-8994; www.historic monitcello.com/chamberofcommerce .html.

Jackson

West of Monticello on Highway 16.

This down-home, turn-of-the-twentieth-century community urges visitors to "come sit on our front porch." Although the town boasts a large historic district of stately old homes, it is best known for several state parks and its easy access to the myriad recreational opportunities at Lake Jackson.

Dauset Trails Nature Center (all ages) 👫 🐘 ♿

360 Mt. Vernon Road (off Highway 42); (770) 775-6798; www.dausettrails.com. Open daily year-round, 9:00 a.m. to 5:00 p.m., except Sunday noon to 5:00 p.m. Closed Thanksgiving, Christmas, and New Year's Days. Free (donations welcome).

A good, kid-friendly place to experience outdoor activities together is this 1,200-acre nature center. In addition to hiking the 6 miles of nature trails and enjoying the several small lakes and creeks, you should check for scheduled programs about ecology issues and plant, tree, and wildlife identification. Little nature lovers will enjoy exploring the various gardens at the center, including the Woodland Garden; the Bog Garden, which features two ponds connected by a waterfall; and the Children's Garden, which is planted to inspire the young ones' senses of smell and taste. They can admire the formal knot garden there and get a worksheet to embark on a pleasure hunt for garden ornaments such as painted mushroom sculptures and a giant caterpillar. For live animal viewing, there are native mammals as well as birds of prey and reptile exhibits. A barnyard exhibit features a large rustic barn with farm animals such as horses, mules, pigs, chickens, goats, cows, and sheep. This is a perfect place to poke around the pens and pet some of these animals—although few of them are truly cuddly. The newest addition at the center is a network of 12 miles of bicycle trails, ranging in difficulty from beginner to expert. Ten miles of the trails are designated for horseback riding (BYOH). The trails are closed if it's rainy or wet. Trails are open from sunrise to midnight. (You must sign the Trail Users Release Form located at the Trail Head Parking Kiosk.) Facilities also include a picnic area, pavilion, and chapel.

High Falls State Park (ages 4 to 12) 🐾 🌊 👟

76 High Falls Park Road (off I-75); (478) 993-3053 or (800) 864-7275; www.gastate parks.org/info/highfall/. Open daily year-round, 7:00 a.m. to 10:00 p.m. Parking $3; camping $.

One of the don't-miss stops in the area is the southernmost falls in Georgia. High Falls marks the Piedmont Fall Line, where the terrain changes from gently rolling hills to the flatlands of the coastal plain. Although caution is advised, intrepid climbers will have fun slipping and sliding as they clamber over the rocks while hiking to the top and bottom of the 100-foot waterfall. Going down is the easy part, but it may take a real cooperative effort of pulling, tugging, pushing, and hauling to get everyone back to the top in one piece. Be sure to take a camera to record the plummeting cascade. You'll get an even more memorable shot for the vacation scrapbook if you can arrange family members in the foreground with the falls as a dramatic backdrop. With a fishing lake (considered to be the best crappie lake in Georgia), boat and canoe rentals, a swimming pool, nature trails, and the magnificent falls themselves, this popular multiuse park is a perfect place for a family frolic. There is no swimming, not even wading, in the lake. Numerous campsites invite you to stay a spell.

Lake Jackson (all ages) 🌊 🐾 ⛺

(770) 775-4753, ext. 3100; www.georgiapower.com/gpclake. Open daily year-round, 7:00 a.m. to 10:00 p.m.; beach at Lloyd Shoals Park open June through Labor Day, weekdays 10:00 a.m. to 5:00 p.m. and weekends 10:00 a.m. to 6:00 p.m. Parking $3.

All the best elements of a memorable vacation are here—particularly swimming, fishing, and boating. Because the lake isn't very deep, the reservoir is warmer than others in the area, making it particularly popular with swimmers. Your own little mermaids or mermen can stay in the water until they're as wrinkled as raisins. Six marinas and several restaurants offer the best in recreational facilities and dining choices.

For More Information

Butts County Chamber of Commerce, 206 East Third Street, Jackson, GA 30233; (770) 775-4839; www.butts countychamber.com.

Notable Georgians **from the Heartland**

- **Sidney Lanier**—famous nineteenth-century poet from Macon

- **Flannery O'Connor**—author from Milledgeville

Indian Springs

South of Jackson on U.S. Highway 23.

Indian Springs State Park (all ages) 🚻 🏖 🎡

678 Lake Clark Road (off Highway 42), Flovilla. For more information on the park, call (770) 504-2277 or (800) 864-7275; www.gastateparks.org/info/indspr; to find out more about the chapel, call (770) 775-2493. Park open daily year-round, 7:00 a.m. to 10:00 p.m. Parking $3; golf $$$; cottages $$; camping $.

Draw spirit and enchantment from the medicinal waters at this natural spring, which was named for the Native Americans who first used it for its healing powers. Located in the oldest state park in the nation, the pure medicinal waters still attract people who come here daily to collect jugfuls of it. A great place to relax with the wee ones for a day or longer, the park's facilities and activities include a lake with a beach, fishing, boat rentals, picnicking, nature trails, and putt-putt golf. The museum features exhibits about the Creek Indians, the resort era, and the Civilian Conservation Corps (CCC). A leisurely way for families to experience the area is to stay at the park's ten fully equipped one- to three-bedroom cottages or ninety RV/tent sites.

Locust Grove

North of Indian Springs on US 23.

Noah's Ark Animal Rehabilitation Center (all ages) 🦒 🐘

712 LG-Griffin Road (off Highway 42); (770) 957-0888; www.noahs-ark.org; noah@noahs-ark.org. Open year-round, Tuesday through Saturday noon to 3:00 p.m. (It's best to call before you come; they close if it's raining.) Donations accepted.

Your herd can't help but have a good time around animals. A real blessing to injured creatures, this center has ministered to more than 16,197 at last count—from turkeys to tigers. Every member in your human family can find a critter that is sure to enchant him or her. Don't forget your camera; pictures of the small fry and animals are always guaranteed to create precious memories. Beautiful nature trails that provide about 1.5 miles of walking allow you to see furry and feathered friends in very natural, peaceful settings. With the wildlife staring back at you, it's hard to tell who's on display.

Hampton

From Locust Grove drive north on Interstate 75 two exits to Highway 20. Head west to Hampton.

Atlanta Motor Speedway (ages 6 to 12)

1900 U.S. Highway 19/41 South; (770) 946-4211; www.atlantamotorspeedway.com. Open year-round; call for a schedule of events. Price varies by event. Tours available through the gift shop.

Something exciting is always happening at the speedway, which hosts two NASCAR Nextel Cup races and the Busch Grand National, as well as several IMSA and ARCA events. The loud, explosive roar of the races and the possibility of serious car crashes may be too scary for small kiddies. On the other hand, uneventful races of endless circling can be extremely boring for the very young. Camping facilities are available.

How to Choose **the Perfect Peach**

- Smell the fruit—the peach is a member of the rose family and should have a sweet fragrance.
- Look for a gold to yellow undercolor—red or blush is an indication of variety, not ripeness.
- The fruit should be soft but not mushy.
- Look for a well-defined crease running from the stem to the point.
- Don't squeeze; peaches bruise easily.
- Place firm peaches on the counter for a day or two to ripen.
- Refrigerate ripe peaches and eat them within a week.
- To peel a peach, dip it into boiling water for thirty seconds, then in cold water.
- To keep peeled peaches from darkening, add lemon juice or ascorbic acid.

Newman Wetlands Center (ages 4 to 12) 🐦 🐷 🐦

2755 Freeman Road; (770) 603-5606; www.ccwa1.com/facilities/wetlands.center.aspx. Trail open March through April daily 7:00 a.m. to 7:00 p.m., November through February daily 7:00 a.m. to 5:00 p.m.; interpretive center open September through May, Monday through Friday 8:00 a.m. to 5:00 p.m., June through August, Tuesday through Saturday 8:00 a.m. to 5:00 p.m. Free.

Get away from the rush of daily life and take the gang on a fun excursion to this wetlands complex, which showcases 130 species of birds, as well as tree frogs, turtles, snakes, deer, mink, beaver, and other native inhabitants. A video prepares visitors before they stroll along the 0.6-mile boardwalk and trail through the wetlands environment. Bird-spotting is an ideal activity to give your little fledglings a sense of purpose while you meander along the paths.

Barnesville

South of Hampton on US 41.

Early in the twentieth century, small Barnesville was the home of four buggy manufacturing factories, earning the town the title Buggy Capital of the South.

Barnesville Buggy Days (all ages)

Third week of September. For more information about the festival, contact the Barnesville–Lamar County Chamber of Commerce: (770) 358-5884; www.barnesville .org/buggy.html. Price varies by event.

Although all the buggy factories are gone, this hamlet still remembers its heritage with a celebrated festival/social extravaganza of the first degree. Let the little ones experience the days of spoke wheels and fringed surrey tops by participating in the celebration that includes a parade of 250 horses and decorated buggies, arts and crafts, antiques, and leisurely old-fashioned horse-drawn buggy rides.

Old Jail Museum and Archives (ages 6 to 12) 🏛 🔎

326 Thomaston Street; (770) 358-0181; http://barnesville.org/tourism.html. Open year-round, Wednesday 10:00 a.m. to 5:00 p.m., Saturday 10:00 a.m. to 2:00 p.m., Sunday 2:00 to 5:00 p.m. $1 donation.

Relics from the city's buggy days include buggies built in Barnesville, a stagecoach, and even the town's last watering trough. (Tell the rug rats it was the filling station of its day.) A selection of antique toys, dolls, and tools are sure to fascinate the high-tech junior set.

For More Information

Barnesville-Lamar County Chamber of Commerce, 100 Commerce Place, Barnesville, GA 30204; (770) 358-5884; www.barnesville.org.

Juliette

From Barnesville take US 41 East to Forsyth. Juliette is east of Forsyth on US 23.

The kids may or may not recognize tiny, one-street Juliette on the banks of Lake Juliette, but you'll surely identify it as the film location of the celebrated Jessica Tandy/Kathy Bates movie *Fried Green Tomatoes*. The old-fashioned turn-of-the-twentieth-century depot, shops, bank, drugstore, and other buildings along McCrackin Street have been resurrected as charming antiques shops, gift and clothing boutiques, and eateries—the most popular of which is the **Whistle Stop Cafe** (the reason most folks come to town in the first place).

Jarrell Plantation Historic Site (ages 4 to 12) 🏛 🐖 🍁

711 Jarrell Plantation Road; (478) 986-5172; www.gastateparks.org/info/jarrell. Open year-round, Tuesday through Saturday 9:00 a.m. to 5:00 p.m. and Sunday 2:00 to 5:30 p.m. (last tour at 4:00 p.m.) Closed Thanksgiving, Christmas, and New Year's Days. $

Ask your sophisticated, worldly offspring if they can imagine completely self-sufficient living where your family would grow or make just about everything you use in everyday life. The concept will boggle their minds. For a lesson in such living, examine the self-contained farm life represented at the plantation. Generations of the Jarrells lived on the farm from the 1840s to the 1940s, after which they donated all the buildings

A Thalimer **Adventure**

As fans of the movie *Fried Green Tomatoes*, we oldsters couldn't wait to see Juliette, where it was filmed, and got a chuckle out of shops such as Towanda's. The grandkids, however, were hungry, somewhat disinterested (although Chris did try to fall into the lake/millpond while skipping stones), and much more intent on the prospect of devouring a gargantuan lunch at the Whistle Stop Cafe, followed by heaping, dripping ice-cream cones afterward. They lost their been-there-done-that attitude immediately, though, when we arrived at nearby Jarrell Plantation Historic Site, where they were absolutely fascinated with the idea that a family could live almost completely isolated for generations out in this wilderness—sawing their own lumber, growing their own food, making their own clothes, and building whatever they needed. Chris was particularly intrigued with the steam-powered gristmill, sawmill, cotton gin, and shingle-making operation, while Tricia, our wannabe veterinarian, fell in love with all the farm animals.

and their contents—the most complete original family collection of artifacts in Georgia—to the state. Although most folks tend to think of Tara in the context of plantation life, this one was simply a self-contained farm complex that allowed family members to produce almost everything they needed. The site includes several simple houses filled with primitive furniture and everyday necessities such as spinning wheels and looms. Little people are even more fascinated by the sawmill, carpenter shop, blacksmith shop, and several beehives and wheat houses, as well as by the farm tools and machinery, such as a cane furnace, steam-powered cotton gin, gristmill, sawmill, and a shingle mill. A barn, farm animals, and a garden lend an air of authenticity. You'll need to spend considerable time here to explore all the farm's offerings—and it's a place where you can comfortably allow independent youngsters to roam on their own. Special events pertaining to farm life—such as sheep shearing—occur throughout the year.

For More Information

Juliette Community, (478) 994-9239 or (888) 642-4628; www.forsyth-monroe chamber.com.

Milledgeville

From Juliette drive south on US 23 to Highway 18. Go east to U.S. Highway 129 North to HIghway 22, then continue east to Milledgeville.

Milledgeville served as Georgia's capital from 1803 to 1868, a period that included the momentous Civil War years. Filled with historic buildings from that era, the town is considered to be the only surviving example of a complete Federal-period city in this country. Make sure to drive by the Old Capitol, now Georgia Military College, to admire its battlements. Monday through Friday 10:00 a.m. to noon and Saturday 2:00 to 4:00 p.m. Mom and Dad can kick back and leave the driving to someone else during a trolley tour of town.

Kids and shivering from fear and bloodcurdling screams create a guaranteed formula for family fun. Milledgeville is so well known for its ghosts, the week of Halloween is highlighted by Haunted Trolley Tours. Actors dressed in appropriate period costumes play the part of the frightening ghosts while imparting their macabre stories to wide-eyed youngsters and parents. Visitors can stroll around the boxwood gardens at Homestead House and perhaps meet up with the ghost of Miss Sue or the banshee. The price of the tour is $12 per person.

The Confederacy's **Bitter End**

Confederate president Jefferson Davis was captured near Irwinton in central Georgia on May 10, 1865. Many believe that the Confederate treasury is buried somewhere nearby, but no one can find it.

Bartram State Forest (ages 4 to 12)

US 441 South; (478) 445-2119; www.milledgevillecvb.com. Open year-round. Free.

Fishing fanatics in your gang will enjoy angling for channel catfish, largemouth bass, and bream in the fifty-one-acre lake. Who knows what a junior fish jockey might hook for a real show-and-tell fish story when school starts? Even the tiniest tot can dangle a line, or you can set them to searching for worms or for flat stones to skip later. Break up your laid-back day with a leisurely picnic or a stroll on one of the three walking trails to see wildlife, wetlands, and an erosion ravine with soil of the ancient shallow sea that covered Georgia 50 to 100 million years ago.

Lockerly Arboretum (all ages)

1534 Irwinton Road; (478) 452-2112; www.lockerlyarboretum.org. Open year-round, Monday through Friday 8:30 a.m. to 4:30 p.m., Saturday from October to May 1:00 to 5:00 p.m. and June through September 10:00 a.m. to 2:00 p.m. Closed on Sunday. Call for the holiday schedule. Grounds Free. Lockerly Hall tour $.

Been in the car too long? Toured one too many museums where the little ones felt restrained? Let them loose to run through the grounds of Lockerly Arboretum, where they can enjoy nature at its best. Comprising nearly fifty acres, naturally the arboretum grounds are filled with trees of many sizes and descriptions, but there's much more—trails, several types of gardens, greenhouses, a stream, and a small (and the operative words are *small* and *informal*) rustic museum. Touring the grounds is free and can be done at your leisure. Oh, and there's one more thing. Those who are in search of the fictional Tara can find the next best thing here. Lockerly Hall, once known as Rose Hill because of the abundance of wild Cherokee roses that grew in the area, is the quintessential Southern Greek Revival many-columned plantation house.

Heartland **Ghosts**

- **The nonexistent child and the black dog**—Ocmulgee National Monument, Macon

- **Sue Peters**—the Homestead, Milledgeville

Built around 1839, it was lived in by only six families. Not only did it survive the Civil War, but its owners treated it with care and never significantly changed or added onto it. If it's Monday and the kids can be enticed inside after letting off some steam, the mansion is open for tours.

Sweetwater Festival (all ages)

102 South Wayne Street; (478) 445-4014; www.sweetwaterfestival.com. First weekend in November. Free.

A popular diversion, this November fair is tons of fun. Sure crowd pleasers—especially with the backseat set—are the food, entertainment, parades, folk music, storytelling, antique car show, and other activities with a family twist. Highlights of the fair include sales of crafts and demonstrations of the skills of yesteryear, such as blacksmithing, painting, pottery, and weaving.

Lake Sinclair (all ages)

North of Milledgeville; Call the Milledgeville CVB at (478) 452-4687; www.milledgeville cvb.com. Open year-round. Free.

Family fun awaits at this popular lake, particularly for boating and fishing fanatics. If you subscribe to the theory that a bad day fishing beats a good day doing just about anything else, finny creatures have been attracting day-trippers and vacationers to Lake Sinclair for years. For dyed-in-the-wool anglers, there are several major fishing tournaments each year, so cast a line. Who knows what state record might await one of you? On the other hand, if the kidlets don't know how to bait a hook yet, this is a fine place to teach them. Everything else you need is here: several recreation areas, restaurants, marinas, and accommodations ranging from primitive camping to luxurious condominiums.

Milledgeville's Trolley Tour (ages 6 to 12)

200 West Hancock Street; (478) 452-4687 or (800) 653-1804; www.milledgevillecvb .com. Tours leave Monday through Friday at 10:00 a.m. and Saturday at 2:00 p.m. Adults $$, children 6 to 16 $.

When the bell clangs, climb aboard a nostalgic trolley for a narrated tour around the charming antebellum town with a stop at one of these attractions: the Old Governor's Mansion, Old State Capitol, St. Stephen's Episcopal Church, Lockerly Hall, and the Stetson-Sanford House (stops rotate daily). If you have the nerve, participate in one of the Haunted Trolley Tours operated two nights in October.

For More Information

Milledgeville Convention and Visitors Bureau, 200 West Hancock Street, Milledgeville, GA 31061; (478) 452-4687 or (800) 653-1804; www.milledgevillecvb.com.

Milledgeville Chamber of Commerce, 130 Jefferson Street, Milledgeville, GA 31061; (478) 453-9311; www.milledgeville ga.com.

Mitchell

East of Milledgeville on Highway 102.

Hamburg State Park (all ages) 🏛️ ⛺ 🧗

6071 Hamburg State Park Road; (478) 552-2393 or (800) 864-7275;
www.gastateparks.org/info/hamburg. Open daily year-round, 7:00 a.m. to 10:00 p.m.
Parking $3; camping $.

History and outdoor fun await visitors to this popular state park. In addition to a historic
1921 gristmill, museum, and country store, your gang will find a lake, fishing, boat ramp,
canoe, and pedal boat rentals, as well as 3.5 miles of nature and hiking trails. After a
strenuous day of activities, vacationers who are too tired and foot weary to move on will
find tent and trailer sites here. When the stars finally blink out, you'll all be fast asleep. A
family favorite, the Hamburg Annual Arts and Crafts Festival is an event held at the park
the third weekend in September.

Macon

From Mitchell take Highway 102 South to Highway 15 South. Take Highway 68 South
to Highway 57 West to Macon.

Sometimes the backseat crowd gets tired of trekking over hill and dale in pursuit of
off-the-beaten-track adventures and would like to settle down in one spot for a day or
two. Or less-than-ideal weather may drive soggy vacationers indoors. Macon, one of
the most gracious cities in Georgia, is filled with the answers to your prayers. The fresh-
ness of spring is the best time to visit the mid-Georgia city, but any time of year will do.
Spared during the Civil War, the city showcases several significant historic structures.
Known as the City of White Columns and Cherry Blossoms, Macon boasts not only a
profusion of antebellum mansions but also thousands of cherry trees. With 275,000
cherry trees, Macon boasts more than any other city in the world. The nation's capital,

Famous Entertainers from Macon

- **Allman Brothers Band**—rock band
- **Lena Horne**—singer/actress
- **Little Richard Penniman**—rock and roll singer
- **Otis Redding**—one of the fathers of soul music

so well known for its cherry trees, has only 5,000. More recently, with its central location in the state, Macon has attracted the Georgia Music Hall of Fame and the Georgia Sports Hall of Fame, making the city a destination with truly something for everyone in your tribe. Nearby Lake Tobesofkee attracts clans with outdoor play in mind. Begin a visit to Macon at the welcome center at 450 Martin Luther King Jr. Boulevard. At the visitor center, you can purchase package attraction tickets and tour on your own or buy tickets that include a guided trolley tour with admission to some attractions. Sports fans can find something to please aficionados of several sports—Macon is home to several teams, including the Macon Trax hockey team, the Macon Blaze basketball team, and the Macon Knights arena football team. A visit timed to coincide with any one of their games should provide plenty of excitement.

Georgia Children's Museum/First Street Arts Center (ages 3 to 12)
382 Cherry Street; museum (478) 755-9539, arts center (478) 745-3760; www.georgia childrensmuseum.org. Open Tuesday through Saturday 9:30 a.m. to 5:00 p.m.; cafe open Tuesday through Saturday 7:30 a.m. to 6:00 p.m.

Designed just for youngsters, the museum joins the Georgia Music Hall of Fame and the Georgia Sports Hall of Fame to create a museum row downtown near the old Union Terminal Station. Although the museum will eventually have six floors of exhibits, it currently offers the Little Learners Play Area, Theater Works—a black-box theater—and the Lost Parents Café, where parents (and their offspring too) can enjoy ice cream, smoothies, shakes, and various kinds of coffees and teas. With the First Street Arts Center next door, both organizations offer summer camps that explore art, theater, journalism, cooking, creative writing, magic, and more.

Georgia Music Hall of Fame (ages 4 to 12)
200 Martin Luther King Jr. Boulevard and Mulberry Street; (478) 750-8555 or (888) GA-ROCKS; www.gamusichall.com; garocks@mindspring.com. Open year-round, Monday through Saturday 9:00 a.m. to 5:00 p.m., Sunday 1:00 to 5:00 p.m. Adults $$, students with ID and children four to sixteen $.

Let the teenyboppers of today's rock/rap generation tune up at this perpetual music fest. They're sure to find whatever turns them on: rock, jazz, rhythm and blues, gospel, country, or classical. A visit here is good foot-stomping, hand-clapping family fun. Located adjacent to Terminal Station, the hall of fame focuses on Georgia's diverse musical heritage through the tunes and memorabilia of Macon artists, as well as other Georgia greats, such as Augusta's James Brown and Jessye Norman; Athens's R.E.M. and the B-52s; Columbus's "Mother of the Blues," Gertrude "Ma" Rainey; and Monticello's Trisha Yearwood. With new members inducted every year,

Georgia's music makers are so varied that everyone in your band—whether musically challenged or a budding rock star or classical artist—can find something to enjoy. Vintage listening rooms, each filled with memorabilia, instruments, costumes, photos, and other artifacts devoted to a different style of music, provide a feast for the ears. Your budding musicians are the stars at the Billy Watson Music Factory, a highly interactive area dedicated to children ages 4 to 9. Designed to introduce tykes to various aspects of music and to spark their interest in musical instruments, techniques, and styles, the Music Factory features the Giant Radio, where starlets can watch themselves on big-screen television as they dance to the sounds of Georgia music; the World of Music, where they listen to bits of music from the far reaches of the globe; the Big Band, where they can experiment with a giant piano, double bass, violin, guitar, drum, xylophone, and tambourine; and Style Matters, where they can hear traditional tunes such as "Twinkle, Twinkle, Little Star" as they are used to hearing but also played as a jazz, salsa, or symphonic tune. For serious aficionados, audio programs intermix music, artists' interviews, and historical context. The grand finale, an extravaganza of music, lights, and laser video in the Gretsch Theater, is guaranteed to get everyone's toes tapping.

Georgia Sports Hall of Fame (ages 4 to 12)

301 Cherry Street; (478) 752-1585, www.gshf.org. Open year-round, Monday through Saturday 9:00 a.m. to 5:00 p.m., Sunday 1:00 to 5:00 p.m. Adults $$, seniors and children under sixteen $; family package $$$.

Play ball! Take all your sports fans to learn about Georgia's storied athletic heritage, which is showcased at this museum. Exhibits honor heroes from the state's top high school, collegian, amateur, and professional teams as well as individual athletes such as Hank Aaron, Herschel Walker, Fran Tarkenton, Bill Elliott, Edwin Moses, and Jackie Robinson with more sports stars inducted every year. Budding sports superstars will love the interactive displays, such as a NASCAR simulator or those that allow wannabe jocks to kick field goals, shoot hoops, or be a wheelchair paralympian. The state-of-the-art theater designed after ballparks of yesteryear is sure to bring back nostalgic memories for Mom and Dad or Grandma and Grandpa.

Museum of Arts and Sciences/Mark Smith Planetarium (all ages)

4182 Forsyth Road; (478) 477-3232; www.masmacon.com. Call for hours of planetarium shows. The museum is open Monday through Saturday 10:00 a.m. to 5:00 P.M, Sunday 1:00 to 5:00 p.m. Closed New Year's Day, Easter, Fourth of July, Thanksgiving, and Christmas Eve and Day. Adults $$, children two and older $.

Only the bright stars light the way to satisfy little stargazers' curiosity about the heavens at this planetarium, which is part of the museum complex. In addition, the Museum of Arts and Sciences features exhibits and programs as well as live animal shows—all of which captivate every age group. The junior set are particularly awed by the forty-million-year-old whale fossil discovered near Macon. Tykes love the three-story Discovery House with its interactive exhibits, scientists' workshop, audio/visual/textural experiences, and adjacent backyard filled with live animals. After exploring all the displays, if any of you have any energy left at all, stroll through the nature trails on the property and visit the Kingfisher Cabin—the former dwelling and work-shop of Macon author Harry Stillwell Edwards. TGIF can apply to both parents and children as they participate in an evening of fun and activities during Jazz Fridays at the museum. For $8 per person, parents can relax while they enjoy food, refresh-ments, and wonderful jazz musicians. Children participate in their own separate activities for $4 each.

Ocmulgee National Monument (ages 4 to 12)

1207 Emory Highway; (478) 752-8257; www.nps.gov/ocmu. Open daily year-round, 9:00 a.m. to 5:00 p.m. except Christmas and New Year's Days. Free; donations accepted; there is a fee if there is a Native American demonstration going on.

Step through a magical doorway to the ancient past at this 700-acre Native American site, where youngsters and oldsters get an excellent lesson in history and archaeol-ogy. Examine 12,000 years of human habitation in the Southeast. A succession of six distinct Native American cultures is documented, but the major concentration is on the Mississippian civilization that flourished here from A.D. 900 to 1100, leaving several Indian mounds including temple and funeral knolls. Exhibits, designed to kindle the small fry's inquisitiveness and spark their imaginations, include an archaeologically re-created ceremonial earth lodge on the exact spot where it existed 1,000 years ago, a museum, and a movie called *Mysteries of the Mound.* The

earth lodge was a ceremonial building that was a meet-ing place for political and religious leaders. Excavations of an old trading post on the site yielded axes, clay pipes, beads, and weapons, which are displayed in the museum. Several nature trails, including the Opelofa Nature Trail through the lowlands of Walnut Creek, wind through the site as well and should keep an active backseat crowd satisfied. Special weekend events held throughout the year add spice to a visit. Modern-day ghostbusters will want to ask the park rangers about some of the spooky occur-rences that have been reported.

It's Cherry Blossom Time

Macon has more cherry trees than any other city in the nation—including Washington, D.C.

Did You **Know?**

The Texas Lone Star state flag was actually designed by Joanna Troutman in Knoxville, Georgia, in 1835 for Georgians to carry in the volunteer fight to help Texans win independence from Mexico.

Old Cannonball House and Museum (ages 6 to 12) 🏛️ ♿

856 Mulberry Street; (478) 745-5982; www.cannonballhouse.org. Open Monday through Saturday, 10:00 a.m. to 5:00 p.m.; closed Sunday. The last guided tour is at 4:00 p.m. Adults and children six and older $.

Just imagine how captivated your youngsters will be when they see the Yankee cannonball still resting on the floor in the parlor of this 1853 Greek Revival mansion—the only structure in the city hit during an 1864 attack. The cannonball actually smashed through a gigantic column before entering the house. Several rooms are furnished as replicas of chambers at the old Wesleyan College, the first women's college in the country and the home of the first national sororities. You might want to breeze through those rooms if the kids' eyes start glazing over. They'll be more interested in the Civil War artifacts such as officers' uniforms, company flags, swords, and guns, which are displayed in a museum located in an adjacent building that was originally a kitchen and servants' quarters.

Starcadia Entertainment Park (ages 3 to 12)

150 Starcadia Circle; (478) 475-9880; www.starcadia.net. Open Tuesday through Thursday 11:00 a.m. to 6:00 p.m. (arcade, batting cages, and minigolf only); Friday 11:00 a.m. to 9:00 p.m. (some activities don't open until 5:00 p.m.), Saturday 11:00 a.m. to 10:00 p.m., Sunday 1:00 to 6:00 p.m. Admission free; activities priced separately.

After a day of touring museums and historic sites, which may tax the attention spans of little ones, active families can't go wrong here. In addition to a kiddie park, the facility offers miniature golf, a rock wall, a trampoline/bungee jump, go-karts for two levels of experience, batting cages, blaster boats, a video arcade, and food concessions.

Tubman African-American Museum (ages 6 to 12) ♿

340 Walnut Street; (478) 743-8544; www.tubmanmuseum.com. Open Monday through Saturday 9:00 a.m. to 5:00 p.m. Adults and children three and older $.

A visit to Macon wouldn't be complete without a visit to Georgia's largest African-American museum. Named for the Maryland native who created the Underground Railroad that helped slaves escape to the North prior to and during the Civil War, the museum will expose your youngsters to African-American history and culture. Artifacts and art in the seven galleries trace the achievements of African Americans from Africa, through slavery in America, through the civil rights movement, and to the present. Art includes paintings and tapestries from Ethiopia; carved ivory from Tanzania; wooden carvings and household implements from Kenya; masks and wall hangings from Liberia; textiles from Ghana; and masks, musical instruments, and textiles from Nigeria as well as American folk and contemporary art by African Americans. Children get the biggest kick, however, out of the gallery devoted to inventions we're used to using in our everyday lives that were created by African Americans—items such as the lowly eyedropper, linoleum, goggles, oxygen tanks, and the wildly popular Super Soaker. Other collections are devoted to African Americans in the military and African-American memorabilia.

For More Information

Macon-Bibb County Convention and Visitors Bureau, 450 Martin Luther King Jr. Boulevard, Macon, GA 31201; (478) 743-3401; www.maconga.org.

Byron

From Macon take I-75 South to Byron.

Although Georgia has slipped to third place in peach production, it is still known as the Peach State, and Byron—a thriving city with a treasured, small-town, Southern feel—is in the heart of peach country. Be sure to take a picture of the Big Peach Monument. To add to the fun, the Powersville Opry performs every Saturday night.

Byron Depot (ages 6 to 12)

101 East Heritage Boulevard; call the Byron Convention and Visitors Bureau (478) 956-3600 or City Hall (888) 686-3496; www.byronga.com. Tours by appointment. Free.

In the nineteenth century, railroads were the sole reason for the existence of many small Georgia towns, and the heart of these hamlets was the often-fancy station. Your crew can relive the glory days of the railroads at this museum, located in a restored 1870s depot. Get on track by examining the extensive collection of photographs and a variety of railroad and local historical memorabilia. For some all-aboard climbing, the kidlets can hang off the back of the caboose, pretending they're conductors or singing their favorite, "Little Red Caboose Behind the Train."

Fort Valley

From Byron take Highway 49 South to Fort Valley.

Fort Valley is the county seat of Peach County, the heart of peach growing and peach packing in Georgia as well as the "birthplace" of the famous Blue Bird school bus. In fact, the city is known as the Peach Capital of Georgia. During the summer season—mid-May through August—your little Georgia peaches can tour some of the packing plants, buy fresh fruit from numerous stands along the roadside, or experience the fun of picking their own succulent, juicy fruit. For more information about touring the plants, call (478) 825-3733. Moms, dads, and the backseat gang might like to visit **Big Six Farms**, 5575 Zenith Mill Road, the second largest grower in the county, or check out the Tailgate Market held at the Old Byron School Auditorium on Main Street.

Lane Packing Company (ages 4 to 12)

50 Lane Road, Highway 96; (478) 825-3362 or (800) 27-PEACH; www.lanepacking.com; lpc@lanepacking.com. Open during peach season, daily 8:00 a.m. to 8:00 p.m., self-guided tours. Free, guided orchard tour $.

Do fresh peaches magically appear at the grocery store? Not! Find out how the fruit gets from the tree to the store by seeing the fascinating behind-the-scenes operations. Uninformed youngsters (and even some parents) can gain an appreciation of what all is involved in the process by touring this plant. During summer watch 300,000 peaches per hour being individually weighed, counted, separated, and packed using computer-controlled equipment and soft-handling techniques to prevent bruising. Half-hour tram tours of the peach and pecan orchards are available. No doubt, seeing all this fruit will get your taste buds drooling, so while you're there, visit the gift shop and wrap your lips around some homemade peach ice cream or the peach or blueberry cobbler. Make sure to have oodles of napkins.

Peachy **Facts**

A medium-size peach has:

- 40 calories
- 0.6 gram of protein
- 10 grams of carbohydrates
- 1.5 grams of fiber
- 47 units of Vitamin A
- Best of all—*no* fat, cholesterol, or sodium

Whoops!

Fort Valley was named accidentally. The town's name was to be Fox Valley because of all the fox hunting done in the area, but the U.S. Post Office misread the application.

Massee Lane Gardens (all ages) 🍁

100 Massee Lane; (478) 967-2358; www.camellias-acs.org. The grounds and gardens are open year-round, Tuesday through Saturday 10:00 a.m. to 4:30 p.m. and Sunday 1:00 to 4:30 p.m. except February daily 10:00 a.m. to 4:30 p.m. Adults and children twelve and older $.

Camellias (which bloom November through March) are as much a feast for the eye as peaches are a treat for the tongue. For a restful family outing, stop at the historic gardens and national headquarters of the American Camellia Society. Your little blossoms will enjoy roaming the acres of pink, red, white, and varicolored camellias that bloom from fall through spring, but they'll get just as much of a kick out of the other brilliant bouquets that flower throughout the year. Ask your little dirt diggers how the Japanese garden is different from a Western garden, and join them on a ramble around the rose garden, daffodil garden, azalea garden, greenhouse, the Stevens Taylor Gallery, and the Fetterman Museum. Depending on the age of your tykes and their attention span for things in glass cases, the gardens have another claim to fame—the world's largest collection of Edward Marshall Boehm porcelain on public display. The lifelike details created in these birds and flowers are breath-taking and would make an excellent wildlife lesson. At least these hold still, unlike their live counterparts. Constructed just for them, the Children's Garden is not only filled with flowering and nonflowering plants, but whimsical sculptures, a playground, and a play area to dig for "fossils." Mom and Dad can relax on the large swings scattered about the grounds. Among the many activities that keep families coming back to the gardens year-round are the Festival of Camellias, the entire month of February, with the gardens open from 10:00 a.m. to 4:30 p.m., and the Day Lily Extravaganza, the entire month of June, with the gardens open regular hours.

Georgia Trivia

The Fetterman Museum at the Massee Lane Gardens in Fort Valley has the world's largest collection of books about camellias and the world's largest and most complete collection of Edward Marshall Boehm porcelain.

Amazing
Georgia Facts

Fort Valley's Blue Bird Body Company is the largest manufacturer of school buses in the world.

For More Information

Peach County Chamber of Commerce, The Troutman House, 201 Oakland Heights Parkway, Fort Valley, GA 31030; (478) 825-3733; www.peachcountyga.com.

Perry

South of Fort Valley on U.S. Highway 341.

Perry, which was named for naval hero Comm. Oliver Hazard Perry, is a well-known agricultural center and the site of several important fairs, festivals, and horse shows. Centrally located in the state, the city is known as the Crossroads of Georgia.

Georgia National Fair (all ages) 🐘 🎵

Georgia National Fairgrounds, 401 Larry Walker Parkway; (478) 987-3247 or (800) YUR-FAIR (Georgia only); www.gnfa.com. October. Adults $$, children ten and free with a paying adult; additional fee for concerts; camping $.

A ten-day October extravaganza, this family-oriented festival is crammed with enough crowd pleasers to keep any activity-craving brood well satisfied. Make a day of enjoying livestock events, horse shows, youth exhibits, home- and fine-arts competitions, midway rides and games, a circus, and rib-stickin' food. The fun doesn't end when the sun goes down, however. Nights filled with concerts, entertainment, and fireworks finish off a busy day with a bang.

Georgia National Fairgrounds and Agricenter (all ages) 🐘 🎵 🎡

401 Larry Walker Parkway; (478) 987-2774 or (800) YUR-FAIR (Georgia only); www.gnfa .com. Gates open 8:00 a.m. to 10:00 p.m. Call for a schedule of events. Free admission to the grounds; special event prices vary.

This mammoth exhibition facility serves not only as the home of the Georgia National Fair but also as a venue for horse and livestock shows, rodeos, concerts, RV rallies, sporting events, and numerous other special events that attract families in search of fun throughout the year. The parklike setting boasts a fountain, lakes, and gardens, making it an excellent family picnic stop even when no special events are in progress. If some of your crowd are old enough to do some reconnoitering on their own, the sky-piercing clock tower not only gives them no excuse for not meeting up with the rest of the gang on time but also makes a perfect gathering place. When the little ones start nodding off, bed down in the RV park.

Mossy Creek Barnyard Festival (all ages)

Highway 96; (478) 922-8265; www.mossycreekfestival.com. Mailing address: 106 Anne Drive, Warner Robins, GA 31093. Open a weekend in mid-April and another weekend in mid-October, Saturday and Sunday 10:00 a.m. to 5:00 p.m. Adults and children $.

Held in both spring and fall, this award-winning festival features pioneer demonstrations that permit the mod squad to get a glimpse into "The Way It Used to Be." In addition, the popular fair features continuous entertainment with plenty of music, arts and crafts, storytelling, a magical ventriloquist, and mule-drawn-wagon hayrides.

Peach Picking (ages 6 to 12)

Fresh off the tree. During the mid-May to mid-August peach season, several orchards along US 41 north of the city invite passersby to pick their own peaches or buy them from numerous roadside stands. Allow your tiny city slickers the pleasure of picking some of the juicy fruit and tasting it fresh off the tree. They'll surely agree with the oldsters that the ones you pick yourself taste the best. Peach picking (and tasting) can be messy business, so plan accordingly if you don't want the backseat gang to get gummed up with peach juice. Save some fruit for the rest of the trip.

For More Information

Perry Area Convention and Visitors Bureau, 101 General Courtney Hodges Boulevard, Perry, GA 31069; (478) 988-8000; www.perryga.com.

Peachy **Trivia**

- There are 130,000 peach trees in Georgia.
- They produce 250 million pounds of peaches annually.

Warner Robins

From Perry take US 41 North to Highway 247C East.

Warner Robins is Georgia's sixth largest city and the home of Robins Air Force Base, but its major claim to fame with the traveling public is the Museum of Aviation.

Museum of Aviation/Georgia Aviation Hall of Fame (ages 4 to 12)

Highway 247 and Russell Parkway; (478) 926-6870; www.museumofaviation.org. Open daily, 9:00 a.m. to 5:00 p.m. Closed Thanksgiving, Christmas, and New Year's Days. Free.

The fun begins for energetic future aviators at the fastest-growing military aviation museum in the Southeast, where they can alternate between indoor and outdoor exhibits. Currently this museum is the fourth largest aviation museum in the country, with 93 aircraft. It is the second largest museum in the U.S. Air Force. Fly-boy displays focus on World War II, Korea, Desert Storm, Flying Tigers, Black Americans in Aviation, Tuskegee Airmen, and CBI Hump Pilots. Wannabe pilots can imagine the thrill of flying the historic aircraft, such as the F-15A from Desert Storm or the fastest plane on Earth—the SR-71 Blackbird. *Windows to the Distant Past* explores Native American heritage (weekends only). In the We the People Theater and Exhibit Hall, Smithsonian movies about government, history, and the constitution are shown on the largest movie screen in middle Georgia. The Georgia Aviation Hall of Fame, housed at the museum, honors living and dead Georgia military and civilian aviators. Photos, documents, and memorabilia describe the lives of such aviation pioneers as Ben Epps Sr., the first man to fly in Georgia; Jacques Bullard, the first black military aviator; and Robert L. Scott, World War II ace and author of *God Is My Co-Pilot*. Little daredevils can imagine their own picture on display there someday.

For More Information

E. L. Greenway Welcome Center, 99 North First Street, Perry, GA 31099; (478) 922-5100 or (888) 288-WRGA; www.warner robinsga.gov.

Dublin

East of Warner Robins on US 441.

Dublin-Laurens Museum (ages 6 to 12) 🏛️
311 Academy Avenue; (478) 272-9242; www.dublin-georgia.com. Open year-round, Tuesday through Friday 1:00 to 4:30 p.m. or by appointment. Free.

If bad weather gets the better of your best-laid plans for outdoor activities, kids will love dropping by this museum, where exhibits include local photographs, vintage dresses, and other local memorabilia highlighting the history of Native American settlements, nineteenth-century plantations, farmsteads, and churches in this part of Georgia.

Dublin-Laurens St. Patrick's Day Festival (all ages)
(478) 272-5766; www.dublin-georgia.com. March. Prices vary by event.

There's a little bit of Irish in all of us—or at least so it's claimed around St. Patrick's Day. A lavish two-week salute to Irish ancestry, Dublin's festival is the second largest St. Paddy's celebration in the state (after Savannah's). Every year the town is blanketed in green as it welcomes 25,000 to 30,000 visitors to events ranging from a leprechaun contest to cooking the world's largest pot of Irish stew. Super Weekend—the weekend of St. Patrick's Day (or the one immediately following it if the holiday falls during the week)—is crammed with activities your little leprechauns will love: beauty pageants, a parade, hot-air balloons, road races, and square dancing.

For More Information

Dublin-Laurens County Chamber of Commerce, 1200 Bellevue Avenue, Dublin, GA 31040; (478) 272-5766; www.dublin-georgia.com.

Why Does Georgia Have More Counties Than Any Other State in the Nation?

Georgia has 159 counties, but originally there were 162—a couple were merged in the twentieth century. The legislature decided that no one should be more than a half-day's ride on horseback from a county seat so that a person could go there, transact his business, and return home the same day. The legacy of this decision is the magnificent collection of courthouses.

Chauncey

US 441 South to Highway 46 West to Highway 165 South to Chauncey.

Jay Bird Springs (all ages)

1221 Jay Bird Springs Road (off US 341S); (229) 868-2728. **Pool open seasonally; other attractions open Wednesday, Thursday, and Sunday 11:00 a.m. to 8:00 p.m.; Friday and Saturday 11:00 a.m. to 11:00 p.m.; roller skating rink open Friday 7:30 to 11:00 p.m., Saturday 11:00 a.m. to 4:00 p.m., Sunday 1:00 to 5:00 p.m. Games cost $; roller skating $; skate rental $$; in-line skate rental $$; miniature golf $. Cabins and motel rooms $–$$$.**

A great country vacation spot for clean, quiet, family-oriented fun, Jay Bird Springs, located 11 miles southwest of Chauncey, offers diversions suitable to children of all ages. Filled with mineral waters from a natural spring, Jay Bird Springs boasts the oldest public swimming pool in Georgia and the only chemical-free pool in the state. Options are the name of the game here: a 150-foot water slide; miniature golf; a game room with pool tables, air hockey, and video games; softball field; and a roller skating rink. A pleasant place to stay while touring the immediate area, the complex also features cabins, a motel, campsites, a country store, a restaurant, and a picnic area.

Hawkinsville

West of Chauncey on US 341.

If your family, like ours, includes any horse lovers, a special treat awaits you in Hawkinsville, the Harness Horse Training Capital of the South. Up to 500 Standardbred horses, which are either pacers or trotters, from the United States and Canada as well as their drivers and trainers are headquartered in Hawkinsville from fall through April.

Lawrence Bennett Harness Training Facility (ages 4 to 12)

US 129 South; (478) 892-9463. **Fall through spring daily daylight hours. Free.**

A visit to the training facility to watch the magnificent Standardbreds at work pulling sulkies around the track or at rest in their stalls makes a superb fun-filled outing. The best time to see the horses gliding around the half-mile and mile-long red clay tracks is very early in the morning (and we do mean when the sun comes up), but you can wander around the dozen stables and visit with the horses, trainers, and drivers anytime. Bright curious eyes, perked-up ears, and soft velvety noses peek out above the half-doors, inviting your little horsefolk to pet them or take their picture.

Hawkinsville Harness Festival and Spring Celebration (all ages)

Hawkinsville-Pulaski Chamber of Commerce; (478) 783-1717; www.hawkinsvillechamber .org/festival.htm. Early April. Prices depend on activity or event.

Just before the horses return to the North to begin their spring-through-fall racing circuit, they have a trial run on the track of the training facility—a racing event that attracts spectators from all over Georgia and the Southeast. Rich red clay, colorful racing silks, high-stepping equines, flying tails and manes, and whirling sulky wheels bring out the shutterbug in almost everyone. (One of our greatest photographic feats was a picture we took here of a racing horse that proves that all four feet can be off the ground at the same time.) A special treat for horse lovers and fairgoers, the lively festival features not only a day of exciting races but also arts and crafts, food booths, a barbecue cook-off, musical entertainment, and an antique car show.

For More Information

Hawkinsville/Pulaski County Chamber of Commerce, 108 North Lumpkin Street, Hawkinsville, GA 31036; (478) 783-1717; www.hawkinsville.org.

Where to Eat in the Heartland

Athens

Harry Bissett's New Orleans Cafe,
279 East Broad Street; (706) 353-7065;
www.harrybissetts.net. A perennial favorite
dining place in a downtown historic building near the UGA campus, the restaurant
fills up hungry explorers with pasta, veal,
chicken, beef, meat loaf, and seafood.
$–$$

**Café Trumps at the State Botanical
Garden of Georgia,** 2450 South Milledge
Avenue; (706) 542-6359. If the little ones
are starving while you're visiting the garden, you and the munchkins can chow
down on soups, sandwiches, and salads at
the garden's tearoom, located in the conservatory. $

Madison

**Granite Shoals Marina Restaurant,
Lodge and Camping,** 3991 Walkers
Church Road, Greensboro; (706) 453-7639.
Bring the whole gang and fill 'em up with
such specialties as fresh shrimp and catfish
hand-battered and fried to perfection, as
well as steaks, burgers, and sandwiches.
$–$$ The economical lodge offers spacious
rooms—many with a deck with a lakeside
view. Campsites are available as well. $

Juliette

Whistle Stop Cafe, 443 McCrackin
Street; (478) 992-8886; www.thewhistle
stopcafe.com. Let's face it, most folks come
to Juliette to feed their face. They want to
sit down amid all the memorabilia left from
the movie set of *Fried Green Tomatoes* for
a plentiful repast of Southern home cookin'
specialties, including, of course, the famous
fried green tomatoes. $

Milledgeville

Chobys Landing Restaurant, 3090
North Columbia Street; (478) 453-9744. A
must-stop dinner-time eatery, this casual
lakeside restaurant is guaranteed to fill in
your hungry holes with the best catfish
around, piles of fried shrimp, or prime rib.
$–$$

Macon

H&H Restaurant, 807 Forsyth Street;
(478) 742-9810; www.mamalouise.com.
Before the Allman Brothers Band became
famous, they'd buy one gargantuan plate
of soul food and all eat off it. For a fixed
price you get enough meat, vegetables,
bread, and beverage to satisfy even the
most ravenous appetites. $

Nu-Way Weiners, 430 Cotton Avenue;
(478) 743-1368; www.nu-wayweiners.com.
"I'd go a long way for a Nu-Way" has been
said by tens of thousands of people since
the original store opened in 1916. Still in
business, with its original neon sign, the
restaurant sells its famous hot dogs with
the secret-recipe chili sauce as well as
sandwiches, hamburgers, and other fast-
food items. Closed Sunday. $

Fort Valley

Lane Packing Company Gift Shop, GA
96; (478) 825-3592; www.lanepacking.com;
lpc@lanepacking.com. For casual fun and
simple, good food, take the gang here for
all types of sandwiches. Reward good
behavior with ice-cream cones or cobbler—plain or a la mode. If you have a
cooler along, take a pint of ice cream with
you when you hit the road. $

Dublin

Ma Hawkins Restaurant, 124 West Jackson Street; (478) 272-0941. For an ample good-ol'-boy country breakfast or a fixed-price lunch or dinner, you can't beat the good ol' down-home Southern cookin' that's been offered here for more than sixty years. $

Where to Stay in the Heartland

Madison

The Brady Inn, 250 North Second Street; (706) 342-4400; www.bradyinn.com. Bed-and-breakfast accommodations are offered in two cozy, turn-of-the-twentieth-century, antiques-filled cottages connected and encircled by vast rocker-lined verandas. $$–$$$

Other Things to See & Do in the Heartland

- **Dan Magill Tennis Complex and ITA Collegiate Tennis Hall of Fame,** Athens; (706) 542-8064

- **Georgia Museum of Art,** Athens; (706) 542-4662; www.uga.edu/ga museum

- **Taylor-Grady House,** Athens; (706) 549-8688; www.taylorgrady house.com

- **Monastery of Our Lady the Holy Spirit,** Conyers; (770) 483-8705; www.trappist.net

- **Greene County Historical Society Museum,** Greensboro; (706) 453-7592 or (800) 886–5253

- **Old Greene County "Gaol" Jail,** Greensboro; (706) 453-7592 or (800) 886–5253

- **Indian Springs Hotel** (museum), Indian Springs; (770) 775-2493; www.gastateparks.org/info/indspr

- **Old Knoxville Jail and Museum,** Knoxville; (478) 836-3825

- **Hay House,** Macon; (478) 742-8155; www.georgiatrust.org

- **Sidney Lanier Cottage,** Macon; (478) 743-3851; www.historic macon.org/slc.html

Eatonton

Cuscowilla on Lake Oconee, 126 Cuscowilla Drive, (706) 484-9616 or (800) 458-5351; www.cuscowilla.com. The resort community offers Mediterranean lake and lodge villas as well as cedar and pine shake golf cottages with all the modern amenities, which are perfect for families with children. The club features two restaurants, golf, a pool, tennis, walking trails, and a Kids Club with table tennis, foosball, and toys for the small fry. $$$$

Juliette

Dames Ferry Park, 9546 GA 87; (478) 994-7945 or (888) GPC-LAKE. Day-use parking $3. Families who've been crammed in the car will appreciate the value of such a place as this all-service campground on the shores of Lake Juliette. In addition to RV and tent sites, the park offers boat launching facilities. $

Milledgeville

Lake Sinclair Villages, 1000 Marigold Road; (555) 444-1212; www.lakesinclair villages.com. In addition to your own brood, bring grandmas, grandpas, uncles, aunts, and cousins to these lakeside condominiums, which can accommodate them all for a family reunion. A three-night minimum is required. $$$$

Little River Park Campground, 3069 North Columbia/US 441 North; (478) 452-1605; www.littleriverpark.com. RV campsites have all the modern amenities and comforts for your casual home away from home. $

Macon

1842 Inn, 353 College Street; (478) 741-1842 or (800) 336-1842; www.the1842inn .com. Get a taste of the past by staying in the lap of luxury in the antebellum Greek Revival main house or in the Victorian cottage. Breakfast is brought to your room on a silver tray—bet the munchkins never started the day this way at home. $$$$

Lake Tobesofkee Recreation Area, 6600 Mosley-Dixon Road; (478) 474-8770; www.co.bibb.ga.us/LakeTobesofkee. Two campgrounds with 113 campsites. $

Perry

New Perry Hotel and Restaurant, 800 Main Street; (478) 987-1000; www.new perryhotel.com. Both the hotel and restaurant are perennial favorites. Although the hotel was built in 1925, it's called "new" because the original was built in 1870; the newest rooms were added in 1956. The menu in the dining room reads like a tribute to Southern Sunday dinners. Lunch and dinner. Restaurant closed Sunday. Rooms $; meals $–$$$

Hawkinsville

Harness Training Facility Campground, US 129 South; (478) 892-9463. Located on the grounds of the training facility, the campground is pretty well filled with owners and trainers during the fall-through-spring season, so don't just show up without a reservation. $–$$

Trotters Inn, 111 North Warren Street; (478) 783-2914. The downtown motel offers basic accommodations. $–$$

Northeast
Georgia

Head for the hills for mountains of fun for everyone. The "Top of Georgia"—the northeast corner of the state—is a vacation waiting to happen. In the highlands the spirit of discovery is alive and well, and every bend in the road opens up new potential. Any multigenerational expedition to this region promises the very best Mother Nature can offer. Natural beauty abounds, perfect for purifying the

Thalimers'
TopPicks in Northeast Georgia

1. Seeing how life used to be at the Foxfire Museum Village, Mountain City

2. Bucking the rapids on the Chattooga Wild and Scenic River, Clayton

3. Biking along the Augusta Canal, Augusta

4. Exploring the world of science at the National Science Center Fort Discovery, Augusta

5. Watching the birth of a Cabbage Patch Kid at Babyland General Hospital, Cleveland

6. Hiking to spectacular Dukes Creek Falls, Helen

7. Huffing it to the top of Brasstown Bald Mountain, Blairsville

8. Venturing deep into the bowels of the earth at Consolidated Gold Mines, Dahlonega

9. Learning Indian lore at Medicine Bow, Dahlonega

10. Cooling off at Lake Lanier Beach and Water Park, Lake Lanier Islands

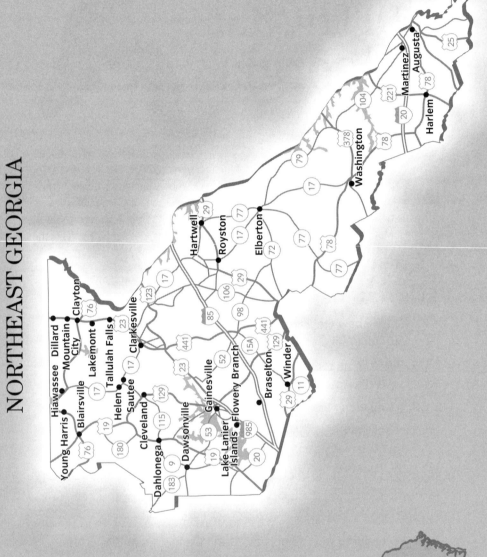

NORTHEAST GEORGIA

Young Harris
Hiawassee
Dillard
Mountain City
Clayton
76
Blairsville
Lakemont
17
Tallulah Falls
23
Clarkesville
17
123
17
Helen
Sautee
129
Cleveland
115
19
180
441
23
Gainesville
52
Dahlonega
9
Dawsonville
53
19
Lake Lanier Islands
985
Flowery Branch
20
183
441
15A
Braselton
129
Winder
11
29
Hartwell
29
Royston
17
77
Elberton
72
77
78
77
17
106
29
98
85
79
378
Washington
17
104
221
78
20
Martinez
Augusta
78
Harlem
25

soul, mind, and body of every member of your brood. Four seasons provide at least four reasons to visit. Halcyon days filled with a profusion of spectacular, wildly wonderful panoramas and an abundance of active outdoor recreational pursuits and wilderness adventures are followed by starlit evenings of hearty dinners at down-home restaurants or around the campfire and then homespun hospitality and quiet comforts at resorts, small inns, bed-and-breakfasts, woodsy cabins, or rustic campgrounds. But this is nothing new. For more than one hundred years, tourists of all ages have flocked to Georgia's northern mountains to escape the heat of the lowlands as well as the hustle and bustle of city life. Vacation-bound folks used to come by train and stay for weeks. Now they flock in by car or RV and may stay as little as a day or as long as the entire summer. Some lucky ones never leave. The pollution-free air and moderate temperatures, coupled with spectacular scenic beauty, numerous glassy lakes, outdoor recreation areas, countless state parks and national forests, boundless sporting opportunities, exceptional fall color, and even occasional soft blankets of snow draw families to the region all year long. Some of the world's best rapids for white-water rafting can be found coursing through northern Georgia's mountain valleys. Everyone isn't an outdoor enthusiast, but those who aren't will enjoy exploring quaint towns, poking through antiques shops, searching for locally made arts and crafts, or browsing through small local history museums—all of which also keep occasional inclement days from being a total loss. The vast region stretches from the state's northern border to the northeastern outskirts of Atlanta and includes the state's only ski resort, a Bavarian village, the birthplace of the Cabbage Patch Kids dolls, and more down-home country cookin' restaurants than you can count.

Dillard

Northeastern Georgia on Highway 246.

Dillard House (all ages) 🍽 😐 🐘 🌲

1158 Franklin Street, Dillard; (706) 746-5348 or (800) 541-0671; www.dillardhouse.com. Meals $–$$, accommodations $$–$$$$; some activities free; others have a fee.

Not just a place to bed down, this year-round mountain resort complex is a perennial favorite with multigenerational travelers. First and foremost is the restaurant. Check your calorie counters at the door before entering. Folks come from miles and miles around just to gorge on the generous helpings of fabulous, farm-fresh, mountain-grown home cooking like Grandma used to fix, served family style. Every table is heaped to overflowing with country ham, country-fried steak, southern fried chicken, pork chops, a dozen vegetables, and much more. Every mouth-watering morsel is prepared from recipes handed down by generations of Dillard House cooks. We have to limit ourselves and the grandchildren so that we'll have room for dessert. No one is allowed to leave the table hungry—that wouldn't be hospitable. Accommodations are offered in the Old Inn—the original Dillard House—as well as chalets, comfortable motel rooms, elegant suites, or cozy cottages that feel like home. One of the chalets will sleep up to eighteen persons. Boasting a one-hundred-year-old working farm and a petting zoo where small, tame beasts can be cuddled and fed, as well as tennis, swimming, horseback riding for children as young as three years old, a waterfall ride and all-day Chattooga Wilderness ride (by special request), an outdoor Jacuzzi, two stocked trout ponds, volleyball, and horseshoe pitching, the Dillard House is always an outstanding place for a family escape.

Notable Georgians

- **Erskine Caldwell**—author
- **Jimmy Carter**—thirty-ninth president of the United States
- **Lewis Grizzard**—humorist, columnist, author
- **Martin Luther King Jr.**—civil rights leader and Nobel Peace Prize winner
- **Gladys Knight**—singer
- **Sidney Lanier**—nineteenth-century poet
- **Margaret Mitchell**—author of *Gone With the Wind*
- **Xavier Roberts**—creator of the Cabbage Patch Kids
- **Sequoyah**—creator of the Cherokee alphabet
- **Ted Turner**—communications mogul and sports franchise owner
- **Joanne Woodward**—Academy Award–winning actress
- **Andrew Young**—former mayor, congressman, and ambassador to the United Nations

Clayton

South on U.S. Highway 441.

Clayton is a mecca for outdoor sports enthusiasts who flock to the area for almost every type of alfresco activity. This section of the Southeast is crisscrossed with trails blazed by Quaker naturalist William Bartram more than 200 years ago. Trekkers can hike approximately 40 well-marked miles of the **Bartram Trail** that wind through northeast Georgia.

Black Rock Mountain State Park (all ages)

3085 Black Rock Mountain Parkway (off US 441); (706) 746-2141 or (800) 864-7275; www.gastateparks.org/info/blackrock. Open daily year-round, 7:00 a.m. to 10:00 p.m. Parking $3; cottages $$–$$$$, camping $.

Tell the gang you're going to see Georgia, North Carolina, South Carolina, and Tennessee without ever leaving Georgia, and then take them to this state park. Known for its mountaintop scenic overlooks, the preserve provides wannabe mountaineers with spectacular vistas of mountain ranges in all four states. On a clear day, junior jaunters can almost see forever—actually 80 miles. If your gang loves hiking, camping, fishing, and having fun in the outdoors, a visit here is sure to please. The highest state park in Georgia (3,640 feet), it was named for its sheer, black biotite gneiss mountain face. A seventeen-acre fishing lake brimming with rainbow trout, smallmouth bass, bream, and catfish is an ideal spot for young anglers. A new wheelchair-accessible pier affords wheelchair-bound fisherfolk very easy access to the water. Hikers are attracted by 11 miles of trails. If you'd like to stay longer, you can lay your sleepyheads down in one of ten fully equipped rental cottages or at the highest campground in the state.

Chattooga Wild and Scenic River (ages 8 to 12)

U.S. Highway 76 East; (706) 782-6097; www.chattoogariver.org.

Daredevils can have a wonderfully wet-and-wild field day while experiencing the heart-pounding excitement of Class II to V white-water rapids on the Chattooga River in the Chattahoochee National Forest. This nationally designated Wild and Scenic River extends 56.9 miles and comprises 39.8 miles designated wild, 2.5 miles designated scenic, and 14.6 miles designated recreational river. During the spring through fall seasons, several outfitters offer guided half-day, full-day, and overnight raft trips on Section III. Section IV, which boasts thirty rapids, is only recommended for advanced rafters. Don't worry about being abandoned after your wild ride down the river. Modern-day voyagers are rescued and returned to their point of origin by bus. Safety is the Thalimer motto, so take note. Because of the dangerous nature of this activity, white water means life jackets and helmets, and some stretches of river are inappropriate for very little would-be rafters. Because there are restrictions on age and size, be sure to check ahead to make sure that none of your intrepid adventurers is disappointed.

Chattahoochee National Forest (ages 6 to 12)

Contact the Chattahoochee-Oconee National Forests in Gainesville at (770) 297-3000; www.fs.fed.us/conf. Always accessible. Free.

Forget civilization and see Mother Nature at her best. This pristine, undeveloped area is laced with wildlife management tracts, recreation areas, and scenic regions. Recreational possibilities for active families include ATVs, mountain biking, horseback riding, hiking, fishing, and camping. The less active can still enjoy leisurely car trips along scenic byways. Although the terrain is extremely rugged, adventure-minded clans will find hunting, fishing, hiking, and primitive camping on the **Coleman River Wildlife Management Area,** Coleman River Road, part of the **Southern Nantahala Wilderness.** Energetic trekkers can hike past large old-growth timber alongside a stream tumbling through high boulders at the **Coleman River Scenic Area,** Forest Service Road 70. Warning: If your brood are all experienced outdoors people, you already know this; if you're not, please check dates for hunting season and restrict recreational hiking during those times.

Mountain Lakes (all ages)

Northeast Georgia's crystal-clear mountain lakes afford numerous family-friendly opportunities for boating, camping, fishing, hiking, and picnicking—all surrounded by spectacular mountain scenery. **Lake Burton,** US 76 or Highway 197, with 2,775 acres and 62 miles of shoreline, offers a public beach and a marina. Although smaller **Lake Rabun,** Lake Rabun Road, has only 835 acres of water and 25 miles of shoreline, its **Rabun Beach Recreation Area,** County Road 10, features not only swimming and boating facilities but also a campground. For camping information call (706) 782-3320. Primitive camping is available at tiny **Lake Seed**—240 acres, 13 miles of shoreline—located off Lake Rabun Road. Minuscule **Tallulah Falls Lake,** US 441, with sixty-three acres and 3.6 miles of shoreline, is a mere sneeze in size. For more information on any of the lakes, call (706) 754-7970.

For More Information

Rabun County Chamber of Commerce and Welcome Center, 232 US 441 North, Clayton, GA 30525; (706) 782-4812 or (706) 782-5113; www.ngeorgia .com (click on Counties, and then select Archives of Rabun County, Georgia, History, Resources, Links, and Events).

Outfitters

These outfitters offer trips on the Ocoee River in Georgia.

- **Nantahala Outdoor Center,** 13077 Highway 19 West, Bryson, NC; (800) 232-7238; www.noc.com; $$$–$$$$

- **Southeastern Expeditions,** 7350 Highway 76 East, Clayton; (800) 868-RAFT; www.southeasternexpeditions.com; $$$$

- **Wildwater, Ltd.,** P.O. Box 309, Long Creek, SC 29658; (864) 647-9587 or (800) 451-9972; www.wildwaterrafting.com; wwltd@carol.net; $$$–$$$$

Mountain City

South on US 441.

Foxfire Museum and Visitor Center (ages 4 to 12)

Information center 2837 US 441 North; Museum, Foxfire Lane; (706) 746-5828; www.foxfire.org/museum.html. Open Monday through Saturday 8:30 a.m. to 4:30 p.m. Closed New Year's Day, Martin Luther King, Jr. Day, Good Friday, Independence Day, Labor Day, Thanksgiving, and Christmas. Information center free, museum $, children ten and younger free.

Youngsters who think they're roughing it if they don't have cable can find out what life was like for the mountaineers who settled the area 150 years ago. From the visitor center you'll be directed to the nearby museum, which is actually a collection of twenty historic and replicated buildings containing artifacts and crafts from early Appalachian life. Cabins, a chapel, a blacksmith shop, barns and sheds, a gristmill, a smokehouse, and other buildings are filled with toys, wagons, tools, and all kinds of handmade and household items. The property also has a scenic nature trail and cabin rentals. Kidlets who are used to video games, cell phones, iPods, Heelies, and hot tubs will marvel at the antique toys, blacksmithing instruments, woodworking tools, shoemaking equipment, and tools needed for hunting, trapping, and farming. One of the wagons was used in the Trail of Tears when Native Americans were forced off the land in north Georgia and sent west to live on reservations.

Believe It **or Not!**

Toccoa Falls is 19 feet taller than Niagara Falls.

Lakemont

South on US 441.

Rabun Beach Recreation Area (all ages) ⊛ ⊛ ⊛ ⊛

5320 Lake Rabun Road; (706) 782-3320. Open mid-April to the end of November, Monday through Friday 7:00 a.m. to 10:00 p.m., weekends until 11:00 p.m. Day-use $; camping $.

If your crew has as many water babies as ours does, this popular day-use beach is a magnet for swimming, boating, fishing, and hiking. The Rabun Beach Trail ends at Angel Falls. If you want to stay longer, there are also campsites.

Tallulah Falls

South on US 441.

Tallulah Gorge State Park (all ages) ⊛ ⊛ ⊛ ⊛

US 441; (706) 754-7970; www.gastateparks.org/info/tallulah. Open daily, 8:00 a.m. to dark. Parking $4; cottages $$; camping $.

You and your offspring can't help but be staggered by the sight of this big hole in the ground—a spectacular gorge carved over time by the river eating its inexorable way through quartzite rock. The view is awesome from gorge overlooks and a suspension bridge: Three falls, the highest of which is 700 feet, plunge to the canyon floor. Several overlooks and a system of trails edge the north rim. Hiking into the ravine, however, is not recommended due to the rugged and treacherous terrain. Twice a year

A Wonder of Georgia

Reputed to be the oldest gorge in the United States, the 2-mile-long, 1,100-foot-deep chasm is second in depth only to the Grand Canyon. Legendary circus patriarch Karl Wallenda once walked a tightrope across Tallulah Gorge.

(the first two weekends in April and the first three weekends in November) Georgia Power releases more water, making the river a tumultuous torrent suitable for advanced white-water kayaking.

The lake, beach, and stream make this park ideal for fishing, hiking, or swimming, but keep an eagle eye on young climbers when you're near the gorge. The danger is obvious to us, but may not be to them. Stop by the interpretive center to see the exhibits and a film about the area. This well-endowed vacation spot features a store, tennis courts, nature trails, more than 20 miles of hiking and biking trails, and a 1.7-mile paved Rails to Trails path, as well as fifty campsites that accommodate tents, RVs, and trailers. Permits are required for hiking to the gorge floor or for rock climbing/rappelling. Pets are not permitted on the gorge floor or trails accessing it, but they are allowed on rim trails. For a budget-minded family on the road, this park can't be beat.

Hartwell

South on Highway 77.

Hartwell Lake (all ages) 🌊 ⛺ 🚣 👫

5625 Anderson Highway; (706) 856-0300 or (888) 893-0678; www.sas.usace.army.mil/lakes/hartwell. Always accessible. Visitor information center open daily 8:00 a.m. to 4:30 p.m. (closed major holidays). Free. Beach use $; boat launching $.

If your brood is into waterborne activities, they won't be satisfied with just one visit to this lake. At 6 miles wide, covering 56,000 acres and boasting 962 miles of shoreline, it's the largest man-made lake east of the Mississippi and not only one of the most popular in the Southeast but also one of the three most popular Army Corps of Engineers lakes in the nation. Fed by two rivers that rise in the Blue Ridge Mountains, the water in the lake is purer than that of many municipal water systems. With a depth of up to 200 feet, it provides a home for more than twenty-one species of fish. The reservoir, part of which is in Georgia and part in South Carolina, offers everything you need for a perfect vacation: more than eighty public park sites, camping, fishing, swimming, boating, picnicking, five marinas, restaurants, an information center, and interpretive services.

The visitor center features displays and information about the lake, including wildlife, water safety, and shoreline management. **Big Oaks Recreation Area,** located next door to the visitor center, offers picnicking facilities, restrooms, a playground, courtesy dock, and boat ramp. There is a $3 boat launching fee. The paved and handicapped-accessible **Hartwell Dam Walking Trail** begins at the visitor center and follows the shoreline 1.37 miles to the Hartwell Dam. Just below the dam is the **Georgia River Recreation Area,** which features picnicking facilities, two fishing piers, and primitive camping.

What's **in a Name?**

The junior set may be amused by a naming tradition in Georgia. The state has the peculiarity of not putting towns in the county of the same or similar name: Lumpkin isn't in Lumpkin County, Clayton isn't in Clayton County. A rarity in Georgia, Hartwell is actually in Hart County. Named in honor of Nancy Hart, a Revolutionary War heroine from this area, Hart County is the only one in the state named for a woman. (Sometime when you're on the road again and the backseat crowd is a little bored, give them a state map and challenge them to find examples of where the county and the town match or don't match.)

Hart State Park (all ages) 🌊 🔺 👫 🦆 330 Hart State Park Road; (706) 376-8756 or (800) 864-7275; www.gastateparks.org/info/hart. Open daily year-round, 7:00 a.m. to 10:00 p.m. Parking $3; cottages $$$–$$$$; camping $.

This state park, which has been a longtime favorite, fills the needs of almost any outdoor lover. Water sports are number one, of course, but there are also hiking and biking trails. Boat ramps and docks offer easy access to the lake. Canoes, johnboats, and pontoon boats are available for rent as well. Gliding silently over the lake is a good method for bird-watching. Back-to-nature types will enjoy the tent, RV, and walk-in campsites; the more comfort-oriented will try to reserve one of the five lakefront cottages. Make your reservations well in advance.

For More Information

Hart County Chamber of Commerce,
31 East Howell Street, Hartwell, GA 30643;
(706) 376-8590; www.hart-chamber.org.

Center **of the World**

Everything is relative. Native Americans not only met at the Cherokee Indian Assembly Ground, which they considered to be the center of their world, for their own councils but also to trade with white settlers. A roadside monument honors the spot.

The Georgia **Peach**

Baseball legend Ty Cobb, who was known in his heyday as the Georgia Peach, won twelve batting titles. Have your baseball fans compare Cobb's feats with current batting phenoms Barry Bonds and Sammy Sosa. There are several memorials to the famous hometown boy around Royston, including the Ty Cobb Museum.

Royston

East on U.S. Highway 29.

Victoria Bryant State Park (all ages) 🌀 🐾 🔺 🏕

1105 Bryant Park Road; (706) 245-6270 or (800) 864-7275, golf (706) 245-6770; www.ga stateparks.org/info/vicbryant. Open daily year-round, 7:00 a.m. to dark. Parking $3; swimming pool $; greens fees $$$$; camping $.

Outdoor enthusiasts belong at this state park, which is surrounded by the rolling hills of the upper Piedmont region. One of only a few of Georgia's state parks that boasts a golf course, these challenging, well-manicured links sport eighteen holes. Anglers enjoy the stocked fish pond, and another fishing pond is reserved for the disabled. A swimming pool and 8 miles of hiking and biking trails round out the amenities. Don't forget to bring some binoculars for your little eagle eyes to do some bird-watching. Travelers who would rather be in the great outdoors will want to make use of the tent, trailer, and RV campsites.

Elberton

Southeast on Highway 17.

What a jewel in the rough. Elberton wasn't even on our list of places to take the family until we got an assignment to write about Georgia's oddities and we heard about the state's Stonehenge. Surprise! Everyone loved this hard-rock town. Elberton is the center of a dynamic granite quarrying industry, so naturally you'll see a lot of granite used in construction and decoration here.

Bobby Brown State Park (all ages) 🔺 🐾 🚣 〰

2509 Bobby Brown State Park Road; (706) 213-2046 or (800) 864-7275; www.gastate parks.org/info/bobbybrown. Open daily 7:00 a.m. to 10:00 p.m. Parking $3. Camping $.

The backseat gang will tumble out of the car in a hurry when the family arrives at this park on the shores of Clarks Hill Lake. There's plenty here to use up lots of pent-up energy: boating, fishing, and two miles of hiking trails. The swimming pool and boat rentals are available seasonally. When it's sleepy time down South, tired campers can lay their heads down at the campground. This park offers yurts (a domed canvas tent on a wooden platform). Mom and Dad might be interested to know that the lake covers the old town of Petersburg. When the water is low, some foundations can be seen.

Elberton Granite Museum and Exhibit

(ages 6 to 12)

1 Granite Plaza (off Highways 17 and 72); (706) 283-2551; www.ega online.com/home/association/museum.shtml. Open year-round, Monday through Saturday 2:00 to 5:00 p.m. Free.

Start the chilluns off on this rock-solid odyssey by watching a film about how Elberton became the Granite Capital of the World. Then your young miners can peruse the displays about granite products and examine antique stone-working tools. Other exhibits explain methods used for quarrying, sawing, polishing, cutting, and carving granite, while still others relate the town's history. Among the unique granite creations is the Confederate statue *Dutchy* (see sidebar). Don't leave without hearing his story.

Georgia Guidestones (ages 6 to 12)

Highway 77 North; no phone; www.thegeorgiaguidestones.com. Always accessible. Free.

Dutchy isn't the only oddity in town by far. Your gang's eyes will bug out when they see this set of gargantuan 19-foot-tall blue granite monoliths connected at the top with capstones sitting alone out in a field. Shades of Stonehenge and the Rosetta stone all in one, the guidestones are carved with a ten-part message for future generations transcribed in twelve languages. The stones appeared mysteriously, and their donor is anonymous.

If you haven't already stopped at the Elberton Granite Museum and Exhibit (previous entry), do so before venturing out to the farmer's field 7.7 miles from town to see the Guidestones. A short video at the museum explains a lot about the Guidestones—how they came to be built, why the site was chosen, something about the mysterious benefactor, and what the various sayings mean. The Guidestone monolith also serves as an astronomical observatory with a sundial—a diagonal hole aligned to Polaris, the North Star, and a slit that marks the sunrise and sunset at the winter and summer solstices. You can also pick up a brochure about the Guidestones at the museum.

The Rise and Fall **of Dutchy**

The first granite statue created in Elberton, it was commissioned as a Civil War memorial. The finished statue of a soldier was met with intense disapproval, being described as a "strange monster . . . a cross between a Pennsylvania Dutchman and a hippopotamus"—hence the name Dutchy. It was also remarked that his hat and uniform looked suspiciously like those worn by the Union. The statue was pulled off its pedestal, lay in state for two days, and then was buried face down—a sign of military disgrace. After eighty-two years, this Rip van Winkle was dug up; a police escort took him to a car wash where decades of Georgia red clay were removed. After some repair, Dutchy resides in the Elberton Granite Museum. Take a picture for show-and-tell.

Richard B. Russell State Park (all ages)

2650 Russell State Park Road; (706) 213-2045 or (800) 864-7275, golf (706) 283-6000; www.gastateparks.org/info/richbruss. Open daily year-round, 7:00 a.m. to 10:00 p.m. Parking $3; Frisbee golf $ (Frisbees provided); golf $$$$; cottages $$$; camping $.

The beach at this park is a popular place from which families can launch a waterborne holiday—tiny tykes can certainly earn their water wings here. The beach swimming area is open year-round (as the rangers say, "Anyone who's crazy enough to swim in February can go for it."), but there are no lifeguards—even in summer. In addition to water sports, the park offers 6 miles of walking trails, two beach volleyball courts, and an eighteen-hole Frisbee golf course. If you haven't tried Frisbee golf, grab the kidlets and give it a try. Even the youngest can play. Whether duffers or experts, families can tee off at the championship eighteen-hole Arrowhead Pointe Golf Course. The course, named for Paleolithic Indians who once lived in the area, skirts one of the state's best boating lakes. The park's facilities, including the swimming beach, are wheelchair accessible. When the sandman comes calling, accommodations are available in seventeen fully furnished and equipped cabins or twenty-eight tent, trailer, or RV campsites.

Hard-Rock Town

Georgia is the number one producer of marble in the United States, and Elberton is known as the Granite Capital of the World. The majority of the production is for gravestones.

Let's **Rock**

The Georgia Guidestones contain the largest granite blocks ever quarried.

- **Overall height:** 19 feet, 3 inches
- **Amount of granite:** 951 cubic feet
- **Total weight:** 119 tons
- **Four upright stones:** each 16 feet, 4 inches tall and 42,437 pounds
- **One center (or gnomon) stone:** 16 feet, 4 inches tall and 20,957 pounds
- **One capstone:** 9 feet, 8 inches long and 24,832 pounds
- **Four support stones (bases):** each 1 foot, 4 inches thick and 4,875 pounds
- **One support stone (base):** 1 foot, 7 inches thick and 2,707 pounds
- **Lettering:** 4,000 sandblasted letters, each 4 inches tall

For More Information

Elbert County Welcome Center, 104 Heard Street, Elberton, GA 30635; (706) 283-5651; www.elbertga.com.

Martinez

South on Highway 104 to Interstate 20, east to Highway 28.

Adventure Crossing (all ages)

4350 Wheeler Road; (706) 863-3087. Open Memorial Day to Labor Day, Monday through Thursday 2:00 to 8:00 p.m., Friday 2:00 to 11:00 p.m., Saturday 10:00 a.m. to 11:00 p.m. Sunday noon to 9:00 p.m. Free admission; each ride or attraction costs $ per person per ride.

If the backseat bunch threatens to gag at one more hiking trail or museum, here's more commercial fun for your horde. The park features the Augusta area's largest arcade, bumper boats, two eighteen-hole miniature golf courses, six amusement rides, three racetracks, batting cages, a carousel, and an indoor playground—enough to satisfy even the most demanding little people from toddler to teen. The small child arcade is in a separate area near the new cafe.

Savannah Rapids Visitor Center (ages 3 to 12)
3300 Evans-to-Lock Road; (706) 868-3349; www.savannahrapids.com. Open Tuesday through Saturday 10:00 a.m. to 4:00 p.m. Free.

The rapids at Bull Sluice mark the fall line between the Piedmont Plateau and the Coastal Plain as well as the end of navigation up the Savannah River from the ocean. A breathtaking view of the rapids is just one of the reasons to visit this park where active families can hike, bike, fish, or set out on a canoe or kayak. From here an 8½-mile trail extends all the way downtown. As an added attraction, the historic lock-keeper's home serves as a visitor center. The bedroom has been re-created, and other exhibits depict the history of Columbia County and describe the significance of the Augusta Canal. A visit here makes a good companion visit to the Augusta Canal Interpretive Center in Augusta.

For More Information

Augusta Visitor Center, 1450 Greene Street, Suite 110, Augusta, GA 30901; (706) 823-6600 or (800) 726-0243; www.augustaga.org.

Georgia State Visitor Information Center—Augusta (access only from I-20 westbound from South Carolina), Martinez, GA 30907; (706) 737-1446.

Augusta

South on U.S. Highway 278/78.

Augusta is the state's second oldest city and the largest in this region. Founded in 1736, only three years after Savannah, Augusta began life as a remote trading post but in one hundred years developed into one of the busiest inland cotton markets in the world. The city served as the state capital from 1783 to 1795. Anyone with even a passing knowledge of golf knows that the renowned Masters Golf Tournament is held here in the spring. It comes as a big disappointment to learn that it's almost impossible to get tickets to watch it, but never fear—there are plenty of other things to do. Begin your visit at the **Augusta Visitor Information Center** (706-724-4067), located inside the Augusta Museum of History at 560 Reynolds Street, to get brochures and advice about what to see in Augusta. Then stay to see the museum (see listing).

All **Aboard**

The first passenger train in the United States ran between Augusta, Georgia, and Charleston, South Carolina.

A Sea of Cotton

When cotton was king, it is said that so many cotton bales surrounded the Cotton Exchange that a child could hop from one bale to another for more than a mile without ever having to touch the ground.

Augusta Canal National Heritage Area (all ages)

Contact: 1450 Greene Street, Suite 400, Augusta 30901; (706) 823-0440 or (888) 659-8926; www.augustacanal.com. Always accessible. Free, except canoe rentals.

For more than one hundred years, the 9-mile canal has provided not only a means of transporting goods but has also served as a source of many outdoor diversions such as canoeing and fishing. In fact, the canal is an ideal spot to introduce first-time fisherfolk to the sport of angling. In addition, the level old towpath that runs alongside the canal provides countless opportunities for hiking, biking, bird-watching, and environmental studies. Bring your own bicycles for some great exercise that even the littlest ones with training wheels can handle.

Augusta Canal Interpretive Center (all ages)

1450 Greene Street, Suite 400; (706) 823-0440/ext.4; www.augustacanal.com. Monday through Saturday year-round 9:30 a.m. to 5:30 p.m., Sunday (March through November only) 1:00 to 5:30 p.m. Adults and children six and older $$. Additonal fee for Petersburg Boat Tours $$$–$$$$ (includes museum admission).

Youngsters can try their hand at all kinds of interactive exhibits at the Augusta Canal Interpretive Center, located in the old Enterprise Mill. They can see working textile looms and learn how canal water makes power. Begin with the film *The Power of a Canal* and then make your way through exhibits that range from a hydropower demonstration turbine that actually operates the paddle fan in the gift shop, to *Braving the Rapids*, *Building the Canal*, *How the Canal Works*, *Mill and Boom Times*, *Hydroelectricity and the Canal*, *Boat Parties and Picnics*, *Workers' Life*, and *New Waters, New Life—The Canal in the Twentieth Century*. Guided canal boat tours are available in season.

Famous Augustans

- **Bobby Jones**—golfer and founder of the Masters Golf Tournament
- **James Brown**—godfather of soul
- **Jessye Norman**—opera diva

Augusta Cutting Horse Futurity and Festival (all ages)

Contact the Atlantic Coast Cutting Horse Association (706) 823-3417; www.augusta futurity.com. Call for a schedule of events. Tickets available from TicketMaster and the Civic Center ($–$$$).

Give your little buckaroos a taste of the old West without having to leave Georgia. Horse lovers will be enthralled by the largest cutting horse competition in the east and one of the top ten in the world. Totally western in flavor, the exciting January event features working bronc competitions, a horse-and-wagon parade, evening shows, and an exposition of cowboy wear and gear.

Augusta Museum of History (ages 4 to 12)

560 Reynolds Street; (706) 722-8454; www.augustamuseum.org. Open Tuesday through Saturday, 10:00 a.m. to 5:00 p.m., Sunday 1:00 to 5:00 p.m. Adults, $$, children $.

Make time travel possible by seeing artifacts from Augusta's past. The museum displays mostly cultural history exhibits about Augusta and the surrounding region from the time of prehistoric Native Americans to the 1970s. Among the star attractions the junior set will get a kick out of are an early filling station with vintage cars pulled up to it, an 1877 fire engine, a horse-drawn hearse, a 56-foot Petersburg boat, and a 1917 steam locomotive. Visitors can clean cotton in a replica cotton gin. Make-believe is what it's all about in the Susan L. Still Children's Discovery Room where they can pack a canoe, sit at the controls of a space shuttle, and dress up and play games of children from throughout Augusta's history.

Georgia Golf Hall of Fame's Botanical Garden (all ages)

1 Eleventh Street; (706) 724-4443; www.gghf.org. Open Tuesday through Saturday 9:00 a.m. to 5:00 p.m., Sunday 1:00 to 5:00 p.m. $

Organize your own scavenger hunt to have the small fry find the life-size bronze sculptures of famous golfers such as Ben Hogan, Bobby Jones, Ray Floyd, Byron Nelson, Jack Nicklaus, and Arnold Palmer scattered throughout the aquatic, Asian, bulb, butterfly, children's, coastal, cottage, formal, gold medal, rose, turf and grass, and xeriscape gardens. The lushly landscaped grounds are peppered with ponds, fountains, and waterfalls. A thoroughly pleasant and relaxing way to spend a few hours.

Water Mania!

Billed as the Water Sports Capital of the World, Augusta is the home of several annual world-class boating events that provide heart-pounding spectator excitement, including the Augusta Spring Regatta, a rowing event, and the Hardee's Augusta Southern National Drag Boat Race, the richest flatbottom boat race in the world of hydroplanes.

Lucy Craft Laney Museum of Black History

(ages 6 to 12) 🖼️

1116 Phillips Street; (706) 724-3526; www.lucycraftlaneymuseum.com. Open year-round, Tuesday through Friday 9:00 a.m. to 5:00 p.m., Saturday 10:00 a.m. to 4:00 p.m., Sunday 2:00 to 5:00 p.m. $

Lucy Craft Laney was born into slavery, but she became one of Georgia's most famous educators. This home, where she lived as an adult, has been transformed into a museum of history and art. Ms. Laney started the first kindergarten for African-American children in Augusta and the first African-American nursing school in Augusta and founded the Haines Normal Industrial Institute. Exhibits focus on Laney's educational legacy as well as the lives of other important local African Americans. Annual exhibits include handmade dolls, quilts, and art created by women as well as traveling exhibits. Be sure to let the young ones expend some energy in the period garden.

National Science Center Fort Discovery (all ages) 🖼️

1 Seventh Street; (706) 821-0200 or (800) 325-5445; www.nscdiscovery.org. Open year-round, Monday through Saturday 10:00 a.m. to 5:00 p.m., Sunday noon to 5:00 p.m. Adults $$, children $.

Your nuclear family can meet the Atom Family at this fascinating science center. A hands-on, kid-friendly place, it offers the perfect opportunity to introduce your little ones to the wonders of science. They'll come out technology fans even if they weren't when they went in. Demonstrations, virtual realities, 250 interactive exhibits, StarLab Planetarium, Martian Towers climbing structure, and a high-tech theater are guaranteed to keep everyone in the family engrossed—even the most blasé preteen. Once the kids (and adults) get involved in the interactive displays, it will be like pulling teeth to drag them away. You can grab a bite at the restaurant and stop in at the science store to stock up on things to keep the backseat gang occupied on the next stretch of your trip.

Phinizy Swamp Nature Park (ages 3 to 12) 🐘 🏛️ 🚶

Lock-and-Dam Road; (706) 828-2109; www.phinizyswamp.org. Open weekdays noon to dusk, weekends dawn to dusk; visitor center open weekends 9:00 a.m. to 5:00 p.m. Free.

Budding naturalists can explore 1,100 acres of swampland, which provide a haven for birds and other wildlife. Bring a bird book and binoculars so that you can hike the miles of trails and boardwalks and climb the observation towers while on the lookout for a variety of wildlife including herons, kingfishers, and red-shouldered hawks as well as tree frogs, bobcats, otters, and alligators.

Confederate **Powder Works**

Located at 1717 Goodrich Street, this 176-foot chimney beside the Augusta Canal is all that remains from the important manufacturer of gunpowder for the Confederate States of America. It is little known that this factory was the only permanent structure begun and completed by the short-lived Confederacy.

For More Information

Augusta Metropolitan Convention and Visitors Bureau, 1450 Greene Street, Suite 110, Augusta, GA 30901; (706) 823-6600 or (800) 726-0243; www.augustaga.org.

Augusta Visitor Information Center (at the Augusta Museum of History), 560 B Reynolds Street, Augusta, GA 30901; (706) 724-4067 or (800) 726-0243; www.augusta ga.org.

Harlem

East on US 78.

Laurel and Hardy Museum of Harlem (ages 2 to 12)

250 North Louisville Street; (706) 556-0401 or (888) 288-9108; www.laurelandhardy museum.org. Open Tuesday through Saturday 10:00 a.m. to 4:00 p.m. (closed major holidays).

Even kids who never heard of the famous comedy team Laurel and Hardy will fall down laughing at the duo's antics in the vintage silent black-and-white films shown at the museum. Oliver Hardy, the more rotund of the two, was born in Harlem in 1892. In 1989 the town began an Oliver Hardy Festival to keep Hardy's legacy alive; the

Haunted **Pillar**

Located at Fifth and Broad Streets, this is all that is left after a minister put a curse on the old marketplace. As the story goes, he was a traveling street preacher who was refused permission to sermonize there and ordered to leave the premises. He flew into a rage and declared that the marketplace would be destroyed. In 1878 a cyclone demolished all of the building except this one pillar. Bad luck is said to come to whoever touches it. The pillar has resisted all attempts to move it from its location on a public sidewalk.

festival is now held the first Saturday of October, with crafts, a carnival, entertainment, a parade, movie mania, and a street dance. Imagine the little ones' amazement as they see dozens of Hardy look-alikes vying to be the winner of the Look-Alike Contest. The many items of Hardy memorabilia the town has accumulated eventually demanded their own museum, and the old post office now serves that purpose. Stop by for a laugh. It will brighten your day.

Washington

Northeast on US 78.

Aonia Pass (ages 4 and up) 🚲 Ⓐ

Georgia Motorplex, 3030 Thomson Road; (706) 678-3737; www.aonia-pass-mx.com. MX and Pee-Wee track open daily at 10:00 a.m. for practice except during event weeks or event weekends. Practice fee $20; camping $.

What adventurous little boy (or girl or mom or dad for that matter) hasn't dreamed of cutting loose on a dirt bike? Here's a place where the smallest ones can watch and older ones can actually try out the wild-and-wooly sport. During several events, off-road racers come from all over the world to compete for money and other prizes. In 2003 Aonia Pass held its first annual Grand National Cross Country Series. Families can bring tents, RVs, or trailers and make it a home away from home. Aonia offers hot showers, plenty of restrooms, concessions, and more.

Callaway Plantation (ages 4 to 12) 🏛 ⓒ

2160 Lexington Road/US 78 West; (706) 678-7060; www.callaway.washingtongeorgia .net. Open year-round, Tuesday through Saturday 10:00 a.m. to 5:00 p.m., Sunday 12:30 to 3:30 p.m. Closed Thanksgiving, Christmas, and New Year's Days. Call for a schedule of special activities. $

The whole clan can take a trip back in time to see what early life in Georgia was really like by visiting this working plantation. Three preserved homes illustrate life in three periods of history. First you can explore the redbrick Greek Revival manor house, which was built in 1869 and remains virtually unchanged. The two-story, four-room Federal Plain–style frame residence was built about 1800 as the home of two-time governor George R. Gilmer. Tykes are even more curious about the hand-hewn log cabin. Built in about 1785, the crude hut probably served as a temporary residence while a more permanent one was under construction. The cabin features one room and a loft and contains primitive furniture and early domestic and agricultural tools. If the younger kiddies aren't into historic homes, you might want to let them play outside (with supervision) while the rest of you tour the houses. Outbuildings were necessary to run a farm. Several examples include a barn, corn crib, smokehouse, blacksmith shop, pigeon house, and schoolhouse. Special events include Mule Days in October and Christmas at Callaway.

Second Time Around Mini Farm (all ages)

146 Hendry Lane (706) 678-4902; www.secondtimearoundminifarm.com. Call for hours. Adults $$, children $.

A visit to this small farm gives animal lovers of all ages an opportunity to get up close and personal with a variety of friendly farm animals. Even tiny tykes can hand-feed potbellied pigs and goats, rub noses with an Old English Baby Doll sheep or a llama, get a leg up on a miniature Bethlehem donkey, or have a conversation with Mo, the African scarlet macaw. (*Note:* The facility is looking for larger property and will be moving, so be sure to call ahead.)

Washington Historical Museum (ages 6 to 12)

308 East Robert Toombs Avenue; (706) 678-2105; www.museum.washingtonga.net. Open Tuesday through Saturday 10:00 a.m. to 5:00 p.m., Sunday 12:30 to 3:30 p.m. Closed Thanksgiving, Christmas, and New Year's Days $.

You won't have to drag the kidlets in kicking and screaming, but they might not be as enthusiastic as you'd like. Once inside this antebellum mansion, however, they'll be fascinated by the Confederate gun collection and the Native American artifacts.

For More Information

Washington-Wilkes Chamber of Commerce, 228 West Square, Washington, GA 30673; (706) 678-5111; www.washington wilkes.com.

Winder

Southeast on Highway 11.

Fort Yargo State Park (all ages) ⓧ △ ▱ ⓒ

210 South Broad Street; (770) 867-3489 or (800) 864-7275; www.gastateparks.org/info/ ftyargo. Open daily year-round, 7:00 a.m. to 10:00 p.m. Parking $3; boat rental $ per hour; cottages $$$; camping $.

A chip off the old block, this park is not just a playground but also a favorite environmental, historical, and recreational opportunity for the whole family. Its log fort, or blockhouse, was built in 1792 by settlers for protection against Creek and Cherokee Indians. A lake with a beach, boating facilities, rental boats, fishing, miniature golf, and 15 miles of nature trail provide diversions for everyone. The park is unique in that it caters to the disabled; Will-a-Way Recreation area features wheelchair-accessible cottages and a swimming pool exclusively for their use.

For More Information

Barrow County Chamber of Commerce, 6 Porter Street, Winder, GA 30680; (770) 867-9444; www.barrowchamber .com.

Braselton

North on Highway 53.

Château Élan Winery and Resort (all ages) ◉ ◒ ⓦ

100 Tour De France; (800) 233-9463; www.chateauelanatlanta.com. Self-guided winery tours Monday through Friday 10:00 a.m. to 6:00 p.m.; guided tours Saturday 10:00 a.m. to 6:00 p.m. Self-guided tours free, $5 to taste four wines; guided tours $5 and includes tasting. Gift shop open daily 10:00 a.m. to 9:00 p.m. Restaurants $–$$$$; lodging $$$$.

A loaf of bread, a jug of wine, and thou (and thou and thou). Imagine a tot's or preteen's surprise when he or she sees a replica of an eighteenth-century French

chateau popping up in a field alongside I-85. Turn off and find out all about it. The romantic castlelike structure houses the wine-making operations of the Château Élan Winery. Everyone in the family can enjoy the tour explaining how wine is made; parents can then sip some of the medal-winning wines. In addition, the chateau contains a museum, a gift shop in the form of a French street market, and several restaurants. Adjacent to the chateau is a luxurious inn, and in a smaller chateau is a European health spa. Other amenities at the resort include gift and pro shops, nature trails, seasonal concerts, three championship eighteen-hole golf courses, a par-3 course, a driving range, tennis courts, swimming pools, and an equestrian and canine center. In other words, you can't be bored here.

Seven miles of all-purpose bike trails meander through the 3,500-acre property. Quiet nature trails wander through forests, around the equestrian center, past the vineyards, along the championship golf courses, and through the exclusive residential community. Bikes are brand-new Mountain Comfort models from Georgia's own Adventure Cycles. A multistory climbing wall and ropes course are available to guests on weekends (reservations required).

As if that's not enough, during the year the chateau comes alive with special events. You never have to leave the property to sample a variety of cuisines and price ranges. There's casual bistro dining at Cafe Élan and prix fixe gourmet dining at Le Clos—both in the winery; casual, healthful spa dining at Fleur-de-Lis in the spa; cafe dining in the Versailles Room at the inn; traditional Irish pub grub in Paddy's Irish Pub—our favorite; and light fare at the golf clubhouse. Treat the family to a luxurious—although pricey—weekend at the resort's elegant hotel.

Mayfield Dairy Visitor Center and Plant Tour (ages 4 to 12)

1160 Broadway Avenue; (888) 298-0396; www.mayfielddairy.com. Visitor center open Monday through Friday 9:00 a.m. to 5:00 p.m., Saturday 9:00 a.m. to 2:00 p.m. Closed Sunday. Plant tours on Monday, Tuesday, Thursday, and Friday every half hour; Saturday, every hour. No tours on Wednesday. Free.

I scream, you scream, we all scream for ice cream. Folks around the South are almost as familiar with the commercials featuring Scottie Mayfield and Maggie the cow as they are with the yellow milk jugs that hold Mayfield milk and with the tasty ice-cream products produced by the dairy. At the visitor center you can watch a video about the dairy and its products, go on a plant tour, and finish up with something delicious back in the welcome center.

Clarkesville

North on Highway 197.

Moccasin Creek State Park (all ages) 🦆🏕️

3655 Highway 197; (706) 947-3194 or (800) 864-7275; www.gastateparks.org/info/moccasin. Open daily year-round, 7:00 a.m. to 10:00 p.m. Parking $3; camping $.

Fisherfolk of all ages love this park located on the shores of Lake Burton—noted for its outstanding trout fishing. A special stream fishing section reserved for angling by physically challenged visitors as well as children younger than twelve and senior citizens is an ideal place for grandparents and grandchildren to do some bonding. Boating and waterskiing are permitted; the only drawback is that there are no swimming areas. A playground, a 1-mile interpretive trail with a wildlife observation tower, and a 2-mile hiking trail please non-anglers. Johnboats and canoes are available for rental seasonally.

Panther Creek Recreation Area–Chattahoochee National Forest
(ages 8 to 12) 🚶

Old US 441; (706) 754-6221; www.fs.fed.us/conf. Open year-round, daylight hours. Parking $2.

High-country adventurers will have to do some real hiking to gaze on spectacular 80-foot **Panther Creek Falls**. It's a 5.5-mile hike one-way, so although it's well worth the effort, this is not a trek you'll want to make with a small child who's likely to get tired and want to be carried. The recreation area features picnic facilities. Fishing is a popular pastime.

For More Information

Habersham County Chamber of Commerce, 668 Clarkesville Street, Cornelia, GA 30531; (706) 778-4654 or (800) 835-2559; www.habershamchamber.com.

The Real **Big Apple**

New York may be known as the Big Apple, but the world's largest apple monument is found in Cornelia's town square outside the railroad depot. Dedicated to area apple growers, the monument weighs an astounding 5,200 pounds. This is definitely a photo op for the scrapbook.

Cleveland

West on Highway 115.

BabyLand General Hospital (all ages) 🖼🔒

73 West Underwood Street; (706) 865-2171; www.cabbagepatchkids.com. Visiting hours are Monday through Saturday 9:00 a.m. to 5:00 p.m. and Sunday 10:00 a.m. to 5:00 p.m. Visits are free; adoption fees for dolls vary from $$ to $$$$.

The moment a kidlet steps into the "hospital," he or she enters a whimsical, magical world of make-believe where the Kids are delivered from Mother Cabbages by licensed Cabbage Patch doctors and nurses and then placed for adoption. When they hear, "There's a cabbage in labor," your little people can let their imaginations run wild as they pass through the father's waiting room, nursery, preemies nursery, bus to Babyland Elementary, a classroom, cafeteria, playground, and finally the Moody Hollow General Store. Each Kid lives for the moment when some child adopts him or her into a loving home. Even adolescents who don't play with dolls can't help but be charmed here. Warning: You'll almost surely end up adopting a Kid. Note: The facility will be moving, so be sure to call first.

Gold 'n' Gem Grubbin' Mine (ages 4 to 12)

75 Gold Nugget Lane; (706) 865-5454; www.goldngem.com. Open daily, 9:00 a.m. to 6:00 p.m. (off season 5:00 p.m.) $$ per bucket; fishing $; camping $.

Your gang can try their luck as gold or gem prospectors at this mine. Kids love learning how to pan with their very own bucket. Whatever they find, they get to keep. Between spring and fall you can also tour the operating mine. If you need to take a break from gold mining, try your luck on the stocked Golden Pond or in historic Town Creek. When exhaustion hits, tent and RV sites await.

For More Information

White County Chamber of Commerce, 122 North Main Street, Cleveland, GA 30528; (800) 392-8279 or (706) 865-5356; www.whitecountychamber.org.

Born Under a Cabbage Leaf

Cleveland is the home of the original BabyLand General Hospital, birthplace of the world-famous, one-of-a-kind, soft-sculpture Cabbage Patch Kids, the brainchildren of local resident Xavier Roberts. Some of the original 1970s Kids now fetch up to $25,000.

Sautee

North on Highway 75.

Old Sautee Store (ages 4 to 12)

2315 Highway 17; (706) 878-2281 or (888) 463-9853; www.sauteestore.com. Open year-round, Monday through Saturday 10:00 a.m. to 5:00 p.m., Sunday noon to 5:00 p.m. (closed Wednesdays in January and February.) Free.

The real thing, this 135-year-old store/museum lets your kidsters delve back into history. Hundreds of old-time items aren't for sale, with its old store fixtures, antique posters, and merchandise from yesteryear, the store conveys a bygone way of life. But now the store sells "new" general store items such as old-time candy, specialty foods, housewares, gifts, apparel, and jewelry.

Stovall Covered Bridge (all ages)

Highway 255; no phone; www.georgiahistory.com/stovallmill.htm. Always accessible. Free.

Cross this bridge when you come to it. Don't leave the valley without stopping to photograph Georgia's smallest covered bridge. Built in 1895, it is only 33 feet long and one span wide. Your little shutterbugs won't even need a panoramic camera or wide-angle lens to immortalize this one for the vacation scrapbook. Ask your little time travelers to close their eyes and imagine the clatter of the horses' hooves as they passed over the loose board flooring of the bridge from yesterday.

Why were they called
covered or "kissing" bridges?

They were enclosed so that horses wouldn't be spooked by passing over a deep chasm or a thundering stream. These spans were affectionately known as kissing bridges because a young couple could steal a kiss inside away from prying eyes.

Helen

North on Highway 75.

Tiny travelers will crow with delight when your crew pulls into the alpine village of Helen. They'll think they've been carried off to a fairytale German or Swiss village, and they won't want to return to reality. Chalets, cobblestone alleyways, and shopkeepers dressed in lederhosen and dirndls create old-world charm. Bavarian favorites such as schnitzel, rouladen, and strudel are served in the many restaurants. More than 200 specialty and import shops purvey Swiss and German merchandise. The newest additions to the shopping scene are factory outlet stores selling everything imaginable. Mom can shop to her heart's content, knowing that the rest of the family can find plenty of other things to occupy themselves. Street entertainers may include jugglers, musicians, and face painters. You may even find yourself recruited to participate in an impromptu maypole dance. The yearly calendar is loaded with more than thirty-five special events. During Oktoberfest and the height of leaf season (late October/early November), Helen is very crowded and traffic can seem as bad as what you left home to get away from, so avoid it altogether or plan accordingly. At those times, don't expect to spend the night without a prepaid reservation with a minimum stay required, and anticipate lines at the restaurants. **Horne's Buggy Rides** (706-878-3658) offers horse-drawn carriage tours.

Alpine Amusement Park (all ages)

419 Edelweiss Strasse; (706) 878-2306; www.helenga.org/alpineamusementpark. During the summer months the park is open daily from 1:00 to 11:00 p.m.; during fall and spring it is open on weekends, Saturday 1:00 to 11:00 p.m. and Sunday 1:00 to 8:00 p.m. Closed November to March. $

Take a magical ride on the Big Wheel, the park's 40-foot Ferris wheel, or on any of the other exciting rides: go-karts, bumper boats, tilt-a-whirl, and kiddie rides. And if that's not enough, the park features miniature golf and arcade games. You'll probably have to set a time limit, or you'll be here forever.

Alpine Extreme Speed (ages 8 to 12)

115 Escowee Drive; (706) 878-8404; www.rememberwhentheatre.com. Call for hours. One race $, three races $$$.

Speed and the roar of zooming motors exert an irresistible attraction to today's fast-track youngsters. They can experience the thrills without the danger at this indoor go-kart track. For those who'd like a somewhat more sedate play time, the facility offers a ten-game arcade center and pool tables.

A Thalimer **Adventure**

Our eldest daughter, Elaine, is a sucker for animals—no matter how inappropriate. Once when we were visiting the Helen area, she was bottle-feeding a lamb she'd rescued and was, therefore, reluctant to leave it at home. So here we were, hiking down to the base of Dukes Creek Falls and back with a lamb still not too steady on its legs. From time to time we'd have to take turns picking it up and carrying it. What amused us most was that folks would stop and ask us what kind of dog it was, could they pet our dog, or could they have their picture taken with our dog. We wondered what planet they were from. Obviously some city slickers have spent their entire lives in the concrete jungle and apparently haven't even looked at many pictures of farm animals.

Anna Ruby Falls (ages 4 to 12) 🧒 🌿

Highway 356; Contact the Chattooga Ranger District of the Chattahoochee-Oconee National Forests (706) 754-6221; www.fs.fed.us/conf/press/arf-hours.htm. Open year-round, summer 9:00 a.m. to 8:00 p.m.; spring and fall closes at 7:00 p.m., winter closes at 6:00 p.m. Admission $.

Make exercising a pleasure by hiking to a double waterfall high on the slopes of Tray Mountain in the Chattahoochee National Forest. Two creeks, the Curtis and the York, flow parallel to each other, dropping as side-by-side cascades. Curtis Falls plummets 150 feet, while York Falls plunges only 50 feet. A 0.5-mile round-trip paved path easy enough for little legs and seniors past their prime leads from the visitor center to the overlook. The Lion's Eye Nature Trail is designed for the visually and mobility impaired.

Black Forest Bear Park and Reptile Exhibit (all ages) 🐻

8160 South Main Street; (706) 878-7043; www.blackforestbearpark.com. Open in summer daily 10:00 a.m. to 6:00 p.m. with hours extended to 7:00 p.m. on Saturday; shorter hours the remainder of the year; closed January through the first weekend in March. $

Let's go hunt bear. A visit to this facility offers families the opportunity to go on a bear hunt—only with a camera instead of a gun. Covered walkways for visitor observation are suspended over the bear enclosures where the nineteen star inhabitants (seventeen adults and two cubs) enjoy swimming pools and climbing trees. Bears in residence include American black, cinnamon black, grizzly, Himalayan, and Syrian brown bears. Visitors can purchase trays of apples, lettuce, and bread to toss down to the bears who will often do tricks for treats. Some slithery snakes also make their home here including the Eastern diamondback rattler and the canebrake or timber rattler. Be on hand for the snake feedings at 3:00 p.m. on Wednesdays.

Charlemagne's Kingdom (all ages) 🛝

8808 North Main Street; (706) 878-2200; www.georgiamodelrailroad.com. Open daily year-round, 10:00 a.m. to 6:00 p.m. (winter hours shorter). Adults and children five and older $.

See the Old World in a new way at this museum. A favorite for all ages, this fascinating exhibit provides an educational and unique trip through a miniature Germany. Stretching from the North Sea to the Alps, the realistic display re-creates the nation with an accurate topological landscape, bridges, autobahns, towns, villages, lakes, and rivers. This isn't just any tabletop display, mind you, but includes mountains 22 feet tall and two levels of viewing—you can actually walk through the country amid 300 buildings, more than 400 feet of HO-scale railroad track, a model railroad with computerized trains, and 800 painted figures. Tykes love the six wooden 4-foot German dancers, which perform at the Glockenspiel in the Gingerbread House three times a day.

Chattahoochee Stables (ages 4 to 12) 🐎

2180 Highway 17; (706) 878-7000. Open daily year-round, 10:00 a.m. to 6:00 p.m. Closed Christmas Day. $$$$ per person.

Young buckaroos can get a taste of cowpoke adventure and create some memories on a one-hour, 3.5-mile horseback ride on this 143-acre ranch located in the beautiful Sautee Nachoochee Valley in the foothills of the north Georgia mountains. Along the way, you city slickers can see lush scenery and perhaps some wildlife brave enough to peek out to watch these strange passersby. All rides are guided by local young people who are trading their time for a chance to ride, so if you feel that your guide has done a particularly good job, don't hesitate to offer a tip. All ages can ride, with no weight limits. Very young cowboys and girls can ride double with a parent. Reservations are suggested but not required.

Dukes Creek Falls and Recreation Area (ages 6 to 12) 🚶 🌿

Highway 348; (706) 754-6221. Open year-round, 8:00 a.m. to 10:00 p.m. Free.

It's all downhill on the steep one-half-mile hike to the base of the falls, which plummets 150 feet into a scenic gorge from the towering cliff above. Don't worry, though; the path is a series of switchbacks, so it's not straight down. Despite its name, the falls themselves are actually on Davis Creek at its confluence with Dukes Creek. The first section of trail is wheelchair accessible to an observation deck that permits a view of the falls. At the foot of the falls, three more observation decks have been built along a boardwalk. Although the new configuration is probably safer for all concerned—especially the tykes—we miss the good old days when we could clamber out onto the huge boulders in the center of the stream for sunbathing or a picnic. After a memorable afternoon, the only problem is that it's all uphill on the return to your car, so don't take small children who are likely to get tired and cranky and demand to be carried.

Haunted Helen (ages 6 to 12)

115 Escowee Street, call the Remember When Theatre (706) 878-SHOW; www.haunted helen.com. Open year round Friday and Saturday 4:00 to 10:00 p.m., Sunday 1:00 to 6:00 p.m. Adults $$$, children $$.

Grab the hand closest to you and hold on tight for this trip through a haunted realm where hi-tech sound and animatronics "Scare the Yell Out of You." Macabre figures tell the story of the Mound Builder (ancient Native Americans) curse concerning the search for gold on the Golden River. Just try to get through without screaming.

Helen Tubing and Helen Water Park (ages 3 to 12) 🌊

9917 Highway 17 North; (706) 878-PINK; www.helentubing.com. Open Memorial Day to Labor Day daily 9:00 a.m. to 6:00 p.m. Adults $$$, children $$.

The sight of bathing-suit-clad folks on pink inner tubes floating down the river alongside the highway is guaranteed to get your backseat bunch to yell for you to pull over. When there's good depth and flow to the river, a river float trip is a great way to spend an afternoon. When the river's low (or just because), families enjoy the four waterslides and the 1,000-foot lazy river at the waterpark.

Remember When Theatre (ages 8 to 12) 🎵

115 Escowee Drive; (706) 878-SHOW; www.rememberwhentheatre.com. Shows Saturday at 8:00 p.m. (once monthly in the winter). Adults $$$, children $$.

Elvis has not left the building. In fact, anyone of any age who enjoys the King's music will have a foot-tapping, hand-clapping good time at Mark Pitt's Tribute to Elvis. Mark has portrayed the King all over the world. Ladies will swoon if they're lucky enough to capture a scarf; the kiddies love the teddy bears.

Unicoi State Park and Lodge (all ages) 🚶 🍴 ⛺ 🍽️

1788 Highway 356; (706) 878-2201 or (800) 864-7275, lodge (800) 573-9659; www.ga stateparks.org/info/unicoi. Open daily year-round, 7:00 a.m. to 10:00 p.m. Parking $3; lodge and cabins $$-$$$$; camping $; meals $-$$$.

In addition to 1,081 acres of forestland, this popular park offers a lake with a beach, canoe and pedal boat rentals, 12 miles of hiking trails, 8 miles of mountain biking trails ($2 trail fee), fishing streams, lighted tennis courts, and children's playgrounds. If your brood loves the out-of-doors but finds roughing it a little too demanding, stay in the comfort of the one-hundred-room lodge or a rental cottage. The lodge's restaurant serves three meals daily at economical prices. Mom will appreciate the gift shop, which showcases handmade quilts and local pottery.

For More Information

Greater Helen Chamber of Commerce, 43 Helen Street, Helen, GA 30545; (706) 878-1619; www.helenchamber.com.

Helen Welcome Center/Helen-White CVB, 726 Brucken Strasse at Edelweiss, Helen, GA 30545; (800) 858-8027; www.helenga.org.

Hiawassee

North on Highway 17.

Most visitors come to Hiawassee for water sports on Lake Chatuge, a 7,000-acre TVA lake, and for hiking in the Chattahoochee National Forest, but in August folks come from miles around and even from neighboring states for the Georgia Mountain Fair.

Funworld at Fieldstone (ages 3 to 12) 🏅

1159 Jack Dayton Drive, Hiawassee; (706) 896-7777; www.funworldga.com. Open 3:00 to 9:00 p.m. Monday through Thursday, 3:00 to 11:00 p.m. Friday, 10:00 a.m. to 11:00 p.m. Saturday, 1:00 to 8:00 p.m. Sunday. Two hours unlimited play $16.95, three hours $24.95, all day $29.95, or pay per play.

Heaven forbid there should ever be a rainy day when you're on vacation, but just in case the unthinkable happens, it's good to know that there's a world of fun awaiting at Funworld—an 83,000-square-foot indoor games and activity center featuring 120 arcade games, laser tag arena, miniature golf course, Slick Track go-kart racing, a four-face rock-climbing wall, batting cages, and Toddler Town with a foam factory, inflatables, and more. If all this activity makes everyone hungry, there's a pizza parlor and an ice cream shop. Adjacent to Funworld is Cinemas Six, a complex with six theaters, stadium seating, and surround sound.

Georgia Mountain Fair/Fred Hamilton Rhododendron Garden
(all ages) 🔒 🍴 🎵

1311 Music Hall Road off US 76; (706) 896-4191; www.georgia-mountain-fair.com. Open Monday through Saturday 8:30 a.m. to 9:00 p.m., Sunday 1:00 to 7:00 p.m. Parking $2; $$ covers everything except food and merchandise; children younger than ten free.

You can hardly top a country fair for memory-making family fun. Little squirts (and let's admit it—grown-ups, too) are enthralled by demonstrations of pioneer skills such as blacksmithing, log splitting, and moonshine stilling. Illustrations of such mountain crafts as woodcarving, pottery making, candle making, and quilting bring folks flocking to the nearly monthlong celebration. Held each August, the fair also features food booths, clogging, and entertainment by Nashville headliners. In the spring stroll along the hillside and lakeside trails to see 3,000 rhododendrons, azaleas, and wildflowers.

Such a wonderful facility can't go to waste the remainder of the year. Many other events are held at the site on **Lake Chatuge** throughout the year, so be sure to check ahead to see what else may be happening during the time you're in the area. Just a few events include the Rhododendron Festival, Bluegrass Festival, Country Music Super Stars Concert Series, and the Georgia Mountain Fall Festival.

Young Harris

West on US 76.

Brasstown Valley Resort (all ages) 😊 😊 😊

6321 US 76; (706) 379-9900 or (800) 201-3205; www.brasstownvalley.com. Accommodations $$$–$$$$.

Although there are oodles of activities within close driving range, families may decide not to leave the property once they settle in. With two restaurants (the Dining Room and McDivots), lobby lounge, 7,100-yard championship Scottish links–style golf course, tennis center with lighted courts, health spa with exercise equipment, indoor/outdoor pool, interpretive hiking trails, stables, and trout fishing, you'll have a hard time fitting everything in. Cradled in a 503-acre forest preserved as a bird sanctuary, the site of the inn was a Cherokee Indian village 10,000 years ago. Acclaimed as a prototype of an "environmentally correct" retreat, the resort carefully preserved the ecological and cultural integrity of the land. Modern, well-appointed accommodations are offered in the hotel or in eight secluded four-bedroom cottages with fully equipped kitchens.

Brasstown Valley Resort Stables (ages 2 to 12) 😊

6321 US 76, (706) 379-9900/ext. 2642; www.brasstownvalley.com. Stables open Wednesday through Sunday 9:00 a.m. to 5:30 p.m.; rides depart at 10:00 A.M, 12:30 and 2:45 p.m. Trail rides $$$$, pony rides $$$.

Whether they want to simply pet a soft nose, take a short pony ride, or take a one- or two-hour trail ride, little cowhands will have a whooping good time at the resort's stables. The under-six crowd can take a pony ride around the training ring; older cowpokes can take a ride through open fields and hardwood forest and alongside crystal-clear trout streams. Thirty Quarter and Walker horses accommodate all levels of experience.

For More Information

Towns County Chamber of Commerce, 1411 Jack Dayton Circle, Young Harris, GA 30582; (706) 896-4966 or (800) 984-1543; www.mountaintopga.com.

Blairsville

West on US 76.

Perfect for an inexpensive outing, the area around Blairsville is peppered with diversions for outdoor enthusiasts: a national forest, waterfalls, lakes, and recreational areas. **Helton Creek Falls,** off U.S. Highway 19/129 (one of our personal favorites), is actually three falls hidden in a deep hardwood forest. **Lakes Nottley** (US 19/129, 706-745-5789) and **Winfield Scott** (Highway 180, 706-745-6928) provide boat docks, camping, fishing, swimming, and picnicking. Recreation areas including **Cooper's Creek Scenic Area** (Forest Service Road 4, 706-632-3031), **High Shoals** (Forest Service Road 283, 706-745-6928), **Sosebee Cove** (Highway 180, 706-745-6928), and **Woody Gap** (Highway 60, 706-864-6173) provide similar activities.

Brasstown Bald Mountain (ages 4 to 12)

Highway 180 Spur; (706) 896-2556; http://ngeorgia.com/travel/brasstown.html. Open daily Memorial Day through the first full weekend in November, as well as spring and fall weekends, depending on the weather, from 10:00 a.m. to 5:30 p.m. Parking fee $2; shuttle $.

Onward and upward. Stalwart climbers are rewarded with a marvelous view of four states from the cloud-tagging summit of the highest spot in Georgia—a sky-piercing 4,784 feet above sea level. Drive most of the way up the mountain to the parking lot. From there it's only 0.5 mile farther by way of a paved path, but the way is steep. Take your time with little hikers; their stubby legs might have a hard time scrambling uphill, but they'll love the feeling of accomplishment when they reach the peak. (There are several benches and rest areas along the way.) Another option is purchasing a ride on the shuttle, seasonally. Either way, once you reach the pinnacle, enjoy the view and then stop in at the visitor information center, where you can see a film and examine several exhibits about flora and fauna. Take jackets—it can be very brisk and breezy in the rarified atmosphere at the summit, where the weather is equivalent to that in the state of Maine. Four other trails of varying degrees of difficulty ranging from 0.5 mile to 6 miles in length branch off from the parking area.

Misty Mountain Model Railroad (all ages)

4381 Misty Mountain Lane on Town Creek Road; (706) 745-9819; www.jwww.com/misty/#train. Open May through December Wednesday, Friday, and Saturday at 2:00 p.m.; February Saturday only. Donations accepted and are given to charity.

Misty Mountain Model Railroad claims to be America's largest O-gauge train display—a 3,400-square-foot layout with fourteen O-gauge Lionel trains operating on a mile of track with twelve bridges, four trestles, and fifteen tunnels. The backdrop represents Georgia communities such as Gainesville, Helen, and Kennesaw; Copper Hill in Tennessee; and even Biltmore Estates in Asheville, North Carolina. The train display is located at Misty Mountain Inn and Cottages (706-745-4786 or 888-MISTY-MN), and packages are available that include a ride on the Blue Ridge Scenic Railway or horseback riding.

Trackrock Stables (all ages)

4890 Trackrock Campground Road; (706) 745-5252 (stable) or (706) 745-2420 (campground); www.trackrock.com/stables.html. The stable is open year-round, but it's best to make a reservation before you arrive. One-hour rides depart at 11:00 a.m.; 1:00, 2:30, and 4:00 p.m.; two-hour rides depart at 10:30 a.m. and 2:30 p.m. Hourly rate adults $$$$, children $$$; hayrides $ per person; camping $; cabins $–$$.

Equestrians can horse around here. In fact, start 'em young—as soon as they can comfortably maintain their seats in the saddle by themselves. For the casual horseman (or woman or juvenile) there's a one-hour ride through mountain meadows and tree-shaded paths alongside gushing streams. More adventurous riders can canter over fields and hillsides and gallop through the pastures. Real horseback riding diehards can spend the night, a week, or longer at the campground or in a rental cabin. Nonriders in your family can go on a hayride or spend their time fishing or swimming.

Vogel State Park (all ages)

7485 Vogel State Park Road off US 19/129; (706) 745-2628 or (800) 864-7275; www.gastateparks.org/info/vogel. Open daily year-round, 7:00 a.m. to 10:00 p.m. Parking $3; pedal boats $; miniature golf $; camping $; cottages $$–$$$$.

Located within the Chattahoochee National Forest, this park is a haven for families. Pedal boats permit little voyagers to skim over the lake like waterbugs. Little duffers will want to challenge you to a round of golf on the miniature course. Seventeen miles of trails, including an access connection to the Appalachian Trail, make the preserve a favorite of both casual and serious hikers. At lullaby time, tuckered-out vacationers can bed down in cottages or unroll their sleeping bags at the tent, trailer, or walk-in campsites.

For More Information

Blairsville-Union County Chamber of Commerce, 385 Welcome Center Lane, Blairsville, GA 30514; (706) 745-5789 or (877) 745-5789; www.blairsvillechamber.com.

Dahlonega

South on US 19.

Our entire family gets gold fever every time we visit this small town. The word *Dahlonega* is from the Cherokee name for "precious yellow metal." Although the area was virtually abandoned by prospectors when a richer seam was discovered in California, millions of dollars worth of ore have been extracted from the mountains—often using primitive methods. Today, Dahlonega's gold is tourism, and the town sits in an advantageous spot north of Atlanta, where it serves as a gateway to the north Georgia mountains. Shops around the town square purvey mountain crafts and gifts, and we never come to town without stopping at ye olde ice-cream and fudge shops.

Appalachian Outfitters (ages 4 to 12)

2084 South Chestatee/Highway 60S; (706) 864-7117 or for reservations (800) 426-7117; www.canoegeorgia.com. March through October. Price depends on activity, $–$$$$. Reservations are strongly suggested.

Thrills and chills and heart-pounding excitement on the Chestatee and Etowah Rivers are guaranteed whether you take a half-hour to overnight guided canoe, kayak, or tube trip.

Chestatee Wildlife Preserve (all ages)

469 Old Dahlonega Highway; (678) 859-6820; www.chestateewildlifepreserve.org. Open daily 10:00 a.m. to 4:00 p.m. Adults $$, children $.

Walk on the wild side at this exotic animal rescue and wildlife preserve in the north Georgia mountains where eager beavers can see one hundred animals, among them tigers, including a white Siberian tiger, lions, wallabies, camels, water buffalo, and deer to name a few. Reptiles include pythons, a corn snake, and a bearded dragon—a central Australian lizard. A popular annual event is an Easter egg hunt for 2,000 eggs.

Consolidated Gold Mines (ages 4 to 12)

185 Consolidated Gold Mine Road; (706) 864-8473; www.consolidatedgoldmine.com. Open daily year-round, 10:00 a.m. to 5:00 p.m. in summer, 10:00 a.m. to 4:00 p.m. in winter. Admission $$, includes tour and gold panning.

Indulge your gang's treasure-seeking spirit at this former mine, where the small fry can get an idea about what extracting gold from the earth was like in the old days. Although the excavation closed in 1900, the mine was the largest east of the Mississippi when it was operating. Visitors are taken 250 feet into the tunnel systems, and afterward your little prospectors can experience the excitement of panning for gold and gem stones.

A Thalimer **Adventure**

One Thanksgiving we rented two cabins to accommodate our adult children, their spouses or significant others, and our grandchildren. Knowing what pet lovers they all are, we specified ahead of time that no pets were allowed and that we could get thrown out if they showed up with any. Naturally vet-at-heart Elaine arrived with a wounded hawk and a lamb that had to be bottle-fed. Just as naturally, we were too soft-hearted to send her and her charges home. The hawk just lay in its box and made no trouble, but the lamb, which had to stay outside, gamboled about on the deck and bleated loudly and frequently. We just hoped that if anyone heard it, they'd think it was baby Chris crying. So this is how it came about that we oldsters were baby-sitting two types of kids while the Gen Xers rented paintball gear and ran around the heavy woods having fun.

Crisson Gold Mine (ages 4 to 12)
2736 Morrison Moore Parkway East; (706) 864-6363; www.crissongoldmine.com. Open daily year-round, weekends and during summer 10:00 a.m. to 6:00 p.m., the rest of the year 10:00 a.m. to 5:00 p.m. $ per pan or $$ for a five-gallon bucket.

For a hands-on field trip, chance-taking kiddies may strike it rich panning for gold and gemstones at this mine that began operation in 1847. Opened in 1970 as a gold panning destination, it is run by the fourth generation of a mining family. See and hear a real stamp mill used in processing gold ore. Oh, and by the way—just so that no one will miss an opportunity to make his or her fortune—indoor panning is offered during the winter season. Just in case this isn't your lucky day, you can purchase gold, gold nuggets, and gold jewelry in the gift shop.

Dahlonega Gold Museum Historic Site (ages 4 to 12) 🏛️ 🧑‍🦽
1 Public Square; (706) 864-2257; www.gastateparks.org/info/dahlonega. Open year-round, Monday through Saturday 9:00 a.m. to 5:00 p.m., Sunday 10:00 a.m. to 5:00 p.m. $

Visiting the museum is an excellent way for young prospectors to learn more about gold mining. Housed in the old courthouse, the repository is the second most visited historic site in the state. A film and exhibits tell the story of the nation's first gold rush and describe mining techniques, as well as lifestyles of old-time miners. Exhibits include gold coins produced when Dahlonega had a U.S. mint and a large hydraulic cannon and nozzle used to blast soil from the mountainsides. Even the most sophisticated pre-adult's mouth will drop open in wonder at the sight of the large gold ingot on display (highly secured, of course).

DeSoto Falls Scenic Area—Chattahoochee National Forest
(ages 4 to 12) 🚶 Ⓐ

US 19/129 North; contact USDA Forest Service, Brasstown Ranger District, (706) 745-6928; www.fs.fed.us/conf/desotocp.htm. Open daily year-round, 7:00 a.m. to 10:00 p.m.; campground open late April through late November. Free; camping $.

If your crew is as waterfall crazy as ours, you'll all want to visit this scenic area. Because the elevation varies between 2,000 and 3,400 feet in a very small area, the streams that flow through the area plunge from the higher level to the lower level in three separate waterfalls. Two are reached by easy hiking trails; the third requires a strenuous hike to see. The adjacent DeSoto Falls Campground is popular for those who want to rough it. The campground offers twenty-four tent pads equipped with tables and grills. With a state fishing license (and a trout stamp, if that's what you're after), anglers can try their luck in Frogtown Creek.

Medicine Bow Wilderness School (ages 6 to 12) Ⓐ 🚶 🌿

104 Medicine Bow Road; (706) 864-5928; www.home.alltel.net/medbow/introduction .htm. Call for a schedule of events. Rates $$$–$$$$ per activity; summer camp $$$$ per week.

Good medicine for your entire tribe, this unique operation offers a very special set of activities sure to capture the imagination of each and every one of you. Essentially an outdoor school imparting the skills of the Native Americans who first resided in the area, Medicine Bow offers such programs as the Weekend of the Bow, Parent/Child Adventures, Nature by Canoe, Weekends with the Earth, Stalking and Tracking, and Spirit Path. Boys and girls ages ten and older can attend exciting summer camps.

That's Gold in Them Thar Hills!

That easily recognized phrase originated during Dahlonega's 1828 gold rush—the nation's first. There was once a U.S. mint here that produced more than $6 million in gold coins in just twenty-three years. The domes of North Georgia College and the Georgia State Capitol in Atlanta are covered with gold leaf mined in Dahlonega. It is believed that enough of the precious ore remains in the area to pave the square around the courthouse 1 foot deep. So grab the kids and start digging.

For More Information

Dahlonega-Lumpkin County Welcome Center, 13 South Park Street on the Dahlonega Historic Square, Dahlonega, GA 30533; (706) 864-3711; www.dahlonega .org.

Dawsonville

South on Highway 9.

Located in an area of scenic beauty, the town is the home of Georgia's own "Awesome Bill from Dawsonville," Bill Elliott, one of the top stock car drivers in the world.

Amicalola Falls State Park (all ages)

418 Amicalola Falls State Park Road off Highway 52; (706) 265-4703 or (800) 864-7275; www.gastateparks.org/info/amicalola/. Open daily year-round, 7:00 a.m. to 10:00 p.m. Parking $3. Meals $–$$; rooms and cabins $$–$$$$; camping $.

Little ones will be awestruck when they crane their necks to gaze up at 729-foot **Amicalola Falls,** one of the tallest waterfalls east of the Rockies and one of the Seven Natural Wonders of Georgia. You can drive close to both the foot and the top of the falls for good viewing from both directions. Alternatively, you can hike up from the bottom or down from the top. Keep an extra-close eye on little (and not-so-little) climbers; anywhere near the falls is definitely not the place to turn them loose. The rocks and banks are slippery, and young risk-takers, who're sure they're immortal, don't always think. In addition to the main attraction, the preserve offers 12 miles of hiking trails, trout fishing, and interpretive programs. One trail leads to Springer Mountain and the southern end of the Appalachian Trail. The newest attraction is the Len Foote Hike Inn, where after a 5-mile hike to the lodge, you have dinner, spend the night, enjoy a hearty breakfast, and then hike out again. We can't imagine that any but the oldest and most serious hikers among the small fry could make this trek, but we've seen pictures of some small fry who've done it. For those more inclined to the creature comforts, a modern fifty-seven-room lodge, nestled on top of the mountain, features modern guest rooms and a restaurant with all-you-can-eat breakfast, lunch, and dinner buffets. The park also offers cabins and camping facilities.

Appalachian Trail (ages 6 to 12)

Contact the Appalachian Trail Conservancy in Harper's Ferry, West Virginia (304) 535-6331 or Amicalola Falls State Park (706) 265-8888; www.appalachiantrail.org. Always accessible. Free.

Sometimes you have to take a walk in the woods to find yourself. This nationally renowned trail, the most hiked track in Georgia, gives you plenty of opportunities to do so. In fact, the southern terminus of the 2,174-mile-plus footpath is in Georgia at

Springer Mountain. Hiking enthusiasts can access Georgia's 78-mile section from an 8-mile approach path from Amicalola Falls State Park and from seven other spots between there and Bly Gap at the North Carolina border.

Burt's Farm (all ages) 🔒

4801 Highway 52 East; (706) 265-3701 or (800) 600-BURT; www.burtsfarm.com. Open daily September through October, 9:00 a.m. to 6:00 p.m. and November 1 through 15, 9:00 a.m. to 5:00 p.m. Free; Fall hayrides $.

Peter, Peter, pumpkin eater, had a wife and couldn't keep her. Okay, okay. So in this case, it's Burt. In autumn children can get lost in the orange (or white or green or speckled) sea of pumpkins at the farm. Folks come from miles around to choose that perfect pumpkin for their Halloween jack-o'-lantern. An even more popular weekend activity, however, is the tractor-pulled hayride—a 2-mile trip past pumpkin fields, over a covered bridge, and within sight of Amicalola Falls. The farm also sells autumn decorations such as gourds, squash, and Indian corn. If you've never seen popcorn being processed, you can watch the process at Burt's, too.

Thalimer **Trail Tips**

1. Make sure it isn't hunting season.

2. Get good directions—perhaps even a map.

3. Wear comfortable clothes and footwear.

4. Take an extra pair of socks.

5. Take your camera and lots of film or memory cards.

6. Avoid holidays.

7. Don't go alone, and let someone know where you are and when you expect to be back.

8. Stay on the trails.

9. Beware of hypothermia.

10. Don't climb rocks around waterfalls or go too close to the edge of rapids.

11. Don't leave a trace of your passing.

12. Have fun.

Kangaroo Conservation Center (ages 8 to 12)

222 Bailey-Waters Road; (706) 265-6100; www.kangaroocenter.com. Open spring through fall (call for exact dates) Tuesday through Saturday. Reservations with a credit card are required. Adults $$$$, children eight to eighteen $$$. Children younger than eight are not permitted.

Your bouncy bunch can get up close and personal with marvelous marsupials without having to go Down Under to experience an outback adventure. Boasting the largest collection of kangaroos outside Australia, the Kangaroo Conservation Center is located in the northeast Georgia mountains. Dedicated to wildlife preservation and environmental concerns, the working farm includes a breeding center. Be sure to bring cameras—your exciting tour includes views of red, Western grey, and Eastern grey kangaroos as well as wallabies, burros, springhaas, kookaburras, dik-diks, cranes, and ducks. You can even learn how to throw a boomerang. Bring rain gear just in case.

Uncle Shuck's Corn Maze and Pumpkin Patch (ages 2 to 12)

Highway 53; (770) 772-6223 or (888) OSHUCKS (674-8257); www.uncleshucks.com. Open in the fall; call for hours and price. Children twelve and younger must be accompanied by an adult.

Uncle Shuck's Maze is a twelve-acre cornfield with 4 miles of trails. The 2006 maze, a race car tribute to NASCAR, was actually two mazes. Who knows what the next fantastic design will be? The average time to complete the maze can be as little as thirty minutes for one maze to two hours for both. Think how long it would take to walk 4 miles in a straight line with no wrong turns or backtracking. On weekends around Halloween, ghosts, goblins, and witches take over the maze from dusk to 10:00 p.m. In fact, scary things can't wait to jump out and give you a scare. This is also the place to buy pumpkins, gourds, Indian corn, and cornstalks.

For More Information

Dawson County Chamber of Commerce and Convention and Visitors Bureau, 6280 GA 53 East, Dawsonville, GA 30534; (706) 265-6278 or (877) 302-9271; www.dawson.org.

Gainesville

Southeast on Highway 53.

Elachee Nature Science Center (ages 3 to 12)

2125 Elachee Drive; (770) 535-1976; www.elachee.org. Open Monday through Saturday 10:00 a.m. to 5:00 p.m. $

Let's dig for dinos. The small fry will be awestruck at the authentic fossilized Mosasaur skeletons. Once enthused about ancient remains, they can become archaeologists themselves at the Dino Dig box where they can hunt for fossils; then they can climb on a one-ton petrified log, make rubbings from fossils, or use goop to create forest animal tracks. Other attractions at the natural history museum and science center include Astronomy Hall, where visitors can learn about the solar system; a live animal room with fish, reptiles, and amphibians; an aviary with red-tailed hawks; native plant and rain demonstration gardens; and 12 miles of hiking trails—one of which is wheelchair accessible. The complex is located at the 1,200-acre Chicopee Woods Nature Preserve, which is among the largest land trusts in north Georgia and one of the biggest within city limits east of the Mississippi. It features pine forests, hardwood ridges, streams, and wetlands. Numerous special events are held throughout the year.

I.N.K.-Interactive Neighborhood for Kids (ages 3 to 10)

999 Chestnut Street; (770) 536-1900; www.inkfun.org. Open Monday through Saturday 10:00 a.m. to 5:00 p.m. $$

Be prepared to stay and stay and stay. The kiddies won't be able to tear themselves away from the dentist office, bank, beauty salon, grocery store, post office, indoor park, 1950s diner, vet clinic, library, playhouse, theater, medical clinic, radiology office, fire truck, sheriff's car, and train. In addition to appropriate props, many of the rooms have costumes to don. For an additional fee, aspiring potters can create a ceramic masterpiece to take home. Tiny tots will enjoy the Preschool Paradise.

Northeast Georgia History Center (ages 3 to 12)

322 Academy Street; (770) 297-5900; www.negahc.org. Open Tuesday through Saturday 10:00 a.m. to 4:00 p.m. $

Your little Indians will be fascinated by **Chief White Path's Cabin,** a typical 1790s Cherokee home. The original cabin, which began more humbly as one room and a

Can You **Believe It?**

Gainesville, the Poultry Capital of the World, has an ordinance prohibiting the use of a knife and fork while eating fried chicken. Kids and kids-at-heart say "Yeah!"

loft, was built by the chief's parents in what is now Ellijay in northwest Georgia. When Cherokee property was taken away from the Native Americans and given to white settlers, the cabin was modified several times over the years until it reached its present form. Artifacts and authentic period furnishings give today's youngsters a glimpse into what life was like more than 200 years ago. Vegetable and herb gardens planted around the cabin are typical of the period. Inside the museum itself are exhibits chronicling the history of the area, black history, industrial history, railroad history, folk pottery, arts and crafts of northeast Georgia, Confederate Gen. James Longstreet, and the Northeast Georgia Hall of Fame. A special exhibit is dedicated to Ed Dodd, who created the environmental preservation comic strip *Mark Trail.*

Walking Tour of Our Solar System (ages 3 to 12)

Downtown Square, contact the North Georgia Astronomers: www.northgeorgia astronomers.org. Free.

In the real world, the distance from the sun to Pluto (Pluto hadn't been demoted as a planet when this tour was devised) is 3.6 billion miles. For this representation, one mile = 2,000,000,000 miles. Beginning at the town square, the 1.8-mile tour leads villagers from the sun, represented by a stainless steel globe, down to Pluto at Longwood Park on Lake Lanier. Informational markers identify Earth, the moon, Mercury, Venus, Mars, the Asteroid Belt, Jupiter, the Galilean Moons, Saturn, Uranus, Neptune and Triton, and Pluto. The last marker points the way to Alpha Centauri.

Flowery Branch

South on Interstate 985.

Atlanta Falcons Headquarters and Training Facility (ages 6 to 12)

4400 Falcon Parkway; (770) 965-3115 or (800) 241-3489; www.atlantafalcons.com. July and August only. Call for hours. Free; off-site parking $.

Fans can watch practices, participate in interactive games, get autographs from players, and tour the Mobile Museum, which is housed in two trailer rigs. The interactive museum chronicles the team's history with videos, photos, replica lockers, and more. Special activities include Junior Falcons Training Camp; punt, pass, and kick competitions; and appearances by the team's mascot, Freddie Falcon. Of course, fans can purchase team memorabilia and collectibles at the store.

Lake Lanier Islands

Continue south on I-985 to Friendship Road exit, west to Lake Lanier Islands.

Bring a world of family fun close to home. An entertainment mecca, Lake Lanier Islands is a full-service resort including 1,200 acres of recreational facilities surrounded by 38,000 acres of waterborne activities. Horseback riding and golf are also popular pursuits. Special events range from scary to merry. Lake Sidney Lanier, named after the Confederate poet, was formed by damming the Chestatee, Little, and Chattahoochee Rivers. Four mountaintops that weren't submerged became Lake Lanier Islands.

Lake Lanier Beach and Water Park (all ages)

7000 Holiday Road; (770) 932-7200 or (800) 840-LAKE; www.lakelanierislands.com. Open May through September, hours vary but are generally 10:00 a.m. to 6:00 p.m. $$$$

Surf's up! This is a fun-filled day-use facility as well as a year-round destination. During the long, hot summer, cool off with the splashiest thrills, spills, twists, and turns around. Youngsters won't have to worry about having enough to do or having to wait in line for a turn at this park, which boasts ten water slides, an 850,000-gallon wave pool with nine types of waves, and a Kiddie Lagoon and Wiggle Waves area for tiny tykes. Hang ten on the Surf Wave, which brings the thrill of surfing on a body board. With the interactive FunDunker, sibling rivalry can achieve some long-overdue revenge. Paddleboats, sailboats, canoes, Wave Runners, fishing guides, and ski boats and ski rental for waterskiing round out the water sports. Landlubbers needn't feel neglected, however, because there's a 1.5-mile sandy beach for sunning, building sand castles, or burying Dad. Type-A personalities can take advantage of seventy-two holes of golf, stables and trail rides, and bicycle rentals—all of which can fill every waking moment. But if that's not enough, there's South Beach with a DJ and live music, summer concerts, and fireworks to provide even more entertainment. Accomodations are in a hotel, lakeside cottages, and houseboats.

For More Information

Lake Lanier Islands, 7000 Holiday Road, Lake Lanier Islands, GA 30518; (800) 840-LAKE; www.lakelanierislands.com.

Where to Eat in Northeast Georgia

Hartwell

The Galley Restaurant, Portman Marina, 1629 Marina Road, Anderson, SC; (864) 287-3215. Tuck a napkin into your collar and dig in at this popular eatery, located on the South Carolina side of the lake. Tuesday through Saturday nights feature all-you-can-eat specials, or ravenous youngsters can fill up on steaks, seafood, and pasta dishes or good burgers. $–$$$

Evans

The Upper Crust, 300 Town Center Drive; (706) 863-3323. This trendy eatery with a clever name serves up good grub: pizza, pasta, wraps, and salad. Kids' menu. $–$$

Martinez

Mimmos Taste of Italy, 362 Furys Ferry Road; (706) 860-0888. Spaghetti and meatballs, ravioli, and other Italian favorites that would do a Roman proud. Kids' menu. $–$$$

Augusta

Boll Weevil Cafe, 10 Ninth Street; (706) 722-7772. Simple eats are on tap here: pizzas, homemade sandwiches, and delicious desserts. $–$$

T-Bonz Gill and Grill, 2856 Washington Road; (706) 737-8325. Voted the best steak in Augusta since 1987, this popular eatery serves up a leisurely dining experience along with the good food. After all, a night out once in a while is well deserved. Kids' menu. $–$$$

Village Deli Sub and Pub, 2803 Wrightsboro Road; (706) 736-3691. This casual eatery serves just the kind of eats munchkins like to devour: hamburgers, corn dogs, grilled-cheese sandwiches, and the like. Be sure to check out the restaurant's fresh soup of the day as well as the prime rib dinner served every Friday evening. $–$$$

Washington

Washington Jockey Club, 5 East Public Square; (706) 678-1672. Fill up the rug rats with salmon, prime rib, other grill items, and desserts you can't say no to. $–$$

Fievet Pharmacy and Soda Shop, 115 East Robert Toombs Avenue; (706) 678-2260. Just like in the good old days, this old-time soda shop fills hungry kids up with burgers, hot dogs, sodas, shakes, and sundaes. $

Home Cafe, 101 North Bypass East; (706) 678-2231. The best in home-style meals and homemade desserts satisfy even the most ravenous hunger. $–$$

Sautee

Edelweiss German Inn and Restaurant, 351 Duncan Bridge Road; (706) 865-7371. Treat your little mountaineers to a taste of Old Bavaria—hearty German fare with an emphasis on brats (not the obnoxious kid kind), wursts, and schnitzels, as well as steaks and barbecued ribs. Lunch $, dinner $$

Stovall House Country Inn and Restaurant, 1526 Highway 255 North; (706) 878-3355; www.stovallhouse.com. Dinner Thursday through Saturday 5:30 to 8:30 p.m. This renowned farmhouse serves gourmet meals of such dishes as manicotti, honey-mustard chicken, citrus trout, or pork scallopini. Also offers bed-and-breakfast accommodations. $–$$ (kids half-price)

Other Things to
See&Do in Northeast Georgia

- **Stephens County Historical Headquarters and Museum,** Toccoa; (706) 282-5055; www.toccoahistory.com

- **Cromer's Mill Covered Bridge,** Carnesville; no phone; www.dot .state.ga.us/specialsubjects/specialinterest/covered/cromers.shtml

- **Hart County Historical Society and Museum,** Hartwell; (706) 376-6330; www.hart-chamber.org

- **Lincoln County Historical Park,** Lincolnton; (706) 359-7970; www .lincolncountyga.org

- **Summer concerts on the lawn of Appleby House,** Augusta; (706) 736-6244

- **Ezekiel Harris House,** Augusta; (706) 737-2820; www.augusta museum.org/harris.htm

- **Fat Man's Forest,** Augusta; (706) 722-0796; www.fatmans.com

- **Gertrude Herbert Institute of Art,** Augusta; (706) 722-5495; www .ghia.org

- **Meadow Garden,** George Walton Historic Site, historic home, Augusta; (706) 724-4174; www.geocities.com/meadowgarden3

- **Morris Museum of Art,** Augusta; (706) 828-7501; www.themorris.org

- **Barrow County Museum,** Winder; (770) 307-1183; cityofwinder.com/ museum.asp

- **George E. Coleman Sr. Planetarium,** Dahlonega; (706) 864-1471; www.ngcsu.edu

Helen

Hofbrauhaus, 1 South Main Street; (706) 878-2248. German dishes lead the menu, but the cuisine is international with French, Italian, and American selections from frog legs to escargot to smoked trout, filet, sauerbraten, steamed mussels, and roast Long Island duck. $$–$$$$

International Cafe, Highway 75/Main Street; (706) 878-3102. We love eating knockwurst, schnitzels, or strudels out on the deck or the covered porch that over-hangs the gurgling stream. $$–$$$

Dahlonega

Smith House, 84 South Chestatee Street; (706) 867-7000 or (800) 852-9577; www .smithhouse.com. Open daily except Mon-day. Lunch 11:00 a.m. to 3:00 p.m. and din-ner 4:00 p.m. to 7:30 p.m. (8:00 p.m. on Friday and Saturday). For a meal beyond belief, take the entire family to the world-renowned restaurant for its bounteous meals of southern fried chicken and honey-cured country ham accompanied by moun-tainous platters of at least a dozen vegetables and other side dishes served family style. $$. B&B accommodations, pool. $$–$$$$

Dawsonville

Dawsonville Pool Room, East First Street; (706) 265-2792. Race right over to the Pool Room for great hamburgers and fries. Collections of memorabilia from local resident Bill Elliott's NASCAR career and relics from early moonshine runners give the Pool Room a one-of-a-kind ambience. $

Where to Stay in North-east Georgia

Dillard

Chalet Village, 3608 Highway 246 North, Dillard; (800) 262-8259 or (706) 746-5301; www.skyvalleyaccom.com. Deluxe chalets come in a variety of sizes—all with kitchens, some with indoor Jacuzzis and fireplaces. There's something for everyone in your brood to do: swimming pool, out-door hot tub, tennis courts, hiking trails, and trout fishing. $$–$$$$

The York House Bed & Breakfast, 416 York House Road, Mountain City; (706) 746-2068 or (800) 231-YORK; www.york houseinn.com. Built in 1896, this simple old hotel welcomes the junior set, who enjoy the freedom of the extensive grounds, two streams, trails, picnic area, and yard games. $$–$$$$

Lakemont

Lake Rabun Hotel, Lake Rabun Road; (706) 782-4946; www.lakerabunhotel.com. Get the feeling of a simple 1920s mountain vacation at this rustic old native-stone-and-wood hotel perched on a tree-shaded hill-side across the street from the lake. Newly renovated rooms feature private baths. Breakfast and use of canoes are included. $$

River Campground and Lodge, 28 Joy Bridge Road; (706) 782-9936; www.river campground.com. Located on the Tallulah River where you can watch resident beavers and ducks, the facility offers cabins, campsites, fishing, covered boat docks, and hiking trails. $

Augusta

Partridge Inn, 2110 Walton Way; (706) 737-8888 or (800) 476-6888; www .partridgeinn.com. Transport your off-spring to a less complicated time by spending the night at this delightful old inn begun in 1879. One of the first all-suite hotels in the country, the inn now offers both suites and rooms, as well as veran-das, pool, restaurant, and complimentary breakfast. $–$$$$

Augusta Marriott Hotel and Suites, 2 Tenth Street; (706) 722-8900. Located right on the river at Riverwalk, the full-service hotel blends well with the historic struc-tures around it and provides a range of guest rooms and suites, restaurant, lounge, and pool. Accommodations $$$$; meals $–$$

Washington

Hill and Hollow Farm, 2090 Thomson Road; (706) 678-4439. If you have any wannabe equestrians, this modern farm/bed-and-breakfast is the best place in Georgia to stay. Horseback riding and lessons, as well as babysitting, are available at an additional cost. $$

Clarkesville

Burton Woods Cabins and Lodging, 56 Ringold Lane; (706) 947-3926 or (706) 219-9027. Staggered up the mountainside near Lake Burton, the modern all-suite lodge and one- to three-bedroom cabins provide maximum privacy and all the comforts of home. On-property family fun includes a recreation building, lawn games, and pontoon boat rentals. $$–$$$

Glen-Ella Springs Country Inn, 1789 Bear Gap Road; (706) 754-7295 or (877) 456-7527; www.glenella.com. A fantastic bed-and-breakfast retreat, the faithfully restored, rustic 1890 inn combines all of today's modern conveniences with the country charm of yesterday. Surrounded by gardens, forest, and nature trails, the hostelry also features a pool and a gourmet restaurant. Room rates $$$$; dinner $$$–$$$$

Sautee

Cherokee Campground, 45 Bethel Road; (706) 878-2267. Outdoorsy types can hunker down for the night at the tent and RV sites or really rough it at the primitive campsites or one of the campground's tepees. $

Helen

Innsbruck Resort and Golf Club, 98 Shwarzwald Strasse; (706) 878-2400; www.innsbruckresort.com. The Bavarian castle–like, luxurious facility offers accommodations ranging from individual guest rooms to spacious four-bedroom homes—with all the modern comforts and amenities from a fireplace to a whirlpool tub. Not just a place to stay, the resort offers an eighteen-hole championship alpine golf course, tennis courts, pool, hot tub, and a bar and grill. $$$–$$$$

Tanglewood Resort Cabins, 3387 Highway 356; (706) 878-3286 or (866) 634-1686; www.northeastgeorgiacabins.com. One- to six-bedroom, fully equipped rustic log cabins tucked away in seventy-five wooded acres adjacent to the Chattahoochee National Forest ensure plenty of privacy. $$$–$$$$

Hiawassee

Bald Mountain Campground and Resort, 751 Gander Gap; (706) 896-2274; www.baldmountainpark.com. Open April 1 through November 1. RV sites with full hookups and cable TV combine with rushing streams, miniature golf, paddleboats, a spring-fed swimming pool, a playground, and planned activities to keep families busy. $

Hickorynut Cove Cabins/Camping, 2500 Hickorynut Cove Road; (706) 896-5341; www.hickorynutcove.com. Three fully equipped cabins have air-conditioning, cable TV, and a fireplace. For those who enjoy roughing it, there are also campsites. Fishing at the trout farm, hiking, and paddleboating on a private lake can fill every waking hour. Cabins $$; camping $

The Ridges Resort, 3499 US 76; (706) 896-2262 or (888) 834-4409; www.the ridgesresort.com. From the minute your family arrives at the upscale inn on the shores of Lake Chatuge, they'll have to start making decisions about the various things to do. The marina has a boat ramp and **free** docking for guests and rents pontoon boats, fishing boats, and aqua-cycles. A restaurant, outdoor pool, exercise room, hot tub, and lighted tennis courts satisfy all those Type-A personalities. Accommodations $$$–$$$$; dinner $–$$$

Blairsville

Blood Mountain Cabins and Country Store, 9894 Gainesville Highway; (706) 745-9454 or (800) 284-6866; www.blood mountain.com. Cabins (which are high up on the mountain, practically right on the Appalachian Trail) sleep four and feature a fully equipped kitchen, bedroom and sleeping loft, fireplace, satellite TV, VCR, and deck. Ask about Green Mansions Cabins for larger families. $$$

Dahlonega

Dockery Lake Recreation Area, Forest Service Road 654; (706) 745-6928; www.fs .fed.us/conf/dkrylkcp.htm. Open May through October. In addition to campsites, the area offers fishing and hiking. $

Lake Lanier Islands

Emerald Pointe Resort, 7000 Holiday Road; (770) 945-8787; www.lakelanier islands.com. Sprawling over a wooded peninsula overlooking the lake, this is a perfect spot for your brood to get away. With 224 rooms and three restaurants, as well as several cottages, the resort offers a wide selection of year-round activities: an eighteen-hole, par-72 championship golf course described by *Golf Digest* magazine as the Pebble Beach of the Southeast; lighted tennis courts; lighted jogging trails; heated pool; health club; whirlpools; steam saunas; boating; fishing; horseback riding; bicycle rentals; scheduled children's activities; and a playground. $$$–$$$$

Harbor Landing Houseboat Rental; (770) 932-7255; www.lakelanierislands .com. Up anchor and sail away for your own waterworld adventure. Sleeping up to ten, these luxurious waterborne homes away from home feature an aft deck with swimming platform, forward deck with grill, and upper deck with sliding board. $$$$

Lake Lanier Islands Development Authority Campground, 7000 Holiday Road; (770) 932-7200; www.lakelanier islands.com. In addition to lakeside tent and RV sites with full hookups, the campground features a fishing pier and boating facilities. $

Northwest Georgia

Twisting, turning country roads can lead to adventure, and here in the high country of northwest Georgia every bend in the byway reveals another opportunity for outdoor fun or a painless history lesson. The region has seen momentous events. At one time northwest Georgia served as the capital of the Cherokee Nation, largest of the Five Civilized Tribes of the Southeast. During the Civil War the Confederacy won one of its most stunning victories in northwest Georgia

Thalimers' Top Picks in Northwest Georgia

1. Exploring Rock City Gardens, Lookout Mountain

2. Hiking to the waterfall at Cloudland Canyon, Rising Fawn

3. Chugging through the mountains on the Blue Ridge Scenic Railway, Blue Ridge

4. Whooping it up at the Chieftains Museum, Rome

5. Digging through the area's history at the Etowah Indian Mounds, Cartersville

6. Rolling along at the Southeast Railway Museum, Duluth

7. Pulling strings at the Center for Puppetry Arts, Atlanta

8. Splashing in Centennial Olympic Park's Fountain of Rings, Atlanta

9. Elevating your sights at Georgia's Stone Mountain Park, Stone Mountain

10. Jousting at the Georgia Renaissance Festival, Palmetto

NORTHWEST GEORGIA

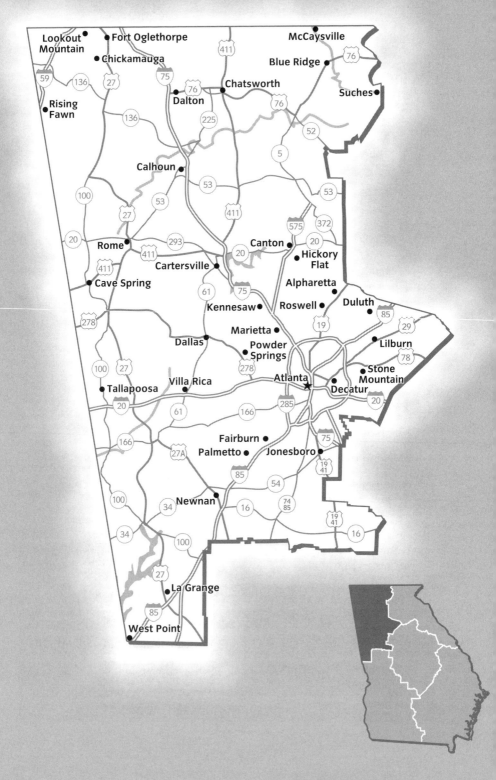

and put up tremendous resistance to advancing Federal troops, although ultimately they were unable to keep the Union from taking Atlanta. In addition to human history, the region abounds with natural attractions tailor-made for a get-out-and-go adventure. The Chattahoochee National Forest encompasses 864,359 acres in north Georgia and provides scenic rivers for fishing, canoeing, rafting, and kayaking. Numerous waterfalls; hiking trails such as the Appalachian, Benton MacKaye, and William Bartram Trails; horseback-riding trails; six state parks; five major lakes; and the Cohutta Wilderness add innumerable possibilities for outdoor recreation. Increased elevation, pollution-free air, and the absence of the glow of city lights make real-life stargazing spectacular. For the most part the region is characterized by diminutive villages, but it also contains small cities such as Dalton, Calhoun, and Rome. In the extreme southern part of this section of Georgia, in the foothills of the Appalachian and Blue Ridge Mountains is vibrant, sophisticated Atlanta—Capital of the New South. All in all, if your clan chooses to explore this area, you'll find a wealth of intriguing historical sites, scenic spots, recreational activities, and high-tech attractions.

Lookout Mountain

West of Rossville on Highway 189.

Rock City Gardens (all ages)
1400 Patten Road; (706) 820-2531 or (800) 854-0675; www.seerockcity.com. Open daily year-round, 8:30 a.m.; summer open until 8:00 p.m.; remainder of the year closing hours vary to as early as 4:00 p.m., so call ahead. (Closed Christmas.) Adults $$$, children $$.

Your gang doesn't have to have rocks in their heads to enjoy exploring this fourteen-acre natural garden, where gigantic boulders strewn about like discarded children's blocks make you feel like a Lilliputian as you clamor through the stony grounds. Lush landscaping, waterfalls, unusual formations, a swinging bridge, deer park, and a legendary view of seven states from Lover's Leap keep munchkins of all ages engrossed, but little squirts are particularly delighted with the underground scenes found in the Fairyland Caverns and the live storybook characters who inhabit Mother Goose Village. Prospector's Point has a gemstone sluice where young chance-takers can try their luck. As if all that weren't enough, the backseat crowd can visit the numerous

Rock City's **Fairy Tale Festival**

This festival, held three weekends in August, is crammed with storytellers, puppeteers, clowns, magicians, and singers to delight story lovers of all ages.

shops and, if tummies start rumbling, eat at one of several restaurants. Special events scheduled throughout the year keep families coming back for more.

Rock City's Enchanted Maize Maze (ages 2 to 12)

Blowing Springs Farm just south of St. Elmo; (706) 820-2531 for information on hours, prices, and directions; (706) 820-0759 for reservations; www.enchantedmaze.com. Open September and October, Thursday noon to 8:00 p.m., Friday through Sunday noon to 10:00 p.m. Adults $$, children $, children younger than four free. Hayrides free with paid admission.

In autumn a cornfield at the foot of Lookout Mountain from Rock City is transformed into an intricate ten-acre labyrinth. A series of stimulating questions will help you find your way. Offering something for everyone, the Enchanted Maize Maze also has hayrides, a kiddie hay maze, a hay pyramid, a pumpkin patch, a Rock City barn, animal barn, refreshments, and more. You can't ever get truly lost. Corn cops are stationed within the maze to help out if necessary. Friday and Saturday nights in October from 6:00 to 10:00 p.m., the maze becomes Spooky Acres—a frightful Halloween destination with haunting spooks wandering the shadowy paths between the rows of rustling corn stalks. There are also pumpkins for sale and trick-or-treat Saturdays for the little ones.

For More Information

Walker County Chamber of Commerce, 10052 U.S. Highway 27 North, Rock Spring, GA 30739; (706) 375-7702; www.walkercochamber.com.

Georgia and **the Civil War**

- Georgia was the site of five major campaigns: the campaign for Chickamauga/Chattanooga, Atlanta campaign, battles for Atlanta, Sherman's March to the Sea, and Wilson's Raid.

- Fifth to secede from the Union (January 19, 1861).

- Sent 125,000 men and boys to fight in the war known variously as the Civil War, the War Between the States, the War of Northern Aggression, and (our favorite) the Recent Unpleasantness.

Fort Oglethorpe/Chickamauga

Southeast of Lookout Mountain on Highway 1; then south on Highway 813.

Chickamauga and Chattanooga National Military Park (all ages)
🚴 🎭 🏛

3370 LaFayette Road, Fort Oglethorpe; (706) 866-9241; www.nps.gov/chch. Visitor center open Memorial Day to Labor Day 8:00 a.m. to 5:00 p.m., remainder of the year 8:00 a.m. to 4:45 p.m. Closed Christmas Day. Free.

One of the most important victories for the Confederacy was at tiny Chickamauga, Georgia, but that conflict was followed by a staggering loss at Chattanooga, Tennessee. The battlegrounds of both campaigns were combined into the Chickamauga and Chattanooga National Military Park, a fascinating place for those who are interested in Civil War history. We will describe only the portion of the park in Georgia.

Even little people who aren't into history yet will find things to be fascinated about here. Begin at the Chickamauga Visitor Center with a multimedia orientation presentation recounting the details of the battle and the origin of the National Military Park System, and then view the Fuller Gun Collection and other exhibits.

Next take your little soldiers out to tour the battlefield, which has a 7-mile driving route as well as walking, hiking, bicycling, and bridle trails (bring your own horse). Numerous historical markers help budding historians understand the progress of the bloody two-day battle, and poignant monuments honor the men of both sides who fought here. You can almost hear the sounds of battle. One log cabin from the era survives, and another has been reconstructed—both of which served as officers' headquarters. Tiny troopers will like the cannons and will want to race you to the top of the observation tower.

Sixth Cavalry Museum (ages 4 to 12) 🏛 🎭

2 Barnhardt Circle, Fort Oglethorpe; (706) 861-2860. Open May through November, Friday and Saturday 10:00 a.m. to 4:00 p.m., Sunday noon to 5:00 p.m. Free.

Shades of F Troop. Fort Oglethorpe was once the home of the Sixth Cavalry of the U.S. Army. Located on the parade field of the former fort, this museum is dedicated to showcasing the lives of mounted military men. Your little troopers can acquaint themselves with that bygone era by examining artifacts including clothing, equipment, pictures, historic documents, and other relics pertaining to the cavalry.

Foreshadowed

Chickamauga is the Indian word for "River of Death," and the site was one of the ten bloodiest battles of the Civil War.

The Fuller **Gun Collection**

This 360-weapon accumulation of military shoulder arms spans the period from the Revolutionary War to World War II and is one of the largest military collections in the world.

Walker County Regional Heritage and Train Museum
(ages 6 to 12)
200 Gordon Street, (706) 375-4488. Open Monday through Saturday 10:00 a.m. to 4:00 p.m. Free.

Once upon a time the town of Chickamauga was called Crawfish Springs (named after the springs that provided water to the Native Americans who lived there and then to the town that sprang up around them). When the town became a stop on the railroad between Chattanooga and Cedartown, a beautiful depot was built of stone with a whimsical Victorian tower. The restored depot now houses displays of Native American artifacts, Civil War and World War I memorabilia, antique guns and furniture, and a working display of Lionel O-gauge model trains that dates back to the 1940s.

Hidden Hollow Resort (all ages)
463 Hidden Hollow Lane, Chickamauga; (706) 539-2372; www.hiddenhollowresort.com. $$–$$$

For a fun-filled weekend, your brood can stay in a country setting at Hidden Hollow Farm, which offers rustic accommodations in a lodge, cabins, and wilderness cabins, as well as fishing, hiking, and canoeing at this 135-acre resort. For even more foot-stompin' fun, the farm offers folk dance entertainment and instruction.

Georgia **by the Numbers**

- 159 counties—more than any other state in the nation
- Largest state east of the Mississippi
- Twenty-first largest state in area (58,876 square miles)
- 315 miles from north to south and 250 miles east to west
- Tenth largest state in population
- Population 8,186,453
- Atlanta metro population—5 million

Remains of the Day

The Gordon-Lee Mansion in Chickamauga, which now operates as a museum house, is one of the few remaining structures used during the battle. The house served as the headquarters of Union general William S. Rosecrans, and its elegant library became a grisly operating room.

Rising Fawn

West of Chickamauga on U.S. Highway 11.

Cloudland Canyon State Park (all ages) 🌊 👫 🏕
122 Cloudland Canyon Park Road; (706) 657-4050 or (800) 864-7275; www.gastateparks .org/info/cloudland/. Open daily year-round, 7:00 a.m. to 10:00 p.m. Parking $3; entry **free** on Wednesday; cottages $$–$$$; camping $.

Fall for this one. A spectacular waterfall erupts over a ledge and bursts with spume and fury into a deep pool with a backdrop of sheer cliffs for ambience. The serene habitat overflowing with natural attractions brings outdoor lovers to Cloudland Canyon. The 3,485-acre park particularly lures those back-to-nature types who appreciate rugged terrain. Paved and dirt hiking trails skirt both rims of the canyon, providing breathtaking views of the deep gorge. In fact, this is one of the most dramatic views in the state. Budding geologists pass through millions of years of the development of Earth's crust during a hike down into the ravine, the only place to take a gander at the awe-inspiring falls. This is a good spot for little shutterbugs to perfect their craft and make a record to take back to school for "What I Did on My Summer Vacation." Parents, listen up: It's all uphill on the way back, so gauge your young trekkers' stamina for completing the round-trip before you start out. Other active pursuits for energetic tykes include fishing, tennis, and swimming—a cool treat on a hot day. When it's time to bed down, accommodations are offered in fully equipped cottages, or, if your gang likes to camp, you can choose tent, trailer, or primitive campsites. For a family reunion, the park also has a large group lodge that sleeps up to forty.

Georgia's **Top Products**

Peanuts, pecans, peaches, poultry, carpet, wood and paper products, and tourism are Georgia's top moneymakers.

Dalton

Southeast of Rising Fawn on Interstate 75 at U.S. Highway 76.

Do you remember with what trepidation you faced being called on the carpet for some misdeed? Tell your kidlets they're going to be called on the carpet, but not to worry—this isn't for a scolding. Dalton, the Carpet Capital of the World, contains an astounding 150 carpet mills and 100 carpet outlet stores, and there are plenty of other attractions and things to do in the immediate area.

Dalton Carpet Mill Tours (ages 4 to 12)
2211 Dug Gap Battle Road; (706) 270-9960 or (800) 331-3258; www.daltoncvb.com. By appointment. Free.

Your little genies don't even need to rub a magic lamp to take a magic carpet ride that satisfies their curiosity about how rugs are created. (Here's a little known fact we were surprised to learn: Bedspread tufting led to the carpet industry.) Simply call the Dalton Convention and Visitors Bureau to schedule a two-and-a-half-hour tour that includes a video presentation, a walk through the research and design department, and a mill tour.

For More Information

Dalton Convention and Visitors Bureau, P.O. Box 6177, Dalton, GA 30722; (706) 270-9960 or (800) 331-3258; www.daltoncvb.com.

Civil War **Memorial**

Despite his assistance to the Southern cause, the statue of Gen. Joseph E. Johnston in Dalton is the only monument in the country dedicated to that fiercely determined Confederate soldier.

Chatsworth

East of Dalton on US 76.

Carters Lake (706-334-2248), one of the state's best recreational reservoirs, impounds the Coosawattee River into 3,220 acres to create a mecca for water sports enthusiasts. Reputed to be the deepest lake east of the Mississippi, it boasts eight public-use parks sure to please any active bunch. But there's more. The area serves as a gateway to the **Cohutta Wilderness,** a 34,000-acre section of the Chatta-hoochee National Forest (706-695-6736) accessible only by footpath. Not only does this almost untouched region contain the southern end of the Appalachian Mountains, but it also embraces the Conasauga and Jack's Rivers—two of the best wild-trout streams in Georgia. Accessible off U.S. Highway 411, the pristine forest is ideal for serious backpackers.

Chief Vann House Historic Site and Museum (ages 4 to 12) 🏛️ 💺

82 Highway 225 North; (706) 695-2598; www.gastateparks.org/info/chiefvan. Open Tuesday through Saturday 9:00 a.m. to 5:00 p.m., Sunday 2:00 to 5:30 p.m., closed Monday. $

Once you have explored the north Georgia mountains, your kids begin to get the picture that Native Americans in the East didn't live in tepees. Your little adventurers will be astonished, however, with the magnificent two-story, Federal-style, redbrick home of Chief James Vann, who—although he was controversial—is credited with bringing education to the Cherokee. The site contains not only the original, humble log cabin in which Vann first lived but also the mansion he built in 1804, the Showplace of the Cherokee Nation. This is the first mansion ever built by a Native American. The imposing brick house, furnished with antiques appropriate to the period, features a superb cantilevered stairway. Tell your little scouts to keep a sharp eye out for the Cherokee roses (Georgia's state flower) carved into the woodwork. A new interpretive center showcases other artifacts from the area.

Fort Mountain State Park (all ages) 🍽️ ⛺ 🚶

181 Fort Mountain Park Road; (706) 422-1932 or (800) 864-7275; www.gastateparks.org/info/fortmt/. Open daily, 7:00 a.m. to 10:00 p.m. Parking $3; cottages $$–$$$; camping $.

Who built the ancient mountaintop fortifications that prompted the park's name and date back more than 1,000 years? Why was it built? No one can answer these questions, but don't let that stop your curious gang from visiting and seeing for themselves. The mysterious wall is just one of this preserve's many attractions. With an elevation higher than 2,800 feet, the park offers a lake with a beach, fishing, and pedal boat rentals. Hiking is a popular endeavor for landlubbers. The Fort Mountain Stables (706-517-4906) offer horseback riding adventures along 37 miles of the park's

The House **the Chief Built**

Vann's estate, Diamond Hill, was a large, prosperous plantation complete with mills, ferries, taverns, and even slaves. It was also a tribal meeting place and a site where Native Americans met with Moravian missionaries.

scenic trails. When the sandman comes calling, accommodations are available in fifteen fully equipped two- and three-bedroom rental cabins; campers can bed down at tent and RV sites.

Carters Lake Marina and Resort (all ages) 🍽️ ⛺ 🚣

575 Marina Road; (706) 276-4891; www.carterslake.com; pontoon boat rentals $$$–$$$$.

Providing something for all your water babies, this resort has boat rentals, beaches, fishing, launch sites, and boat and fishing supplies, as well as accommodations in family cabins and luxury cabins for up to six people.

For More Information

Chatsworth-Murray County Chamber of Commerce Welcome Center, 126 North Third Avenue, Chatsworth, GA 30705; (706) 695-6060 or (800) 969-9490; www.murraycountychamber.org/tourism .htm.

Fannin County (Blue Ridge/ McCaysville/Suches)

North on US 76.

A haven for outdoor devotees, the mountainous Blue Ridge area abounds in active back-to-nature pursuits—primary among them is trout fly fishing, considered an art in north Georgia. An angler's dream come true, fishing for both native and stocked trout is available in more than 100 miles of trout fishing streams, including the **Jack's** and **Conasauga Rivers.** McCaysville sits right on the Georgia/Tennessee border. In fact, on one side of the main street you're in McCaysville, Georgia, and on the other side of the street you're in Copperhill, Tennessee. Jokesters among your clan will want a gag photo with one foot in each state. The **Aska Trails Area** of the Chattahoochee National Forest is a 17-mile hiking and mountain-biking trail system near Deep Gap on Aska Road. Trails, some of which descend 3,200 feet to the shores of Lake Blue Ridge, are 1 to 5.5 miles long. The **Toccoa River Canoe Trail** utilizes

17.3 miles of the Toccoa River from the put in at Deep Hole Recreation Area west and north to near its entry into Lake Blue Ridge. Beautiful views, laurel and rhododendron thickets, wildlife, good fishing, and some rapids make a perfect canoe trip, especially for beginning paddlers. Thrill seekers find white-water rafting on the Class III and IV rapids of the **Ocoee River,** site of the 1996 Slalom/Canoe/Kayak Olympic competitions, an exciting challenge from March through October. Professional guides offer trips of varying length. The Ocoee Whitewater Center is presently being used as an information center with displays from the Olympic events.

Adventure Trail Rides (ages 7 to 12)

Call for directions, (706) 258-BARN (258-2276); www.adventuretrailrides.com. Open daily for two-hour rides at 10:00 a.m., 1:00 p.m., and 4:00 p.m., reservations secured by credit card required. $$$$

Have your buckaroos saddle up for guided rides along easy scenic trails (Bum Level 1). Those cowboys and cowgirls with more experience can try advanced steep terrain and winding trails (Bum Level 2 and 3). To avoid a charge on your credit card, cancellation must be made at least twenty-four hours in advance. Other requirements: No riders younger than seven; all riders younger than sixteen must wear a helmet; no double riding. Tip: Read the Web site for hilarious rules and thoughts from the horses.

Blue Ridge Scenic Railway (all ages)

241 Depot Street, Blue Ridge; (706) 632-9833 or (800) 934-1898; www.brscenic.com. Trains depart March through November Friday, Saturday, and Monday at 11:00 a.m. and Sunday at 1:00 p.m. Adults $$$$, children ages three to twelve $$$.

All aboard! Introduce the kiddies to the joys of riding the rails just as in bygone days during this 26-mile three-and-a-half hour round-trip that chugs through historic Murphy Junction and along the Toccoa River to McCaysville, where there is a one-hour stop. Sit back, relax, and enjoy the views. Every season puts on a new and different show outside your window. The Web site offers a discount coupon.

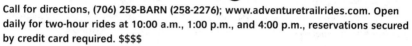

Amazing Georgia Facts

- Forty state parks and forty wildlife management areas
- 60,000 lakes and ponds
- 40,000 acres of large lakes
- No natural large lakes
- Seventeen major rivers covering 2,218 miles

Chattahoochee National Fish Hatchery (all ages) 🐟

4739 Rock Creek Road, Suches; (706) 838-4723; www.fs.fed.us.conf/. Open Monday through Friday 7:30 a.m. to 4:00 p.m., weekends 8:00 a.m. to 8:30 p.m. Free.

If little fish live in fish bowls, where do big fish live? Spawn some interest in how nature propagates the species by taking your little tadpoles to see all stages of fish culture and thousands of fish being raised. As an extra treat, fishing is allowed on the grounds. There's nothing like success to serve as an inspiration for little anglers, so start them out here, where they're sure to hook something.

Eagle Adventure Company (ages 8 to 12) △ 🐟

375 Eagle Ranch Road, Copperhill, TN; (423) 496-1843 or (800) 288-3245; www.eagle adventures.com. Open daily, 9:00 a.m. until the last trip returns. Rafting $$$$.

Vigorous clans who like a challenge will want to try some of the unparalleled array of exploits offered by this purveyor of dreams. Although the company is based across the state line in Tennessee, many of the adventures are in north Georgia. Exhilarating activities include white-water rafting, canoeing, kayaking, and guided trout fishing expeditions. Visit for the day or stay for the week.

Lake Blue Ridge (all ages) △ △

Old US 76, Blue Ridge; (800) 899-MTNS; www.blueridgemountains.com. Open year-round. Free.

Heaven on Earth—this lake is one of the most beautiful and pristine spots in the state. With 3,290 acres of deep blue mountain water and 100 miles of mostly public shoreline, the impoundment boasts ninety national forest campsites, several boat ramps, a full-service marina, and public swimming areas. There are also two Forest Service campgrounds that border the lake. Warning: This is a true mountain lake—the water's very cold even in the middle of summer, but that probably won't deter little polar bears. We remember when our eldest daughter Elaine would insist that she wasn't cold—despite blue lips and goose bumps the size of goose eggs. End a perfect day by camping out under the stars.

Sugar Creek Alpaca Farm (ages 6 to 12) 🐑 ⊖

1050 Cox Road, (706) 258-4494 or (888) 662-8253; www.sugarcreekfarmandinn.com. Guided tours by reservation. Free.

Most modern-day kidlets (and even their parents) have never seen an alpaca. In fact, can you tell the difference between an alpaca and a llama? Well it turns out that camels, llamas, and alpacas are all related, and camels are the largest and alpacas the smallest. Alpacas are renowned for their high-quality, silky fleece, which is used for making sweaters and shawls among other things. Visit with a herd of suri alpacas at this friendly farm where you can also cavort with adorable babydoll sheep. Their wool is in the same class as cashmere and is highly desirable when blended with

Angora rabbit or goat wool. Sugar Creek supplies fleece and wool for yarn to creators of hand-woven and machine-knit clothing. The farm also offers bed-and-breakfast accommodations.

Swan Drive-In (ages 6 to 12)

651 Summit Street; (888) 469-1955; www.swan-drivein.com. Open nights year round. $

Many kidlets these days may never have experienced a drive-in movie, but don't despair. First-run, family-oriented movies are offered year round at one of the last four drive-in movies in Georgia. This one has been around since 1955—perhaps attended by the parents or even the grandparents of today's moppets.

For More Information

Fannin County Chamber of Commerce, 3990 Appalachian Highway, Blue Ridge, GA 30513; (706) 632-5680 or (800) 899-MTNS; www.blueridgemountains.com.

Calhoun

West on Highway 53 at the intersection of Highways 156 and 225.

Battle of Resaca Festival (ages 4 to 12)

300 South Wall Street; (706) 625-3200 or (800) 887-3811; www.georgiadivision.org/ gdra_main.html. Third weekend in May, Saturday 9:00 a.m. to 8:30 p.m., Sunday 9:00 a.m. to 3:00 p.m. Admission $, younger than twelve free.

"The Yankees are comin', the Yankees are comin'." Don't forget some one-use cameras for your budding photojournalists when you take your battalion to see this Civil War living-history lesson, where the Battle of Resaca is reenacted on the old battlefield between Calhoun and Resaca. The junior set are encouraged to question the hundreds of authentically costumed soldiers and camp followers who bivouac on the grounds.

New Echota State Historic Site (all ages) 🏛 🚗 ♿

1211 Chatsworth Highway; (706) 624-1321; www.gastateparks.org/info/echota. Open Tuesday through Saturday 9:00 a.m. to 5:00 p.m., Sunday 2:00 to 5:30 p.m. Adults and children ages six to eighteen $, younger than six free. If you are interested in a guided tour, ask when the next one is scheduled (tours take about two hours).

History comes alive at this site, which from 1825 to 1838 served as the last capital of the Cherokee Nation, an independent realm that covered north Georgia and parts of four other southeastern states. Once Native Americans tilled these fields and established a village here. Now your tribe can follow in their footsteps as you explore this historic site.

In 1838 the Cherokee Indians were rounded up and removed to Oklahoma via the Trail of Tears, a lamentable period in U.S. history. After the Native Americans were removed, the village completely disappeared, but today reconstructed buildings allow you to see how these early Americans lived. Rather than the stereotypical Indian village, New Echota was a traditional American town of frame homes and farm buildings, a newspaper printing office, and a tavern. The council house, which could just as well have been a courthouse in any Southern town, also served as a school. The visitor center offers a film about the site and houses an interpretive museum. Special events throughout the year include living-history demonstrations.

For More Information

Calhoun-Gordon County Convention and Visitors Bureau, 300 South Wall Street, Calhoun, GA 30701; (706) 625-3200; www.gordonchamber.org.

Cherokee **Lore**

- New Echota was the capital of the Cherokee Nation and was recognized by the federal government.

- The Cherokees had their own alphabet, the Sequoyah syllabary.

- The Cherokee at New Echota published the *Cherokee Phoenix*, the only Native American newspaper ever printed in nineteenth-century North America.

Official Georgia

- **Flower:** Cherokee rose
- **Gem:** quartz
- **Mineral:** staurolite
- **Motto:** Wisdom, Justice, Moderation
- **Songs:** "Our Georgia" (waltz) and "Georgia on My Mind" (blues)

Rome

South on US 27.

Early European settlers to the area of seven hills noted the similarity to Rome, Italy, and so the town was named in its honor. In recognition of that distinction, the old-world city presented a replica of the *Etruscan Wolf* statue (the twins Romulus and Remus with their she-wolf mother) to its American counterpart. Founded in 1834, Rome quickly became a thriving commercial center. Start your excursion with a stop at the welcome center to pick up a map and information about this fascinating town.

Chieftains Museum (ages 4 to 12)

501 Riverside Parkway; (706) 291-9494; www.chieftainsmuseum.org. Open Tuesday through Friday 9:00 a.m. to 3:00 p.m., Saturday 10:00 a.m. to 4:00 p.m. Admission $, children younger than six free.

Whoop it up at this Native American history museum, housed in the 1794 home of Major Ridge, another important Cherokee leader and one of the signers of the Treaty of New Echota. Major Ridge struggled to adapt to white men's ways, mediated disputes with other tribes, and earned his rank in the War of 1812 at the Battle of Horseshoe Bend in Alabama. He and his kin were ferryboat masters, storekeepers, and slave-holding planters. The museum contains exhibits pertaining to Cherokee history, Ridge's life, and the chronicles of the area.

Chiaha

Native American residents called the region around Rome *Chiaha*, their word for "meeting of the hills and rivers."

You Can't Judge a Book **by Its Cover**

The beautiful 1870 brick-enclosed clock tower that dominates Rome's skyline is really a water tower containing the town's water supply. It also houses a small museum and is a wonderful vantage point from which to get a bird's-eye view of downtown Rome. Bring the camera.

Zion Farms (ages 6 to 12) 🅰 🚫 👥
2979 Big Texas Valley Road NW; (706) 235-8002 or (706) 232-4323; www.zionfarms .com. Prices vary.

Zion, meaning "the place where God dwells," is the perfect name for this oasis in the north Georgia mountains. The family-owned and -operated estate features 340 acres of pastures, mountain trails, ponds, and secluded picnic areas, but it is primarily an equestrian facility. Riding lessons are available for beginner to intermediate riders in both English and Western, as are one- to three-hour trail rides and therapeutic riding for children. Birthday parties include horseback riding, a hayride, "Barn Talk," and barn games. Summer equestrian camps are available for beginner to advanced riders. There are day camps for ages five through eight and overnight camps for ages eight though sixteen. You can even learn to be a certified riding instructor. Families can stay in guest cottages. Breakfast is included, and private dinners and picnics can be arranged.

For More Information

Rome Welcome Center, 402 Civic Center Drive, Rome, GA 30161; (800) 444-1834 or (706) 295-5576; www.romegeorgia.com.

Civil War **Trivia**

The Confederate Women's Monument in Rome was the first one to pay homage to the women of the Civil War era.

Cave Spring

Southwest on US 411.

The town of Cave Spring was named for a huge limestone cavern and the pure natural spring that flows from it. Legend says that Native Americans first discovered the spring and held tribal meetings and competitions near the cave. Considered to have medicinal properties, the waters drew many visitors to the small town at the turn of the twentieth century. Mom and Dad or Grammy and Gramps will be interested to know that the quaint town has ninety homes listed on the National Register of Historic Places and is filled with quaint antiques and gift shops. We never pass through town without stopping at the great ice-cream parlor.

Rolater Park (all ages) 😎 🏛

Park Square; (706) 777-3382; www.romegeorgia.com/cavespg. Open daily, 7:00 a.m. to 9:00 p.m.; cave 10:00 a.m. to 5:00 p.m. Monday through Friday; pool noon to 6:00 p.m. daily. Park free; cave $; swimming $.

During summer the rug rats delight in venturing into the recesses of the dark, mysterious cave like modern-day Tom Sawyers, Huck Finns, and Becky Thatchers. Reputed to be 300,000 years old, the cavern is not particularly large but does offer some impressive stalagmites. Excess water from the spring flows into a Georgia-shaped, spring-filled swimming pool (the largest spring-fed pool in the state). (Warn your little tadpoles, this is not a pool for the fainthearted—the water is always cold.) Significant buildings in the park include a church built in 1851 and a classroom building left from the former Cave Spring Manual Labor School, which later became the Hearn Academy.

For More Information

City of Cave Spring, P.O. Box 365, Cave Spring, GA 30124; (706) 777-3382 or (800) 444-1834; www.romegeorgia.com/cavespg.

Cartersville/Cassville/White

East on US 411, then south on U.S. Highway 41.

These small north Georgia towns have a little bit of everything and a little bit extra: a major lake for fishing, swimming, boating, and other water sports; Civil War historic sites; Mississippian Indian mounds; early furnaces that smelted iron ore; a mineral museum; a pair of covered bridges; and a state park complete with cottages and a lodge.

The First **Decoration Day**

The country's first Confederate Memorial Day observance was held at the Kingston Confederate Cemetery.

Booth Museum of Western Art (ages 4 to 12)

501 Museum Drive, Cartersville; (770) 387-1300; www.boothmuseum.org. Open Tuesday, Wednesday, Friday, and Saturday from 10:00 a.m. to 5:00 p.m. Thursday 10:00 a.m. to 8:00 p.m. Sunday 1:00 to 5:00 p.m. Closed Monday and Thanksgiving, Christmas, New Year's, and Independence Days. Adults $, children younger than twelve free.

Your little cowboys and cowgirls will want to mosey on over to Cartersville's newest attraction. The ultramodern museum in the heart of downtown houses a collection of contemporary Western American art featuring representations of Indians, settlers, and animals in Western settings. Galleries are devoted to illustrations, movie posters, Civil War art, and presidential letters and portraits. Get in the mood by viewing the orientation film, *The American West*. Of particular interest to young buckaroos is Sagebrush Ranch, an interactive gallery where they can climb aboard a stagecoach, sit on a still-life horse, draw a buffalo, or brand a cow (not for real). Organized like a ranch, the gallery features a farmhouse, barn, bunkhouse, and corral. Rodeo Joe, the ranch foreman, guides your cowpokes to more than thirty fun and educational stations.

Etowah Indian Mounds Historic Site (ages 4 to 12)

813 Indian Mounds Road SW, Cartersville; (770) 387-3747; www.gastateparks.org/info/etowah. Open Tuesday through Saturday 9:00 a.m. to 5:00 p.m., Sunday 2:00 to 5:30 p.m. Closed Monday except those included in holiday weekends and Thanksgiving, Christmas, and New Year's Days. Adults and children ages six to twelve $. Parking $3.

Ancient Mississippian-era Native Americans occupied northwest Georgia between A.D. 950 and 1450, when they constructed huge ceremonial and burial mounds. Take your time travelers back to the era of that culture by visiting these gigantic remnants of their society, which make up one of the most intact Mississippian sites in the Southeast. Although your little explorers will want to see the video presentation and explore the interpretive museum to learn more about the Mississippian civilization, their biggest treat is climbing to the flat tops of the three major ceremonial protuberances. In fact, they'll probably want to race you to the top up the wooden stairways that protect the slopes. No one is certain exactly why the mounds were built or how long each took—maybe your Indiana Jones–in-training will catch the archaeology bug and be the one to solve the mystery.

Lake Allatoona (all ages) ⊗ 🏛 🕮

1138 GA Highway 20 Spur, Cartersville; (678) 721-6700; http://allatoona.sam.usace.army.mil. **Visitor center open 8:00 a.m. to 4:30 p.m. Free.**

Allatoona Dam impounds the Etowah River into Lake Allatoona, a 12,000-acre playground with 270 miles of shoreline. A perfect place for a day's (week's) escape, the reservoir and its thirty-six public-use areas abound with numerous land-based and water sports activities. Long before the impoundment was created by man, Native Americans lived in the area. Later miners extracted precious ores from beneath the ground. Junior jaunters can investigate both these historic periods and others at the visitor center atop the dam, where a film and exhibits interpret the natural and cultural history of Bartow County and the lake.

Noble Hill-Wheeler Memorial Center (ages 6 to 12) 🏛 🕮

2361 Joe Frank Harris Parkway, Cassville; (770) 382-3392. **Open Tuesday through Saturday 9:00 a.m. to 4:00 p.m. Free.**

Brighten up a dog-day afternoon and learn something about African-American heritage with a visit to this history museum and cultural center, which is housed in the former Noble Hill Rosenwald School. Built in 1923, it was the first institution in northwest Georgia constructed with Rosenwald funds for the education of African-American children. Among the artifacts from those early school days are kettles, washboards, desks, and wooden carvings, as well as old photographs. In the old days a student could go to the head of the class without a computer in sight.

Pettit Creek Farms (all ages) 🐘 ⊛ 🔒

337 Cassville Road; (770) 386-8688; www.PettitCreekFarms.com. **Open October through December; call for hours and admission fees.**

When Halloween's a-comin' what's better for your little ghouls than pickin' their own pumpkin for the best jack-o'-lantern ever? October is not only the time for the farm's Pumpkin Pickin' Patch, but also for Pumpkinfest—an arts and crafts festival. Starting the day after Thanksgiving, back-to-nature-type families can choose their own Christmas tree, take a hayride of the farm, and enjoy a drive-through holiday lights display. Whenever you visit, the rug rats can enjoy getting up close and personal with a camel, zebra, Patagonian cavy, emu, ponies, buffalo, and traditional farm animals.

Red Top Mountain State Park (all ages) 🌊 ⊛ ⊗

50 Lodge Road, Cartersville; (770) 975-0055; www.gastateparks.org/info/redtop. **Open daily, 7:00 a.m. to 10:00 p.m. Parking $3; cottages $$–$$$; lodge $$–$$$; camping $; meals $–$$.**

Named for Georgia's red, iron-rich soil, this park is one of the state's most visited. Located on a wooded peninsula overlooking Lake Allatoona, Red Top is a haven for nature lovers and wildlife observers, as well as for water babies, fisherfolk, and hikers.

Youngsters will be busy from the moment you get here. When it's lullaby time down South, accommodations are available in a lodge or cabins. Rough-it types can plop a tent or RV into one of many campsites. One word of warning: If you arrive early in the morning, watch for deer on the roadway.

Tellus Northwest Georgia Science Museum (ages 4 to 12)

Formerly the William Weinman Mineral Museum, the museum will be closed July 31st 2007 for expansion and should reopen in 2008 with its new name. 51 Mineral Museum (I-75, exit 126), White; (770) 386-0576; www.chara.gsu.edu/~weinman; weinman@ innerx.net. Open Tuesday through Saturday 10:00 a.m. to 4:30 p.m., Sunday 1:00 to 4:00 p.m. Admission $, younger than six free.

Young rock hounds can spend hours in this museum, examining the minerals, fossils, and gemstones from northwest Georgia, the Southeast, and all over the world. Another highlight sure to tickle the fancy of young explorers is a man-made cave. Dan's father was a lapidarist, so this was a must-stop while he was alive; now it's the new generation who insist that we stop. Twenty-first-century Stone Agers look forward to the Rock Swap and Festival held the second weekend in June. The new expansion will include a digital planetarium with 125,000 square feet of galleries dedicated to fossils, transportation technology, and hands-on science experiences.

For More Information

Cartersville Bartow Country CVB, 1 Friendship Plaza, Cartersville, GA 30120; (770) 387-1357 or (800) 733-2280; www.notatlanta.org.

Canton/Hickory Flat

East on Highway 20, then south on Highway 140.

Cagle's Dairy (ages 2 to 12)

362 Stringer Road, Canton; (770) 345–5591; www.caglesdairy.com, click on Tours, then Family Tours. Farm tour days and times vary greatly. Check the calendar on the Web site or call and then e-mail your reservation to Scott@CaglesDairy.com. $

Cagle's is a working dairy farm located not far outside Atlanta with lots of things for visiting families to do. Several days a month the Cagle family offers farm tours that start with a tractor-pulled hayride and a herding demonstration by award-winning Border collies. Your kids (as opposed to the goat kids they'll see) can get up close and personal by bottle-feeding calves and seeing how a cow is milked. You'll visit the processing facility and learn how the milk gets from the cow to the dairy case. Everyone even gets some plain or chocolate milk. Friday through Sunday from early September through late November, the farm operates the Cagle's Farm Maze with its 3 miles of twists, turns, and decision points. (Reservations aren't required for the maze or other tours during this time.) Parents will appreciate the new Cow Wagon Train for taking small children through the maze. Other special activities throughout the year include stock trials one weekend in April, where Border collies compete in herding sheep, cattle, and ducks; the Spring Farm Days Festival; and the Fall Harvest Festival.

Alpharetta

South on Highway 140 to Hardscrabble Road, then east.

Autrey Mill Nature Preserve and Heritage Center (all ages)

9770 Autrey Mill Road; (678) 366-3511; www.autreymill.org. Preserve open daily daylight hours; visitor center open weekdays 10:00 a.m. to 4:00 p.m., Sunday 2:00 to 4:00 p.m. Free.

Once a forty-six-acre cotton plantation, the preserve features creeks, shoals, springs, cliffs, forest, native plants, wildflowers, and wildlife as well as a 1½-mile hiking trail. The Tenant Farmhouse contains antique tools and furnishings. The rustic visitor center houses other exhibits. Special events and programs occur throughout the year.

Kroger School of Cooking (ages 6 to 13)

12460 Crabapple Road; (404) 892-1250, ext. 246. Class times vary. $$$$ per child.

Aspiring chefs among the small fry can brush up on their cooking skills with classes designed just for them at this brainchild of Chef Bernard Kinsella, who began his own culinary career at age ten. Sessions, which include student participation, are geared for ages six through nine and ages ten through thirteen. While teaching fun ways to prepare nutritious foods, Chef Bernard directs tasty assignments that range from creating basic pretzels to making fruit-filled pancakes. Make sure the munchkins go to class hungry; part of the fun is sampling the finished products.

The Cooler/Alpharetta Family Skate Center (ages 6 to 12)

10800 Davis Drive; (770) 649-6600; www.cooler.com. Open daily 5:30 to 1:00 a.m.; all sessions two hours; afternoon ice-skating and in-line skating $; evening sessions $$; skate rentals $.

Skate through life with an outing to this three-rink ice and in-line skating center, which is certainly not the ho-hum skating rink Mom and Dad might have been used to in their youth. The state-of-the-art facility sports two NHL-regulation ice hockey arenas, figure skating, an in-line roller arena, food service, and a pro shop. So strap on the blades and head for the ice.

Wills Park Equestrian Center (all ages)

11915 Wills Road; (678) 297-6120; www.alpharetta.ga.us/main.city.parks.parkfacilities
.html. Park always open; call for a schedule of horse shows and other events. Park
free; horse show admission varies.

If you have horse lovers in your herd, they'll be thrilled with the numerous equestrian
events that take place almost every weekend at this City of Alpharetta park. Outdoor
and covered show rings set the stage for Western and English events such as rodeos
and dressage competitions. It's a pleasure simply wandering around the 300 stalls
visiting horses and getting to know both the steeds and their owners. Baseball fields,
tennis courts, an Olympic-size outdoor pool, football field, playground, and a Frisbee
golf course at adjacent Wills Park provide enough excitement to keep any energetic
youngster satisfied. A popular new event, dog agility trials, are held several times a
year. Get on your hobby horse and ride on over.

For More Information

Alpharetta Visitors Bureau, 3060 Royal
Boulevard South, Suite 145, Alpharetta, GA
30022; (678) 297-2811 or (800) 294-0923;
www.alpharettacvb.com.

Duluth

West on Highway 120.

Southeastern Railway Museum (ages 6 to 12)

3595 South Old Peachtree Road; (770) 476-2013; www.southeasternrailwaymuseum
.org. April through December, open Thursday through Saturday 10:00 a.m. to 5:00
p.m.; January through March, open Saturday only 10:00 a.m. to 5:00 p.m. Adults $8,
seniors $6, children two through twelve $4.

All aboard! Railroad buffs can stay on track with a visit to the largest railroad
museum in Georgia, operated and maintained by the Atlanta Chapter of the National
Railway Historical Society. Your little cabooses can wander around and through
acres of restored and unrestored railway cars, tracks, signals, and engines. Curious
wannabe engineers can watch cars and engines undergoing restoration. Hop on
board a real train for a ride around the property on the third weekend of each
month.

Roswell

West on Highway 120.

Our kind of town, Roswell is where we hung our hats for more than twenty years. This charming Southern town has several historic districts dating from 1839. Roswell was one of the only hamlets near Atlanta that didn't suffer major damage during the Atlanta Campaign of the Civil War, although its textile mills were burned because they were making gray fabric for Confederate uniforms, and the women and children who were running them were taken prisoner. Begin your tour with a visit to the **Historic Roswell Visitor Center,** located across from the Town Square (617 Atlanta Street; 770-640-3253 or 800-776-7935; www.cvb.roswell.ga.us; open Monday through Friday 9:00 a.m. to 5:00 p.m., Saturday 10:00 a.m. to 4:00 p.m., Sunday noon to 3:00 p.m. **Free**). Here you can watch a video, view historic exhibits, and pick up a brochure for a self-guided walking or driving tour past two dozen historic sites. Guided tours offered by the Roswell Historical Society leave from the visitor center on Wednesday at 10:00 a.m. and Saturday at 1:00 p.m. $.

Bulloch Hall (ages 6 to 12)

180 Bulloch Avenue; (770) 992-1731; www.bullochhall.org. Guided tours on the hour Monday through Saturday 10:00 a.m. to 3:00 p.m., Sunday 1:00 to 3:00 p.m. Special holiday tours are self-guided. Adults $$, children $.

Take your little historians to Bulloch Hall, a grand 1840 Greek Revival mansion that was the home of Theodore Roosevelt's mother, Mittie Bulloch—who was also the grandmother of Eleanor Roosevelt. Teddy visited the house while he was president. By the way, do your little bear lovers know that the name "teddy bear" honors Teddy Roosevelt? Docents regale curious kidlets with anecdotes about the house, the family, and its most famous visitor. One of the bedrooms, known as Mittie's Room, is furnished as it would have been when Roosevelt's mother lived there. Unusual for an antebellum house, the kitchen is located in the basement rather than away from the structure for fear of fires. A reconstructed slave cottage portrays the life of African Americans. Periodic special events, such as the monthlong Christmas at Bulloch Hall, various summer camps for children, Civil War encampments, and Halloween and storytelling festivals keep things lively. A combination ticket is also available, which also allows admission to Barrington Hall and Smith Plantation.

Chattahoochee Nature Center (all ages)

9135 Willeo Road; (770) 992-2055; www.chattnaturecenter.com. Open Monday through Saturday 9:00 a.m. to 5:00 p.m., Sunday noon to 5:00 p.m. Closed Thanksgiving, Christmas, and New Year's Days. $

Miles of freshwater ponds, wooded uplands, river marshes, nature trails, a river boardwalk, a Georgia wetlands exhibit, a Discovery Center, and a beaver exhibit attract active families to this 127-acre environmental education center on the Chattahoochee

River. But what your fledglings will probably like best are the raptor aviaries where they can see many rehabilitated birds of prey—including bald eagles—that can't be returned to the wild. There are camps, nature programs, and other activities throughout the year.

Roswell Fire and Rescue Museum (all ages) 🔥

1002 Alpharetta Street; (770) 641-3730. Open daily 9:00 a.m. to 6:00 p.m. unless personnel are responding to a call. Free.

Located inside an active fire station, the museum displays antique fire equipment showing how firefighting progressed through the years.

Roswell Ghost Tour (ages 6 to 12)

(770) 649-9422 or (404) 644-8051; www.roswellghosttour.com. Friday and Saturday at 7:00 p.m. (sometimes 8:00 p.m.). $$$

The youngsters will squeal with shivery delight at these spine-tingling tales about the other-worldly spirits who once inhabited the area (and perhaps still do). Those who are brave enough meet at the bandstand in the square across from the visitor center at 617 Atlanta Street for a spooktacular two-hour tour of the historic district. Wear comfortable shoes and bring a flashlight—an umbrella, too, in inclement weather. Note: A minimum of six people is required for a tour to depart, but they don't have to all be in the same party, so call to see if you can join an existing group.

The Missing Roswell
Women and Children

During the Civil War, the Roswell mills were making gray cloth for Confederate uniforms as well as making rope for the Confederate army. Union general William T. Sherman's troops came to Roswell, burned the mills, and arrested the few men and all the women and children who had been working at the mills. They were charged with treason, taken to Marietta, Georgia, and put on trains for the North. There some were imprisoned and others were basically under house arrest—made to work for Northerners for little or no wages. After the war some made their way back to Roswell, but others were never seen or heard from again. A monument to these workers has been erected near the site of the mills. An excellent fictional work about the episode that young readers might enjoy is *Turn Homeward, Hannalee,* by Patricia Beatty, which tells the story of a young girl and her brother who were not only taken but also separated from each other.

Roswell Trail System and River Walk (ages 3 to 12) 🏕️ 🚵 👫 🏛️

(770) 640-3253 or (770) 641-3705 or (800) 776-7935. Open daily dawn to dusk. Free.

The kids can expend plenty of energy exploring the city's 16 miles of trails that wind through developed and undeveloped areas and along the Chattahoochee River. Some trails provide access to the Chattahoochee River National Recreation Area. Maps are available at the visitor center at 617 Atlanta Street. Seven miles along the Chattahoochee River have been incorporated into a linear park dotted with parks and recreational facilities such as playgrounds, picnic facilities, boat ramps, places to fish, and restrooms.

Smith Plantation (ages 4 to 12) 🏛️ 🛍️

935 Alpharetta Street; (770) 641-3978; www.archibaldsmithplantation .org. Open Monday through Saturday 10:00 a.m. to 4:00 p.m., Sunday 1:00 to 4:00 p.m. (last tour at 3:00 p.m.) $$ adults, $ children.

Youngsters can step back in time at the 1840s Archibald Smith Plantation Home—once a simple farm. Although the three-acre site is now completely surrounded by the City of Roswell, the Smith family first lived here in isolation. One of the things that's interesting about this farm is that is was continuously occupied by the same family for three generations spanning more than one hundred years. Many of the outbuildings, such as a separate kitchen, corncrib, barns, and other structures typical of early farms, still survive to intrigue small visitors.

StarTime Entertainment Complex (ages 6 to 12) 🎢

608 Holcomb Bridge Road; (770) 993-5411; www.startimeentertainment.com. Open Monday through Saturday 11:00 a.m. to 2:00 a.m., 11:00 to midnight Sunday. $–$$

Anyone who can't find something to do here isn't looking very hard. The complex, which features plenty to do for the small fry as well as the young at heart, features two miniature golf courses, two go-kart tracks, bumper cars, batting cages, a fourteen-seat motion simulator, an arcade with 200 video/skill games, and a ten-screen movie theater as well as the Studio Café. For the bigger kids among you, there are also billiards, the Funny Farm comedy club, and the StarTime Sports Bar. Prices are dependent on the activity.

Teaching Museum—North (ages 4 to 12) 🛍️

791 Mimosa Boulevard; (770) 552-6339; www.fulton.k12.ga.us/dept/teachingmuseum north. Open Monday through Friday 8:00 a.m. to 3:00 p.m. $

Interesting exhibits feature U.S. presidents, Georgia authors, women in the White House, transportation, World War II, and more. The museum stands on the site of the first academy in Roswell.

Bulloch Hall **Guilds**

The Open Hearth, Weaving, Garden, and Quilting Guilds at Bulloch Hall give demonstrations of nineteenth-century skills and crafts such as fireplace cooking, weaving, and quilting as they work on their projects. Some of their wares are for sale in the museum shop.

Vickery Creek Unit of the Chattahoochee National Recreation Area (ages 6 to 12) (🏃)(♿)(🚻)

Riverside Drive; (770) 399-8070; www.nps.gov/chat. Open daily 9:00 a.m. to 5:00 p.m. Parking $2.

Come a little closer—we want to whisper in your ear. This wilderness preserve is one of the metropolitan area's best-kept secrets, so if we let you in on it, promise you won't tell anyone. We don't want the word to get out and spoil this great uncrowded spot. The topography in the heavily wooded park includes steep cliffs and rugged rocky outcroppings, as well as level terrain along gurgling streams—adding up to 11.5 miles of hiking trails of varying degrees of difficulty. A great place to let the little people run free to burn off lots of energy, this untamed forest amazingly exists within Roswell's city limits. In addition, the refuge provides plenty of opportunities for little squirts to fish, rock climb, or explore the historic 1860s mill dam and several mill ruins.

For More Information

Historic Roswell Convention and Visitors Bureau, 617 Atlanta Street, Roswell, GA 30075; (770) 640-3253 or (800) 776-7935; www.cvb.roswell.ga.us.

Marietta

West on Highway 120.

Marietta Fire Museum (ages 3 to 12) (🔥)

112 Haynes Street; (770) 794-5460. Open weekdays 8:00 a.m. to 5:00 p.m. Free.

Your wanna-be firefighters will be fascinated by the range of usual and unusual equipment from the 1800s to the present housed at the Marietta Fire Station. The star attraction is *Aurora*, a horse-drawn Silsby Steamer fire engine in service from 1879 to 1921.

Mountasia Family Fun Center (ages 6 to 12) ⚙

175 Ernest Bennett Parkway; (770) 422-7227; www.mountasia.com. Open Monday through Thursday 10:00 a.m. to 10:00 p.m., Friday and Saturday 10:00 a.m. to midnight, Sunday noon to 9:00 p.m. $$

Kidlets can hardly decide between the go-karts, bumper boats, miniature golf, or the sixty video arcade games. Stave off hunger pangs at the snack bar. Prices vary by activity; specials and ride combination packages are available.

Six Flags/American Adventures (all ages) ⚙ 🍴

250 North Cobb Parkway; (770) 948-9290; www.sixflags.com/parks/aadventures. Open weekends March through May, daily June through mid-August, weekends mid-August through October. Closed November through February. Call for exact hours, or check online. Weekend fun pass (all attractions) $$$ ages four to fifteen, $ younger than four and adults (rates vary by season and there are specials going on all the time, so call before visiting to check). Parking $.

For a gung-ho, all-out day of family-oriented entertainment suitable for all ages, including tiny tots, revel in this park's foam factory, go-kart racing, miniature golf, bumper cars, mini roller coaster, carousel, kiddie's play area, arcade, and more. If hunger strikes, as it surely will after all this activity, an on-site restaurant can temporarily fill those hungry holes.

Six Flags/White Water (all ages) 🏊 ⚙ 🚗

250 North Cobb Parkway; (770) 948-9290; www.sixflags.com/parks/whitewater. Open daily Memorial Day through Labor Day, 10:00 a.m. to 8:00 p.m. with extended evening hours on weekends and holidays; weekends only in May. $$$$ over 4 feet tall, $$$ 4 feet tall and less. Parking $5.

For the aquatically inclined this is the ultimate in swimming holes. Named the most scenic water park in the nation, the splashtacular complex provides all the necessary ingredients to cool off on hot summer days: forty attractions ranging from relaxing to high-thrill, including tree-shaded waterfalls, lazy rivers, family raft rides, the four-story Tree House Island, and Atlanta's only "ocean," plus five restaurants, picnic tables, and plenty of beach chairs for the older generation to kick back in when they get exhausted. For the more high-risk minded of the water rats, the Cliffhanger is one of the tallest free falls in the world—it's like plummeting from a nine-story building. When darkness falls, settle in for the Dive-In Movie.

U.S. Play (ages 6 to 12) ⚙

775 Cobb Place Boulevard; (770) 427-7679; www.bowlbrunswick.com. Hours vary widely, so call ahead. $$

This games emporium for kids of all ages boasts cosmic bowling, billiards, karaoke, and video games. Prices vary by activity.

For More Information

Marietta Welcome Center and Visitors Bureau, 4 Depot Street, Marietta, GA 30060; (770) 429-1115 or (800) 835-0445; www.mariettasquare.com.

Kennesaw

North on US 41.

The General, a Confederate locomotive, was abducted by Yankees from Kennesaw, then known as Big Shanty, chased, and rescued by railroad employees—but that wasn't the end of Kennesaw's involvement in the Civil War. In 1864 Confederate soldiers held off Union troops for several weeks at Kennesaw Mountain.

IceForum at Town Center (ages 6 to 12) ⊚

3061 George Busbee Parkway; (770) 218-1010; www.iceforum.com. Hours for public skating sessions vary widely, so call ahead. $$

Help the kiddies lace up the skates for a rare treat in the South—ice skating on regulation NHL-size surfaces. Everything for skaters is available here: pro shop, skate rentals (figure and hockey), skate repairs and sharpening, and instruction for all ages and levels of ability. In addition, the facility offers a full-service snack bar, video games, and seating for spectators.

Southern Museum of Civil War and Locomotive History
(ages 4 to 12) 🏛 🎦

2829 Cherokee Avenue; (770) 427-2117; www.southernmuseum.org. Open Monday through Saturday 9:30 a.m. to 5:00 p.m., Sunday noon to 5:00 p.m. Closed Easter and Thanksgiving, Christmas, and New Year's Days. $

Rain, rain, go away? Well, if that song doesn't work on nasty weather, chug on over to this museum and let junior adventurers relive the excitement of the Great Locomotive Chase by seeing the famous abducted engine, *The General,* up close and personal. Watching excerpts from a movie about the daring escapade and examining the numerous Civil War artifacts will keep all the gang engrossed for a while. The museum also houses the Glover Iron Works collection and Smithsonian traveling exhibits.

The Great **Locomotive Chase**

One of the most colorful incidents during the Civil War was the Great Locomotive Chase, which has been immortalized in two movies. A group of daring Yankees infiltrated the South and hijacked a train pulled by the locomotive *The General.* Determined Southerners chased it with a series of engines; the last one, *The Texas*, was commandeered in Adairsville. Although the Southerners were ultimately successful in catching the train and the hijackers, the Yankees were later awarded this nation's first Congressional Medals of Honor.

Kennesaw Mountain National Battlefield Park (ages 6 to 12)

900 Kennesaw National Drive; (770) 427-4686; www.nps.gov/kemo. Park open daily dawn to dusk; visitor center open year-round, 8:30 a.m. to 5:00 p.m. weekdays, 8:30 a.m. to 6:00 p.m. weekends, evening hours extended in summer. Closed Thanksgiving and Christmas. **Free.**

Out-manned Confederate soldiers kept the Union at bay for weeks at the Kennesaw Mountain battle line until they were forced to give up the positions because of the Union army's flanking action. On these hallowed grounds an interpretive museum offers exhibits and a video presentation, so start here. Then vigorous young troopers can hike up the mountain by way of paved trails that pass well-preserved breastworks. Numerous cannons and historic markers line the route. On weekends the less energetic can ride a shuttle bus almost to the summit; then it's only a hop, skip, and a jump to the top. From the peak on a clear day, little kiddies will see one of the best panoramas there is of downtown Atlanta. Sixteen miles of additional hiking trails beckon vigorous broods bent on exercise.

Dallas/Villa Rica

West on U.S. Highway 278 then south on Highway 61.

Pickett's Mill State Historic Site (ages 4 to 12)

4432 Mt. Tabor Road, Dallas; (770) 443-7850; www.gastateparks.org/info/picketts. Open Tuesday through Saturday 9:00 a.m. to 5:00 p.m., Sunday noon to 5:30 p.m. Closed Monday (except holidays), Thanksgiving, Christmas, and New Year's Days. Adults and children ages five to eighteen $.

Thirsting for more Civil War history? Take your battalion to the site of one of the Confederacy's most dramatic victories. Three self-guided hiking trails through one of the best-preserved Civil War battlefields in the country permit little soldiers to view the surviving breastworks. If they still want to know more, the interpretive center features exhibits and a film about the battle. Your little troopers can learn the most, however, from the living-history programs that are presented the first and third weekends of each month by costumed reenactors.

For More Information

Douglas County Local Welcome Center, 2145 Slater Mill Road, Douglasville, GA 30135; (770) 942-5022; www.douglas countygeorgia.com.

Tallapoosa

West on Interstate 20, north on Highway 100.

West Georgia Museum (ages 4 to 12)

185 Mann Street; (770) 574-3125; www.westgeorgiamuseum.com. Open Tuesday through Friday 9:00 a.m. to 4:00 p.m., Saturday 9:00 a.m. to 5:00 p.m. Closed Sunday, Monday, and holidays. $

A rainy afternoon spent in this unusual museum spans all of time. To begin with, replicas of huge grinning dinosaurs, including a 30-foot *Tyrannosaurus rex* looming over seven smaller dinosaurs, greet visitors. Now that we have everyone's attention, let's proceed. Still representing the prehistoric era are a real dinosaur egg from China and a 600-pound, 300-million-year-old fossilized tree from Alabama. In the next section a mannequin of an Indian astride a taxidermied horse chases a mounted buffalo.

Arrowheads and other artifacts fill this area. Next proceed to the fully stocked General Store and fully furnished log cabin. Other displays from this era include stores, a barber shop, and a bank. The Lithia Springs Hotel was once the largest wooden structure east of the Mississippi. Artifacts from the hotel and a miniature model of it recall a bygone affluent era. Transportation History contains buggies, wagons, and early motorized vehicles. Natural history displays include mounted animals representing the wildlife of Haralson County. Young and old will be amazed by the intricate animals and other sculptures created by folk artist Max Morris from grapevines, magnolia pops, pinecones, and nuts.

Atlanta Metro

Southeast at I-75, Interstate 85, and I-20.

Atlanta, not only the capital of Georgia but considered the Capital of the New South, is on the fast track. It's the home of Coca-Cola, the world's most popular soft drink; Cable News Network (CNN); and Delta Air Lines among others. The megalopolis hosted the 1994 and 2000 Super Bowls and the 1996 Summer Olympic Games. Atlanta is a popular tourism destination and the number-two convention spot in the country—a vibrant city that abounds in family attractions ranging from simple diversions to highly sophisticated entertainment. And the fun doesn't end when the sun goes down. We suggest beginning a visit with a guided tour such as those offered by **Gray Line of Atlanta** (404-767-0594 or 800-965-6665). Such an excursion orients your gang to the metropolitan area and its attractions, from which you can plan what to see in more detail. The best way to avoid the city's infamous traffic is via the trains and buses of the **Metropolitan Atlanta Rapid Transit Authority** (MARTA) (404-848-5000 or 404-848-4711; www.itsmarta.com), which offers 1,500 miles of bus routes and 39 miles of rapid rail lines. Many of the attractions listed in this section are accessible by MARTA, as is the airport. Here's another important tidbit: Provisions are made on the last car of each train for transporting bicycles. Fares are $1.75 per person per ride. One of the city's newest attractions is a world-class aquarium. We've described the kid-friendly Atlanta attractions in alphabetical order for convenience in finding them. An economical way for families to see some of the major attractions in Atlanta is to purchase the **CityPass.** The pass allows nine days to see the Georgia Aquarium, World of Coca-Cola, High Museum of Art, Inside CNN Atlanta Studio Tour, Fernbank Museum of Natural History or Atlanta Botanical Garden, and Zoo Atlanta or the Atlanta History Center at a savings of almost 50 percent. Purchase it from any of the Atlanta Convention and Visitors Bureau Welcome Centers or any of the listed attractions. $$$$ (but remember you get to see six attractions).

Art & Soul: An Arts and Crafts Cafe! (ages 3 to 12)

4920 Roswell Road NE; (404) 303-9956. Open Sunday through Tuesday 12:00 to 7:00 p.m., Wednesday and Thursday 11:00 a.m. to 8:00 p.m., Friday and Saturday 11:00 a.m. to 9:00 p.m. Prices range from $ to $$ in addition to $$ for painting.

Eat, drink, and be merry at this paint-your-own pottery studio, which sells the joys of participating in the creative process. Billed as fun for those three to ninety-three, the studio allows your little artists to select a piece of white, unglazed pottery and lets their impish imaginations run riot as they create their own masterpieces. Even the artistically challenged klutz can adorn plates, mugs, bowls, candlesticks, platters, pitchers, and the like with colorful glazes. Leave your creations to be kiln fired and pick them up a few days later. Crafters-in-training can try out other projects as well:

mosaics, glass painting, beaded jewelry, painting terra-cotta pots and birdhouses, making sand castles, and tie-dyeing fabrics. All this creative energy is bound to work up an appetite, but fortunately the studio has thought of everything. It serves munchies, cookies, coffee, tea, and sodas.

Atlanta Cyclorama and Civil War Museum (ages 4 to 12) 🏛️ 🎟️

800-C Cherokee Avenue SE, Grant Park; (404) 624-1071 or (404) 658-7625; www.webguide .com/cyclorama.html. Open Tuesday through Sunday, until 5:30 p.m. in summer. Closed Martin Luther King Jr. Day, Thanksgiving, and Christmas.

The word *unique* is grossly overused, but we've only seen one other cyclorama paint-ing during our world travels (in the Netherlands). If the idea of seeing a circular painting doesn't impress the young set, just tell them you're going to see *The Texas*—the engine that finally caught up with the stolen *General* in the great locomotive chase (it's on display here)—then ease them in to see the painting. They'll thank you later. Atlanta's masterpiece depicts the fiercely fought Civil War Battle of Atlanta in July 1864, aided by a revolving seating section where you actually sit in the middle of the paint-ing, a three-dimensional diorama with music and dramatic lighting and sound effects. The cyclorama is right next door to the Atlanta zoo, so plan your excursion to include both kid pleasers.

Atlanta History Center (ages 6 to 12) 🏛️ 🎟️ 🍴

130 West Paces Ferry Road; (404) 814-4000; www.atlantahistorycenter.com. Open Mon-day through Saturday 10:00 a.m. to 5:30 p.m., Sunday noon to 5:30 p.m. Closed Thanks-giving, Christmas Eve and Day, and New Year's Day. Holiday hours (noon to 5:30 p.m.) on several other holidays. Adults $$$, children ages six to seventeen $$; lunch $–$$.

This is the source for learning about Atlanta's and Georgia's history, as well as being a fun place to visit. Displays include artifacts from Atlanta's history, folk crafts, and African-American history memorabilia, but the center is most noted for its extensive collection of Civil War artifacts. Be sure to have your little soldiers try to lift the typi-cal Civil War backpack and thirteen-pound-plus musket that was carried by each infantryman (North and South) during the long war. They'll be staggered by the weight—literally. The complex includes the museum itself, two historic houses, for-mal and informal gardens, acres of woodland, a snack bar, and a restaurant in the old carriage house. Although the oldsters may appreciate a tour of the opulent 1928 Italianate villa called the Swan House, the kiddies are more likely to enjoy the 1840s Tullie Smith Farm's farmhouse and outbuildings complete with farm animals. Every would-be athlete (or even couch potato) in the world was glued to the television set during the seventeen days of the Centennial Olympic Games held in Atlanta in 1996. In remembrance of those games and their tremendous legacy to the city of Atlanta, the new 27,500-square-foot Fentener van Vissingen Family Wing has been con-structed to house the **Centennial Olympic Games Museum.** The spectacular col-lection of multimedia presentations, artifacts, images, and interactive displays

Now That's **Big**

Atlanta-Hartsfield International Airport is not only the biggest terminal complex in the world with 138 gates, but it is consistently among the top two busiest in the world as well.

comprises one of the most significant exhibitions on Olympic sports and history in the entire world.

Visitors enter the museum over actual maple flooring from the 1996 Olympic basketball court where both the U.S. men's and women's teams won gold. The full story of the Centennial Olympic Games is explored including how the city won the games, how the games changed Atlanta, day-to-day chronology, heroes and special moments, event results and records, the global impact of the games, and their legacy.

Eight sections, thirteen interactive computer kiosks, and the Olympic Mania trivia game create a different experience for each visitor. Exhibits include participation medals, posters, the only complete collection of Olympic torches from 1936-1996, examples of licensed merchandise, gifts from among the 197 delegations that participated in the games, puppets, costumes, country signs, sports artifacts, and uniforms, among other memorabilia. The second floor houses the interactive Sports Lab—a high-energy area where visitors test their strength and skill compared to the world's greatest athletes. An assisted long jump, two side-by-side sculls, and two bikes engage participants.

Atlanta Sports Teams (ages 6 to 12)

Sports fans, listen up. Name the sport and Atlanta probably has at least one professional team. The **Atlanta Braves** baseball team plays at Turner Field (755 Hank Aaron Drive; 404-522-7630; www.atlantabravesmlb.com; $ to $$$$); the **Atlanta Falcons** football team plays at the Georgia Dome (1 Georgia Dome Drive; 404-223-8000; www.atlantafalcons.com; $$$$); the **Atlanta Hawks** basketball team plays at the Phillips Arena (1 Phillips Drive; 866-715-1500; www.nba.com/hawks; $$$$); and the **Atlanta Thrashers** (404-878-3300; www.atlantathrashers.com; $$$$) NHL hockey team plays at the Phillips Arena.

A Capital **Idea**

Atlanta became the fifth capital of Georgia in 1868 and has served in that capacity ever since.

Sayings from the Past

Do the small fry know where these folk phrases came from: "sleep tight," "don't let the bedbugs bite," "hush puppy," "pop goes the weasel," or "whistle while you work"? Docents/reenactors at the **Tullie Smith Farm** explain their origins.

Centennial Olympic Park (all ages) 🏛️ 🍴

265 Park Avenue West Northwest; (404) 223-4412 or (404) 222-PARK (recorded information); www.centennialolympicpark.com. Always accessible. Free.

As the name announces, Centennial Olympic Park was created for the 1996 Summer Olympics and was the center of the action during the games. If your crew contributed to the construction of the park by buying a brick, turn eagle-eyed young detectives loose to look for it—or if you want to cheat, go into the pavilion and look up its location on the computer terminal. In hot weather bring dry clothes for the little squirts; they're bound to get into the **Fountain of Rings**—body and soul. Designed in the form of the Olympic Rings, the fountain is the largest depiction of the Olympic logo in the world. Different heights of water jet out of the ground all the time, but hourly there is a dancing water show set to music. You might just decide to join the munchkins in the refreshing spray of Atlanta's fountain of youth. During the Christmas season, an outdoor ice skating rink and a spectacular lights display are big hits.

Center for Puppetry Arts (all ages) 🎵

1404 Spring Street NW; (404) 873-3391; www.puppet.org. Museum open Tuesday through Saturday 9:00 a.m. to 5:00 p.m., Sunday 11:00 a.m. to 5:00 p.m. Call for performance times. Adults and children ages four to thirteen $$.

String along with your little dolls to this magical place. Not just a performance venue, the center has the largest collection of puppets in the world. Tiny tykes are agog with the tremendous variety of puppets. An interactive exhibit is called *Puppets—the Power of Wonder.* As an added bonus, future puppeteers older than three can create their own puppets at periodic workshops.

Chattahoochee River National Recreation Area (ages 4 to 12) 🥾 🐟 ⛺

Headquarters: 1978 Island Ford Parkway; (678) 538-1200; www.nps.gov/chat. Open one hour after sunrise to one hour after sunset. Free.

As the Chattahoochee River flows languidly from the north Georgia mountains to the Georgia/Florida border, 48 miles of it meander through the metro Atlanta area, providing endless opportunities for family fun: rafting, canoeing, kayaking, rowing, fishing, hiking, mountain biking, horseback riding, and wildlife observation at fourteen units of the park. The number one activity in Atlanta on a hot summer day is drifting down the Hooch on a raft.

Federal Reserve Bank of Atlanta Visitors Center and Monetary Museum (ages 6 to 12)

Federal Reserve Bank, 1000 Peachtree Street NE; (404) 498-8764; www.frbatlanta.org. Open Monday through Friday 9:00 a.m. to 4:00 p.m. Free.

Can there be anything much more fascinating for junior consumers than learning about how money is made? Let your young Rockefellers learn the history of money and see a gold bar (like the ones in Fort Knox), gold coins minted in Dahlonega, Georgia, and other rare coins. The museum shows a twenty-minute video on how the Federal Reserve works. It's probably over the heads of most youngsters, but who knows? Maybe one of your offspring will become the next Alan Greenspan.

Georgia Aquarium (all ages)

225 Baker Street; (404) 581-4000; www.georgiaaquarium.org. Open Monday through Thursday 10:00 a.m. to 5:00 p.m., Friday through Sunday 9:00 a.m. to 6:00 p.m.; hours extended one hour in the summer and during holiday periods. Note: Tickets are for a specific entrance time. $$$$

Obviously, landlocked Atlantans have been starving for an ocean. Now they have the next best thing—the Georgia Aquarium. So far in only a little more than one-and-half years of operation, the world's largest aquarium has attracted more than five million visitors. Located near Centennial Olympic Park and the new World of Coca-Cola, the facility resembles a huge ship (some have called it a modern-day Noah's Ark). Children (and parents too) will be totally awed by its five million gallons of water brimming with 55,000 animals representing 500 species. Favorites among visitors are the huge fearsome whale sharks and the sweet-faced Beluga whales as well as the comical penguins and otters. Innovative technologies and interactive and interdisciplinary techniques educate and entertain visitors while impressing on them the need for protection and preservation. Other attractions include a 4-D theater, behind-the-scenes tours, Deepo's Undersea 3-D Show, and Café Aquaria. Several ticketing packages are available.

Cyclorama

One of only twenty cycloramas left in the world, Atlanta's gargantuan 358-foot (that's longer than a football field) by 50-foot, 900-pound treasure (completed in 1885) is the biggest painting in America and one of only two in this country that are circular.

Georgia Dome (ages 4 to 12) 🏈

1 Georgia Dome Drive NW; (404) 223-TOUR; www.gadome.com. Tours on the hour Tuesday through Saturday 10:00 a.m. to 4:00 p.m. (last tour at 3:00 p.m.) $

Whether the members of your team are sports fans or not, everyone will find the architecture of the Georgia Dome awe inspiring. Public tours of the world's largest cable-supported dome explore the facility that hosted the 1994 and 2000 Super Bowls and the gymnastic and basketball events during the 1996 Summer Olympic Games. Young and not-so-young sports fans visit the observation level, press box, exclusive Dome suites, and the locker room. The finale is a visit to the field where they can toss a football. In addition, a section of the floor level contains several mini museums (really showcases) dedicated to the Atlanta Falcons, SEC football and basketball championships, the Chick-fil-A Bowl, and the Bank of America Football Classic.

Imagine It! The Children's Museum of Atlanta (ages 2 to 8) 🎨

275 Centennial Olympic Park Drive NW; (404) 659-KIDS (5437); www.imagineit-cma.org. Open daily 10:00 a.m. to 4:00 p.m., 10:00 a.m. to 5:00 p.m. weekends except Thanksgiving and Christmas Days. $$

Kids will never hear "Don't touch" in this high-energy hands-on environment where learning and fun are seamlessly intertwined. Larger-than-life, out-of-the-ordinary exhibits encourage children to explore and discover for themselves. Exhibits include Fundamentally Food, which celebrates food in many ways; Let Your Creativity Flow, which involves art, music, and dance; Tools for Solutions, where youngsters engage in creative problem solving; and Leaping into Learning, where toddlers and preschoolers can explore a friendly forest, splash in a stream, and get a fish's-eye view of the world. The Town Square is a place for performances and featured activities. Daily activities are ever changing and may occur in any of the exhibit areas. The Morph Gallery features changing exhibits.

Inside CNN Atlanta Studio Tour (ages 6 to 12)

1 CNN Center, Marietta Street at Centennial Olympic Park Drive; (404) 827-2300 or (877) 4CNN-TOUR; www.cnn.com/studiotour. Open daily, 8:30 a.m. to 5:00 p.m. with tours every 20 minutes. Adults $$, children ages six to twelve $, children under six are not admitted. Ninety-minute VIP tour $$$$.

The high-tech, fast-paced, state-of-the-art, twenty-four-hour-a-day Cable News Network and Headline News have changed the face of news broadcasting worldwide. Your news crew can tour the center via specially constructed, glass-enclosed overhead walkways from which wannabe newscasters can actually watch as up-to-the-minute news events are reported.

Jimmy Carter Presidential Library and Museum (ages 6 to 12)

441 Freedom Parkway; (404) 865-7101; www.cartercenter.org; carterweb@emory.edu.
Open Monday through Saturday 9:00 a.m. to 4:45 p.m., Sunday noon to 4:45 p.m.
Adults $, children under sixteen free.

Many junior patriots will never get the opportunity to visit the White House in Washington, D.C., but at the Carter Center they can see a life-size replica of part of the presidential Oval Office as it existed during the Carter administration. The repository of the former president's library and documents pertaining to his term in office, the museum interprets his life and presidency through numerous exhibits, gifts received during his tenure in the White House, and an interactive town meeting. Hidden to the rear of the building is an exquisite Japanese garden in which Mom and Dad can enjoy a leisurely stroll and admire a splendid vista of the downtown skyline, while the small fry rip and race to their hearts' content.

Martin Luther King Jr. National Historic Site (ages 4 to 12)

450 Auburn Avenue NE; (404) 331-5190 or (404) 331-6922 (recorded information); www.nps.gov/malu. Open daily 9:00 a.m. to 5:00 p.m.; hours extended to 8:00 p.m. June 15 to August 15. Free.

Martin Luther King Jr.'s links to Atlanta are long and deep. He was born here, and his grandfather and father preached at Ebenezer Baptist Church before he did. The most visited attraction in the state, the historic site is a must-see. Three sites relate to Dr. King's life: the house where he was born; the church where he preached; and the Freedom Hall Complex, which contains the Martin Luther King Jr. Center for Nonviolent Social Change and the reflecting pool in which Dr. King's burial crypt rests. Begin with the Park Information Office at 522 Auburn Avenue for guided tours that make history come alive.

Varsity Facts

- In one day The Varsity (an Atlanta drive-in restaurant) serves 2 miles of hot dogs, 300 gallons of chili, a ton of onions, 2,500 pounds of potatoes, and 5,000 fried pies and serves 12,000 to 15,000 hungry people.

- Super-fast inside counter clerks bellow, "Have your order in mind and your money in your hand."

- Carhops and clerks have a language all their own: "Walk a dog sideways, bag of rags" is a hot dog with onions on the side and chips.

Piedmont Park (all ages) (🏕) (🎠)

Piedmont Park, Fourteenth and Piedmont in Midtown; (404) 875-7275; www.piedmont park.org. Always accessible. Free.

When the backseat gang needs a break from it all, pack up a picnic and head for the wide-open spaces. Piedmont Park was created for the 1898 Cotton States Exposition by famed landscape architect Frederick Law Olmstead, creator of New York's Central Park. Today the 180-acre meadow attracts walkers, joggers, roller skaters, and picnickers and also offers tennis and softball, as well as frequent festivals and special events.

Six Flags Over Georgia (ages 4 to 12) (🎡) (🍴)

275 Riverside Parkway, Austell; (770) 948-9290; www.sixflags.com/parks/overgeorgia. Open daily, Memorial Day through August 10:00 a.m. to 9:00 p.m. with evening hours extended to midnight on Friday and Saturday, weekends only mid-March through Memorial Day and in September and October. Admission $$$$, two-day tickets and family season passes available. Restaurants $–$$$$.

An excitement seeker's passport to fun, this gargantuan playground, the Southeast's premier amusement park, has ten themed areas, 100 rides, eight thrills-and-chills roller coasters, water adventures, and dozens of other rides from mild to wild. In addition to enough heart-pounding rides to please any daring-doers, there are plenty of activities for little squirts of all ages to try. Adding to the entertainment mix, the complex offers shows, other performances, games, multiple restaurants, and shopping. Batman the Ride challenges even the bravest fun seekers with its dizzying 105-foot height, breakneck speed of 50 miles per hour, four times the force of gravity, weightlessness, corkscrews, and vertical loops. The Superman-Ultimate Flight is the South's only flying coaster. Goliath, the newest coaster, is a 200-foot-tall, 4,400-foot-long monster coaster that reaches 70 mph and covers eight-and-a-half acres. In October the park is transformed into a spine-tingling Fright Fest when Dr. Fright and Arania the Black Widow Bride host one of Atlanta's creepiest Halloween parties. Your little hobgoblins will love it.

Turner Field Tours (🏈)

755 Hank Aaron Drive; (404) 614-2311; www.bravesmuseum.com. Call for a schedule of games. No tours when there's an afternoon or Sunday game. Tours Monday through Saturday 9:00 a.m. to 3:00 p.m., Sunday 1:00 to 3:00 p.m.; noon to 3:00 p.m. on game days. Adults $$, children thirteen and under $. Museum-only tours $.

Take me out to the ball game. If you and your teammates love the national pastime, the adrenaline rush of the enthusiastic crowd, the thrill of the organ music, the aroma of hot dogs and popcorn, the satisfying taste of thirst-quenching drinks, and you have a long-running love affair with America's team—the Atlanta Braves—then a game at Atlanta's new stadium may be just the ticket. You'll find much more to do than just watching a game—it can be a full day's experience.

Before you enter the stadium, pay tribute to the Home Run King at the **Hank Aaron Statue** and admire the **Olympic cauldron**—a legacy of the 1996 Centennial Olympic Summer Games. Visit the **Ivan Allen Jr. Braves Museum and Hall of Fame** (404-614-2311), located beyond left field (aisle 134), where your little ballplayers can go on an exciting journey from the Braves' humble beginnings in Boston in 1871. Your little sluggers will see more than 200 one-of-a-kind, rarely seen memorabilia. Spend some time shopping for Braves memorabilia in the **Braves Clubhouse Store,** where you'll find everything imaginable emblazoned with the team logo. Then your teammates can test their skills at a collection of interactive electronic pitching and batting games in **Scout's Alley** that allows wannabe sluggers to bat against a computer playing the other team or against pitching machines set up to reproduce the pitches of famous Braves players. They can get the speed of their pitch measured with a radar gun. Maybe a real team talent scout will catch their impressive moves. **Turner Field Tours** begin at the Braves Museum and include the Coca-Cola Sky Field, a luxury suite, press box, broadcast booth, clubhouse and dugout, Scouts Alley, the Plaza, and the Braves Clubhouse store. When you hear the exultant strains of the "Star Spangled Banner," you'll know it's almost time for the umpire to shout "Play ball," so hustle to your seats for an exciting afternoon or evening.

When it comes to eating, high tech has come to the ballpark, so lunch will be a cinch without missing a minute of the game. Seatside food service for standard ballpark grub is available to those seated in the dugout level (field-level infield sections). Fans make their choices from menus located in cup holders attached to the seatbacks, flag down an attendant, place an order that is transmitted via a tiny computer, and then pay by cash or credit card. Your meal arrives in minutes as if by magic. If you're not seated in those sections or you'd rather get up and move around, food service for pizza, barbecue, Mexican food, and almost any sports-related cuisine is available at more traditional food booths. Get an ultimate dining experience in a two-level restaurant next to the Braves bull pen in right center field. Downstairs in the **Braves Chop House,** you can get chicken wings, burgers, and barbecue. In the upstairs sit-down restaurant (404-614-2100), called the **755 Club** because Hank Aaron had 755 career homeruns, you can sample salads, entrees, and desserts. Reservations aren't accepted, so arrive early. If you want to just sit and soak up the sun, Turner Beach opens two hours before each game. Located in right field, the beach features hospitality lifeguards, tropical palm trees, a cabana bar, food concessions, a picnic area, and lounge chairs.

On game days, if you're staying at a downtown hotel or have easy access to any of the MARTA bus/rail system stations from an outlying hotel, you can avoid traffic hassles and the expense of parking at the stadium by riding the Braves Stadium Shuttle from the Five Points Station to Turner Field. The shuttle begins operation ninety minutes before game time and continues until the stadium is empty. Each passenger will need a rail-to-bus or bus-to-bus transfer or a standard fare in order to ride the shuttle.

Practical **Notes**

Avoid traffic jams and parking fees by taking the MARTA shuttle (**free** with MARTA rail or bus fare of $1.75 each way per person), which runs from the Five Points Station to the ballpark and starts ninety minutes before each game. Alternately, take the train west to the Georgia State station and walk 4 blocks south to the stadium. You'll be especially glad you're not driving when the spectators start spilling out of the parking lots into total gridlock after the game. For those adventurous enough to take their chances on getting the $1.00 tickets, there are 178 "skyline" (translation: nosebleed) seats along the far ends of the upper decks, which are sold only on the day of the game. Some spectators report that these seats are so high, they have to duck to keep from bumping their heads into the blimps hovering overhead, but the price is right. Don't forget the sunscreen, insect repellent, and a hat.

Underground Atlanta (ages 4 to 12) 🍴 🔒

50 Upper Alabama Street SW; (404) 523-2311 or (866) 494-6187, ext.1494; www.underground-atlanta.com. Open Monday through Saturday 10:00 a.m. to 9:00 p.m., Sunday noon to 6:00 p.m. Restaurant and summer hours may vary. Free; restaurants $–$$$$.

It's not just little people who fall in love with a hidden, perpetually twilit city beneath the streets. Encompassing 6 blocks covering twelve acres, the underground and aboveground area is crammed with shops, eateries, nightspots, street vendors, and entertainment. "Is it really underground?" the kiddies will ask. Well, yes and no. In the old days trains and horses and buggies caused Atlanta's first traffic jams until some clever engineer solved the problem by building viaducts over the tracks. Adjacent business owners were left with their first floors below the new street level (thus underground). Not to worry, they simply opened new entrances on the second story. That's why there's an Upper and Lower Alabama Street and an Upper and Lower Pryor Street. Hours vary at the restaurants and nightspots, but in general they're open until late evening or even into the wee hours of the morning.

World of Coca-Cola (ages 4 to 12) 🥤

121 Baker Street; (404) 676-5151 or (800) 676-COKE; www.worldofcocacola.com. Open daily 9:00 a.m. to 5:00 p.m., June through August, Monday through Saturday 8:00 a.m. to 6:00 p.m.; last entry one hour before closing. Closed Easter, Thanksgiving, and Christmas Days; early 3:00 p.m. closing on Christmas and New Year's Eves. Advance reservations strongly recommended. Adults $$, seniors fifty-five years and older and children ages six to eleven $.

Now That's a **Big Thirst**

Seven thousand Coca-Cola beverages are consumed around the globe every second!

Just opened on May 24, 2007, the new facility (located near the Georgia Aquarium and Centennial Olympic Park) is twice as big as the old museum. This Atlanta landmark offers a mesmerizing fantasy for every thirsty sightseer. Atlanta is the home and world headquarters of the legendary giant of the soft drink industry, so it's only fitting that a shrine to the magical elixir should be here. You and the small fry can trace the beverage's history from its development as an 1886 drugstore drink to its present position as a worldwide phenomenon. Examine more than 1,000 items of Coca-Cola memorabilia (the largest collection in existence) that chronicle the one-hundred-year-plus history of the world's most preferred soft drink. However, the most popular exhibits are an old-fashioned soda fountain and a futuristic tasting center where you can sample twenty-two soft drink flavors available only regionally, twenty-two exotic flavors made around the world but not available in America, and far-out experimental flavors. The new facility adds several theaters, including a 4-D theater, and a real bottling line.

Wren's Nest House Museum (ages 6 to 12)

1050 Ralph David Abernathy Boulevard SW; (404) 753-7735; www.wrensnestonline .com. Open Tuesday through Saturday 10:00 a.m. to 2:30 p.m. Adults $$, children ages four to twelve $. Storytelling is extra.

Many of today's parents and grandparents grew up on the Uncle Remus tales—stories adapted from old slave tales recounted by author/journalist Joel Chandler Harris. Gather up all your little bunnies and visit Harris's "briar patch"—a Victorian home called the Wren's Nest. This cozy house where the author lived most of his adult life, furnished with original pieces and Uncle Remus memorabilia, provides a glimpse into his family life. So faithfully re-created is the setting that it looks as if the famous author just stepped out for a walk. Periodic storytelling events re-create the famous tales for today's children. Be prepared for your critters to want some of the books and Br'er Rabbit memorabilia in the gift shop.

Zoo Atlanta (ages 2 to 12)

Grant Park at 800 Cherokee Avenue SE; (404) 624-5600 or (888) 945-5432; www.zoo atlanta.org. Open daily year-round, 9:30 a.m. to 4:30 p.m.; hours extended to 5:30 p.m. on summer weekends. Closed Thanksgiving, Christmas, and New Year's Days. $$$

Wild fun for everyone. Take your house apes on safari to visit their distant relatives at the Atlanta zoo. One of the best in the country, the zoo is especially noted for its pair of pandas and their endearing baby as well as for its primate collection. Among the most popular residents are the pandas, gorillas, a comical gang of orangutans. More than a thousand animals roam freely in natural habitats as diverse as an Asian rain forest or an African savanna. There's an exemplary reptile collection and a petting zoo. In good weather a miniature train chugs around the property carrying small passengers. The regular #97 MARTA bus route offers access to the zoo from the Five Points Station.

For More Information

Atlanta Convention and Visitors Bureau, 233 Peachtree Street, Suite 100, Atlanta, GA 30303; (404) 521-6688 or (800) ATLANTA (285-2682); www.atlanta.net/acvb.

Decatur

East on U.S. Highway 78.

Fernbank Museum of Natural History (ages 3 to 12)

767 Clifton Road NE; for recorded information (404) 929-6300, for ticket sales (404) 929-6400; www.fernbank.edu/museum. Open Monday through Saturday 10:00 a.m. to 5:00 p.m., Sunday noon to 5:00 p.m. Closed Thanksgiving and Christmas. Adults and children three to twelve $$$. IMAX: adults and children ages three to twelve $$.

Take the moppets to visit Barney's ancestors at the natural history museum's impressive dinosaur gallery. Then your whole clan can increase its knowledge of the earth sciences at the largest museum of its type in the Southeast. One major exhibit, *A Walk Through Time in Georgia,* uses the state of Georgia as a microcosm to tell the story of Earth. Two major children's environments include the *Georgia Adventure* for six- to ten-year-old children and the *Fantasy Forest* for three- to five-year-old children. The IMAX Theatre offers spectacular movies on a five-story-tall screen.

Fernbank Science Center (ages 3 to 12)

156 Heaton Park Drive NE; (678) 874-7102; www.fsc.fernbank.edu. Open Monday and Wednesday 8:30 a.m. to 5:00 p.m., Thursday and Friday 8:30 a.m. to 10:00 p.m., Saturday 10:00 a.m. to 5:00 p.m., Sunday 1:00 to 5:00 p.m. Fernbank Forest is accessible Sunday through Friday 2:00 to 5:00 p.m., Saturday 10:00 a.m. to 5:00 p.m. Closed many major holidays. Call if in doubt. Adults and students $, seniors free. Children younger than five years of age are not admitted to the planetarium. The complex is accessible by MARTA.

Are the stars out tonight? Well, it doesn't matter whether it's cloudy or bright at the science center's planetarium, one of the country's largest. On nice days turn the

Seeing **Stars**

The planetarium at the Fernbank Science Center is the third largest in the country.

kiddies loose to explore the greenhouse, botanical garden, and a sixty-five-acre old-growth forest with paved walking trails—some adapted for heart patients and the visually impaired.

For More Information

DeKalb Convention and Visitors Bureau, 1957 Lakeside Parkway, Tucker, GA 30084; (770) 492-5000 or (800) 999-6055; www.dcvb.org.

DeKalb Historical Society Museum, Library, and Archives/DeKalb Welcome Center, 101 East Court Square, Decatur, GA 30030; (404) 373-1088; www.dekalbhistory.org.

Stone Mountain/Lilburn

East on US 78.

Stone Mountain Park (all ages) 🌐 🏛

US 78, Stone Mountain; (770) 498-5690 or (800) 317-2006; www.stonemountainpark .com. Gates open 6:00 a.m. to midnight; attractions open June through August 10:00 a.m. to 8:00 p.m., the remainder of the year 10:00 a.m. to 5:00 p.m.; laser show nightly at 9:30 p.m. June through September and weekends in May and October. Closed Christmas Eve and Day. Many attractions are closed November through February, so check ahead. Parking $8; all-attractions pass $$$. Individual attractions range from $ to $$.

Stone Mountain Park has enough facilities and activities to keep your brood busy for an afternoon, a day, or a week. We try to visit at least two to three times a year because there are always fun new things to do in addition to our old favorites. The focal point of the preserve is the gargantuan bas-relief sculpture of confederate heroes carved on the face of the huge granite mass. During summer and on weekends in spring and fall, the mountain serves as the backdrop for the spectacular laser light show, the highlight of which is when the mounted heroes come to life and circumnavigate the mound to the poignant strains of "Dixie." Other attractions at the 3,200-acre complex include a skylift to the top of the mountain, a complete antebellum plantation with farmyard animals, a train ride around the mountain pulled by a diesel locomotive, a paddle wheel riverboat, an antique-car museum, a large lake, an eighteen-hole golf course, hiking trails, a water slide, boat and bicycle rentals, batting cages, and miniature golf. Crossroads re-creates a Southern town of the 1870s through authentic architecture as well as colorful costumed characters and crafters. Bustling with family fun, the village contains Georgia's only 4-D theater, Tall Tales of the South, and Atlanta's largest children's indoor play experience, The Great Barn, which features four stories of gigantic mazes, climbing structures, super slides, and Harvest Quest—sixty-five interactive play stations. In addition, the village features gold panning, a boardinghouse-style restaurant featuring Southern cuisine, a bakery, several shops where old-time items are produced and sold, a tintype photography studio that will create your own 1800s-style costumed family portrait, entertainment throughout the day, and much, much more. Admission to Crossroads is included in the park's Daily All Attractions Pass. Other popular attractions include Ride the Ducks, land-to-water 1945-era Army DUKWs (770-498-5600), and Treehouse Challenge, three dozen interactive activities in two treehouses. Energetic hikers can follow a trail to the top of the mountain. We have to admit we're wimps. We ride the skylift up and walk down. Numerous special events and festivals keep things hopping. Whew! We're exhausted just listing the attractions, and there are even more. Two hotels, camping facilities, and several restaurants mean never having to leave the park.

Stone Mountain **Fun Facts**

- Stone Mountain is the largest mass of exposed granite in the world, covering 583 acres and rising 825 feet above ground.

- The mountain's base below ground underlies half of Georgia and part of North Carolina.

- The bas-relief sculpture of Confederate heroes President Jefferson Davis and generals Robert E. Lee and Stonewall Jackson is the largest such sculpture in the world, covering three acres.

- The carving is recessed 42 feet into the mountain; the deepest point is Lee's elbow, which is 12 feet to the surface.

- Workers could stand in a horse's ear or inside its mouth to get out of a sudden shower.

- A tour bus could fit on the rump of one of the horses.

Yellow River Game Ranch (ages 3 to 12) 🐾🧺

4525 US 78, Lilburn; (770) 972-6643; www.yellowrivergameranch.com. Open daily, 9:30 a.m. to 6:00 p.m. Closed Thanksgiving, Christmas Eve and Day, and New Year's Day. Adults and children ages three to eleven $$.

Let your wild bunch get to know more than 600 species of birds and animals native to Georgia up close and personal—everything from ferrets to black bears and including one of the largest herds of buffalo east of the Mississippi River. Walk the trails and experience wildlife firsthand at this unique petting zoo and feeding preserve. After being supplied with food for the beasts, visitors walk along a 1-mile trail to feed many of the critters that live in the sprawling sanctuary. Some special events include sheep shearing and wilderness hayrides. Oh, and by the way, the ranch is the home of the famous Gen. Beauregard Lee, the groundhog who predicts spring's arrival in the South. This famous prognosticator lives in a pint-size Tara-like plantation house. Move over Punxatawny Phil.

Jonesboro

South on U.S. Highway 41/19.

Located just a few miles south of Atlanta, sleepy Jonesboro was the site of a major Civil War battle during the Atlanta campaign. Six hundred to one thousand Confederate soldiers are buried in the Patrick R. Cleburne Confederate Memorial Cemetery at McDonough and Johnson Streets. Jonesboro was also the home of author Margaret Mitchell's grandparents. She based many of the locations and characters in *Gone With the Wind* on people and places she knew in Jonesboro. Today the book and movie are prominent reasons to visit Jonesboro.

Beach at Clayton County International Park (all ages)
🌊🏊👪🛝

2300 Highway 138 SE; (770) 473-5425; www.thebeachccip.com. Open Tuesday through Sunday 8:00 a.m. to 8:00 p.m. Memorial Day weekend through early August, then weekends only through Labor Day weekend. $$

Kids won't ever be bored at this multiuse park where there's a Beach Waterpark with a sandy beach, adventure kiddie pool, waterslides, a water trampoline, and a sundeck; as well as a tennis center; fitness center called Muscle Beach Fitness; hiking and biking trails; volleyball courts (the 1996 Centennial Olympic Games volleyball events were held here); and fishing lakes (a proper fishing license is required). Several concession stands keep the moppets from fainting from hunger after all the activity.

Margaret Mitchell Playhouse (ages 3 to 6) 🔆

168 North McDonough Street; (770) 478-7211. Available to view daily daylight hours. Free.

When the famous author of *Gone With the Wind* was a little girl, she often visited her grandparents at Fitzgerald Plantation near Jonesboro. To keep the active tomboy busy, her grandparents built her a Victorian playhouse. Today the fully decorated and furnished playhouse has been relocated to the grassy lawns in the rear of the Pope-Dixon Funeral Home. Visitors of all ages will enjoy going up onto the porch and peeking in the windows to see a slice of young Peggy's life. Youngsters also have a macabre sense of curiosity, so before leaving, drive by the rear of the funeral home to see a glass-enclosed bay that contains the **Antique Funeral Museum**—the only drive-by museum we know of. You'll see a pre-Civil War casket, Civil War embalming equipment, and the horse-drawn hearse used for the funeral of A. H. Stephens, the Georgian who served as the vice president of the Confederacy.

Road to Tara Museum (ages 4 to 12) 🔆

104 North Main Street; (770) 478-4800 or (800) 662-7829; www.visitscarlet.com. Open Monday through Friday 8:30 a.m. to 5:30 p.m., Saturday 10:00 a.m. to 4:00 p.m. $

Gone With the Wind groupies can peruse memorabilia from Atlanta's best-known story at this museum, located in a historic railroad depot. This is the largest permanent public collection of such memorabilia anywhere. A hit with the young and not-so-young ladies in your crowd is the collection of gowns that are replicas of those in the movie.

Also located in the depot is the Jonesboro Depot Welcome Center, where you can get a brochure for a driving tour past the many historic homes and structures of Jonesboro.

Stately Oaks Historic Home and Plantation Community
(ages 6 to 12) 🏛🔆

100 Carriage Lane; (770) 473-0197; www.jonesboroga.com/history_tourism or www.historicaljonesboro.org. Open Monday and Friday 10:00 a.m. to 4:00 p.m. and most Saturdays (check ahead). Adults $$, children five to eleven and seniors $.

Poke into the past and let the mod squad see what life in Georgia was like more than 150 years ago. The authentically restored, white-columned home, circa 1839, was a landmark for both Confederate and Union troops. In fact, Yankees camped around the dwelling during the Battle of Jonesboro. Tours of the home are conducted by costumed docents who interpret customs and lifestyles of the rural south. Among the plantation outbuildings curious tykes can poke their heads into are a one-room school and a tiny country store. Living history demonstrations are conducted periodically and festivals and special events occur year-round. It is believed that Margaret Mitchell used Stately Oaks as one of her inspirations for *Gone With the Wind.*

A Thalimer **Adventure**

When we and the grandkids visited Serenbe B&B in Palmetto, owner Steve Nygren suggested we get the feel of the property by hiking down to the lake and stopping in the barnyard to check out a potbellied pig. Steve lifted up the lean-to pig house and out shot what appeared to be hundreds of squealing piglets (actually there were probably only about fifteen). We were surrounded with tiny pigs running in every direction. The kids loved it so much it took us about an hour to get them out of the barnyard. Between the piglets, the baby goats, chickens, cows, and a miniature pony, they were captivated. Out of the kids' hearing we asked Steve if the piglets were going to end up on the breakfast table. He assured us that "every animal on the farm gets a name, and you can't eat what you've named."

For More Information

Clayton County Convention and Visitors Bureau, 104 North Main Street, Jonesboro, GA 30236; (770) 478-4800 or (800) 662-STAY; www.visitscarlett.com.

Fairburn/Palmetto

Southwest on I-85.

Georgia Renaissance Festival (all ages)

6905 Virlyn B. Smith Road, Fairburn; (770) 964-8575; www.georgiarenaissancefestival .com. Open spring weekends April through early June and Memorial Day, 10:30 a.m. to 6:00 p.m. Check Web site for admission rates. Many discounts available, such as from Kroger stores and on the Web site.

Our gang has been attending Rennfests for more than twenty years, and we all love these time-travel excursions into the days of fair maidens, damsels in distress, and knights in shining armor—not to mention characters such as the rat catcher, kissing wench, mud wrestlers, musicians, acting troupes, his Royal Majesty King Henry the Eighth, and one of his queens (they change from year to year, just as they did in real life). Located in a field and forest situated at exit 61 off I-85, the medieval village comes to life like Brigadoon for several weekends in spring. Watch knights battle it out in a joust, admire and purchase contemporary and medieval crafts, become part of the hilarious entertainment, and participate in games of the period. Savor typical food and drink such as huge turkey drumsticks, meat pies, sausage on a stick, dill pickles, wine, ale, and lemonade. The millennium set enjoys losing themselves in the sights, sounds, smells, and tastes of another era.

Newnan

Southwest on US 27A.

Male Academy Museum

30 Temple Avenue; (770) 251-0207; http://historicalsociety.org/mam.htm. Open Tuesday, Wednesday, and Thursday 10:00 a.m. to noon and 1:00 to 3:00 p.m., weekends 2:00 to 5:00 p.m. $

Little scholars are enveloped in history at this repository, which is located in one of the first schools in the area. You might want to point out to your modern girls that in the old days only boys got a formal education. Among the exhibits are Civil War artifacts, an outstanding collection of period clothing that allows today's fashion trendsetters to see how vastly styles have changed over many years, and a display of *Gone With the Wind* memorabilia. Don't leave without picking up a brochure for a walking/driving tour of this lovely Southern town.

LaGrange

Southwest on U.S. Highway 29.

Explorations Antiquity Center (ages 6 to 12)

130 Gordon Commercial Drive; (706) 885-0363 or (866) 903-2139; www.explorationsinantiuity.com. Open Wednesday through Saturday 10:00 a.m. to 6:00 p.m., Sunday noon to 6:00 p.m. $

Every family may not get the opportunity to visit the Holy Land, so this interfaith museum presents an interpretation of daily life in Biblical times through full-scale archaeological replicas of an aqueduct, an Israelite altar, a tomb, a stone stable and nativity cave, ancient house of worship, and an ancestral cemetery, among other structures. The Time Tunnel traces 2,000 years of civilization. Budding archaeologists and historians can explore the lives of a shepherd, a farmer, and a villager in designated areas. In the shepherd's area they can sit on camel-hair rugs in a goat-hair tent and learn how to make Bedouin bread, and in several areas they can dig for "artifacts."

Hills and Dales/Ferrell Gardens (ages 6 to 12) 🍁

1916 Hills and Dales Drive; (706) 882-3242; www.hillsanddalesestate.org. Open Tuesday through Saturday 10:00 a.m. to 6:00 p.m., Sunday 1:00 to 5:00 p.m. March through September; one hour less the remainder of the year. Admission to house and gardens $$, admission to gardens alone $.

Although the centerpiece of the estate is the opulent 1916 Italian-style villa, active kids may be more interested in exploring the gardens, which date back to 1841. You can make a scavenger hunt out of sending the kidlets on a search for topiaries trimmed in religious shapes or even spelling out words, which are scattered among the extensive boxwood plantings arranged in Italian Renaissance and baroque designs. They'll also enjoy finding the fountains, statuary, and specialty gardens. Tours of the first floor of the house showcase magnificent architectural detailing and furnishings. (If you decide to tour the mansion, keep in mind that children younger than six are not admitted.) At the visitor center you can see educational exhibits and a film about Sarah Ferrell, who designed the gardens, and two generations of the Callaway family who had the home built and then lived there.

West Point

Southwest on US 29 at the Georgia-Alabama border.

West Point Lake 🔺 🛟 👨‍👩‍👧 🏕️

(706) 645-2937; http://westpt.sam.usace.army.mil/. Always accessible; visitor center/ museum open March through September, Monday through Friday 8:00 a.m. to 5:00 p.m., weekends 9:30 a.m. to 5:30 p.m.; remainder of the year, Monday through Friday 8:00 a.m. to 4:00 p.m. Free.

A bonanza for active crews, this 25,900-acre lake, created by damming the Chatta-hoochee River, offers excellent fishing and recreational activities. Along the 500 miles of forested shoreline are twenty-five day-use areas, three public swimming beaches (open early May to Labor Day), eleven campgrounds, two marinas, and a 10,000-acre wildlife management area—together providing boating, swimming, fishing, and hiking. The visitor center and museum located in the Resource Manager's office interpret Native American history and the 1817 battle between Native Americans and U.S. soldiers.

Where to Eat in Northwest Georgia

Blue Ridge

Toccoa Riverside Restaurant, 8055 Aska Road; (706) 632-7891; www.toccoa riverside.com. Active kiddies won't know whether to skip rocks in the babbling Toccoa River or feast on steaks, trout, seafood, and ribs or pig out on the area's most unique and extensive salad bar. $$$

Other Things to
See&Do in Northwest Georgia

- **John Ross House,** Rossville; (706) 375-7702; www.mindspring.com/~rwall/johnross.htm; open June through September

- **Lake Winnepesauka Amusement Park,** Rossville; (706) 866-5681 or (877) 525-3946; www.lakewinnie.com; open April through September

- **Crown Gardens and Archives,** Dalton; (706) 278-0217; www.dalton cvb.com/cvb/attractions.htm

- **Oakleigh,** Calhoun; (706) 629-1515

- **Sunrise Planetarium,** Fairmount; (706) 337-2775

- **James H. "Sloppy" Floyd State Park,** Summerville; (706) 857-0826; www.gastateparks.org/info/sloppy

- **Berry College Campus,** Rome; (706) 232-5374; www.berry.edu

- **Oakhill/Martha Berry Museum and Art Gallery,** Rome; (706) 291-1860 or (800) 220-5504; www.berry.edu/oakhill

- **The Bartow History Center,** Cartersville; (770) 382-3818

- **Great Locomotive Chase Festival,** Adairsville; (770) 773-3451, ext. 26

- **Lake Arrowhead,** Waleska; (770) 479-5505

- **John Tanner State Park,** Carrollton; (770) 830-2222; www.gastate parks.com/info/jtanner

- **Bud Jones Taxidermy and Wildlife Museum,** Tallapoosa; (770) 574-7480; www.budjonestaxidermy.com

- **Atlanta Botanical Garden,** Atlanta; (404) 876-5859; www.atlanta botanicalgarden.org

- **Hartsfield-Jackson Atlanta International Airport,** Atlanta; (404) 530-6600 or (800) 897-1910; www.atlanta-airport.com

- **Georgia State Capitol,** Atlanta; (404) 656-2844; www.sos.state.ga.us/onlinetour

- **Pioneer Museum,** Atlanta; (404) 529-0971; www.bellsouthgapioneers .org/Museumtemp.htm

Cartersville

The Four Way, corner of Main and Gilmer Streets, Cartersville; (no phone). Kids will be intrigued by the tiny size of this eatery (it's got to be one of the world's smallest restaurants), which is currently painted a brilliant red so that it's impossible to miss. For more than fifty years, The Four Way has been dishing up Southern specialties such as hamburger with gravy and the world's sloppiest chili dogs. There are so few seats; take-out is a much better option. $

Cave Spring

Corner on the Square, 2 Alabama Street; (706) 777-8599. Choose from pastries and eight flavors of ice cream for dessert. $

Roswell

CiCi's Pizza, 10516 Alpharetta Highway; (770) 645-1550. You can't beat this casual place for an all-you-can-eat pizza, salad, and dessert buffet. $

Dreamland Barbecue, 10730 Alpharetta Highway, (678) 352-7999, www.dreamland bbq.com. The Tuscaloosa, Alabama, institution has made it to Roswell where diners can fill up on ribs, barbecue sandwiches, cole slaw, and baked beans. Fortunately, there are always mountains of napkins to catch the inevitable drips. $$

Greenwoods on Green Street, 1087 Green Street; (770) 992-5383. You'll say, "Mmm, mmm, good"—Southern cookin' and to-die-for pies. $$

Southern Skillet, 1037 Alpharetta Street; (770) 993-7700; www.theskillet .com. Stoke up on energy with generous helpings served at this down-home eatery. A breakfast of biscuits and gravy, bacon, sausage, grits, and pancakes could keep the munchkins going all day. $–$$

Marietta/Cobb

The Big Chicken KFC, 12 North Cobb Parkway, Marietta; (770) 422-4716. It's not just fried chicken, it's a beloved landmark that'll have the rug rats' eyes popping out. $

Dave and Buster's, 2215 Dave & Buster's Drive, Marietta; (770) 951-5554; www.daveandbusters.com. Eat and play the night away at this eatery, which also has state-of-the-art interactive games and entertainment. $–$$

Kennesaw

My Country Kitchen, 2740 Summers Street; (770) 423-9448. Fuel your clan's flagging energy level by chowing down on Southern comfort foods washed down with sweet tea. $

Atlanta Metro Area

Flying Biscuit Cafe, 1655 McLendon Avenue, Atlanta; (404) 687-8888; www .flyingbiscuit.com. Although the casual eatery's motto is "no pig, no cow, no human," it isn't totally vegetarian—it serves some fish and chicken. Fragrant aromas of homemade biscuits and other goodies make a wait at the cool-hip-funky spot worthwhile. $–$$

Hard Rock Cafe, 215 Peachtree Street NE, Atlanta; (404) 688-7625. Pop/rock decor, souvenirs, and, oh yes, food. Juicy burgers, fries, soups, salads, and sand-wiches. $–$$$

Mary Mac's Tea Room, 224 Ponce de Leon Avenue NE, Atlanta; (404) 876-1800; www.marymacs.com. An Atlanta tradition since 1945, the restaurant serves heaping portions of Southern food like Mom used to fix, all accompanied by generous help-ings of Southern hospitality. $–$$

Six Feet Under, 415 Memorial Drive, (404) 523-6664; www.sixfeetunderatlanta .com. Folks are "just dying to get into" this casual eatery directly across the street from Historic Oakland Cemetery. A wide variety of seafood, burgers, and fried green tomatoes, as well as a view of the cemetery attract diners of all ages. Mom and Dad might enjoy sampling some of the twenty-one kinds of beer. $$$

The Varsity, 61 North Avenue NW, Atlanta; (404) 881-1706; www.thevarsity .com. Yep, they still have carhops here who'll take your order for chili cheese dogs and other fast foods accompanied by a mound of onion rings. Billed as the World's Largest Drive-In, the eatery has been a popular stop since 1928. $

Decatur

Cafe Antico, Emory University Carlos Museum, 571 South Kilgo; (404) 727-0695. Binge on fill-'em-up good eats—pita clubs, wraps, pasta salads, and more—at this great place to grab an inexpensive breakfast or lunch. $

Where to Stay in Northwest Georgia

Lookout Mountain

Chanticleer Inn, 1300 Mockingbird Lane; (706) 820-2015. Stay within walking distance of Rock City Gardens at this simple bed-and-breakfast, which occupies charming stone cottages built in the 1930s. $–$$

Fort Oglethorpe/Chickamauga

Captain's Quarters Bed & Breakfast, 13 Barnhardt Circle, Fort Oglethorpe; (706) 858-0624 or (800) 710-6816; www.cqinn .com. Lay your head on a soft pillow in an upscale two-room family suite at these original officers' quarters. $$$–$$$$

Chatsworth

Cohutta Lodge, 500 Cochise Trail; (706) 695-9601 or (800) 394-9790; www.cohutta lodge.com. Located high atop Fort Mountain, the rustic lodge provides not only accommodations but also a restaurant with a sweeping view of the mountain, horseback riding, hiking, and a pool. $–$$$$

Blue Ridge

Black Bear Cabin Rentals, rental office 21 High Park Drive, Suite 7; (706) 632-4794 or (888) 902-2246; www.blackbearcabin rentals.com. These privately owned cabins make a perfect place for young cubs to hibernate. Choose a mountain cabin with a spectacular view or a cabin nestled in the forest by a babbling brook. $$$$

My Mountain Cabin Rentals, rental office 3945 Old Loving Road, Morganton; (706) 374-4111 or (800) 844-4939; www .1MyMountain.com. Luxury log cabins in the mountains make a great base from which active families can launch outdoor activities, but feature every modern convenience, such as satellite TV, indoor and outdoor hot tubs, pool tables, decks, screened porches, and even fire pits for roasting hot dogs and marshmallows. $$$$

Rome

Mayo's Lock and Dam Park, 181 Lock and Dam Road; (706) 234-5001. Future river pilots will be fascinated by how boats are "locked" up and down the river. The dam, which has always been important to navigation on the Coosa River, is also a great recreation area that offers plenty of outdoor fun—especially boating and fishing. RV camping sites. $

Cave Spring

Hearn Inn, Rolater Park; (706) 777-8865. Formerly the academy's 1839 dormitory and now a bed-and-breakfast, the inn sits inside the park grounds close to the cave and the swimming pool. $$

Marietta/Cobb

Marietta Conference Center and Resort, 500 Powder Springs Street, Marietta; (770) 427-2500 or (888) 685-2500; www.mariettaresort.com. Designed to resemble grand resorts of yore, the hostelry offers rooms and suites, a restaurant, a lounge, golf, tennis, a pool, and gardens. Kids free in the room with parents. $$$–$$$$

Atlanta Metro area

Georgian Terrace, 659 Peachtree Street; (404) 897-1991; www.thegeorgianterrace .com. Stay in a spacious suite where the stars stayed and partied during the world premiere of *Gone With the Wind*. Rooms $$$$; meals $$–$$$.

Stone Mountain/Lilburn

Evergreen Resort and Conference Center, 4021 Lakeview Drive, Stone Mountain; (770) 879-9900; www.evergreenresort .com. Located within the grounds of Georgia's Stone Mountain Park, the hotel's spacious, beautifully furnished rooms have gorgeous views of the lake or woods from their balconies. Indoor and outdoor pools, tennis courts, and jogging trails make this an attractive place to stay. $$$$

Fairburn/Palmetto

Inn at Serenbe, 10950 Hutcheson Ferry Road, Palmetto; (770) 463-2610; www .serenbe.com. For an upscale bed-and-breakfast farm vacation, ask for the room with the three double beds, one of the cottages, or the lake house, then head for the pool and the hot tub. Several miles of trails, three streams, two waterfalls, a lake, hayrides, marshmallow roasts around a campfire, and dozens of farm animals keep the wee folk entertained. The newest addition is a gourmet restaurant. $$$$

Southeast Georgia

C reek and Guale (pronounced "wally") Indians were the first inhabitants of Georgia's barrier islands. Covered with dense vegetation and crisscrossed with winding waterways, the islands were much disputed territory among warring European countries trying to establish a foothold there. The Spanish, who

Thalimers'
TopPicks in Southeast Georgia

1. Flying with eagles at the Center for Wildlife Education and Lamar Q. Ball Jr. Raptor Center, Statesboro

2. Participating in a simulated bombing mission at the Mighty Eighth Air Force Heritage Museum, Pooler

3. Cruising the Savannah River aboard the paddle wheeler *Savannah River Queen,* Savannah

4. Reaching new heights at the Tybee Island Lighthouse, Tybee Island

5. Exploring Georgia's Tory past at the Fort King George Historic Site, Darien

6. Illuminating Georgia's coastal past at the St. Simons Island Lighthouse Museum, St. Simons Island

7. Playing at The Cloister Sea Island, Sea Island

8. Really, really getting away from it all at the Lodge at Little St. Simons, Little St. Simons Island

9. Discovering the recesses of the Okefenokee Swamp

10. Experiencing the good life at Millionaire's Village, Jekyll Island

SOUTHEAST GEORGIA

believed they would find gold there, called the islands Islas de Oro. As if the constant little wars weren't enough commotion, plundering pirates used the islands as a refuge. The English finally prevailed in 1742, and life settled down. Later the islands and coastal region attracted hardworking fishermen and beauty-seeking millionaires, captivating each in their turn. Today on the Golden Isles, quaint seaside villages dotted with sunny resorts are caressed by soft sea breezes. Gracious Savannah, Queen City of the South, contains a timeless bounty of architectural treasures. In complete contrast, the eerie stillness of the dark, brooding primeval Okefenokee Swamp is found not too far inland. Wherever you go in the state's southeastern corner, life moves at a gentle pace. Families seeking a quiet getaway couldn't make a better choice than to spend considerable time in this bewitching region, exploring its profusion of absorbing historical sites, numerous state parks, breathtaking scenic spots, and outstanding beaches.

Millen

At U.S. Highway 25 and Highway 23.

Magnolia Springs State Park (all ages) 🚶 🎣 🏕 🏛

1053 Magnolia Springs Drive off US 25; (478) 982-1660 or (800) 864-7275; www.gastate parks.org/info/magspr/. Open daily year-round, 7:00 a.m. to 10:00 p.m. Parking $3; swimming pool $; campsites $; cottages $$.

If your crew loves the out-of-doors, you'll relish spending a day or a week at this state park, which offers enough to keep even the most energetic youngsters satisfied. On hot summer days the kidsters can cool off by hitting the water in the swimming pool or lake, and this is the perfect place for little anglers to cast a line. Young hikers can explore three hiking trails to their hearts' content—they're easy, even for little legs. A historic site, the area served as a Civil War prison camp; budding historians can see the few remains that were left after Union general William Tecumseh Sherman burned the camp. Amateur naturalists enjoy the interpretive center, which features alligators and turtles, as well as a fresh-water aquarium filled with fish native to the Southeast. And if you can't tear yourselves away, accommodations are offered at campsites and two- to three-bedroom cottages.

Official Georgia

- **Character:** Pogo the Okefenokee Swamp possum (from the comic strip)
- **Fish:** largemouth bass
- **Fossil:** shark's tooth
- **Marine mammal:** right whale
- **Reptile:** gopher tortoise
- **Seashell:** knobbed whelk
- **Tree:** live oak
- **Vegetable:** Vidalia onion

Twin City

South on Highway 23.

George L. Smith State Park (all ages)
371 George L. Smith State Park Road off Highway 23; (478) 763-2759 or (800) 864-7275; www.gastateparks.org/info/georgels/. Open daily year-round, 7:00 a.m. to 10:00 p.m. Parking $3; campsites $; cottages $$.

On a day when visits to museums and other indoor pursuits have created some pent-up energy, take the whole gang to this state park, where the midgets will probably be happier anyway. Young visitors naturally want to scout the grounds on their own, so turn the kidlets loose and sit back and relax or join in the fun in and around twenty-three-acre Cypress Lake. A covered bridge and an 1880 millhouse serve as glimpses of how life used to be. As a perfect end to a perfect day, you can camp under the stars or, if your clan likes a roof over its head, stay in a two-bedroom cottage.

Amazing Georgia Facts

Every year six million pounds of rich fruitcake are baked and distributed internationally from the Claxton Bakery, Inc., in Claxton.

Statesboro

South on U.S. Highway 80.

Center for Wildlife Education and The Lamar Q. Ball Jr. Raptor Center (all ages) 🐦

Old Register Road, Georgia Southern University; (912) 681-0831; www.ceps.georgia southern.edu/wildlife/. Open Monday through Friday 9:00 a.m. to 5:00 p.m., Saturday and Sunday September to May 1:00 to 5:00 p.m. Closed holidays and summer weekends. Free.

Tell your fledglings this place is for the birds—birds of prey, that is. Sure to excite the imaginations of your flock is a visit to this wing-ding of a four-acre woodland nature center, where eagles, hawks, owls, kestrels, and seven other species nest in natural niches linked by elevated boardwalks for your viewing pleasure. Your little chickadees will revel in the challenge of finding fifty animals hidden in the Down-to-Earth Encounter display as well as the seventeen stations along the Children's Discovery Trail, where they'll find snake eggs and sheds, bird nests, feathers, skeletons, antlers, insects, turtle shells, and an animal tracks sand table. The highlight of the trail is Fly In and Perch—a life-size eagle nest into which your eaglets may climb. Two programs the family won't want to miss are the weekend reptile programs at 2:00 p.m. followed by the raptor flights at 3:00 p.m.

For More Information

Statesboro Convention and Visitors Bureau, 332 South Main Street, States- boro, GA 30458; (912) 489-1869 or (800) 568-3301; www.visit-statesboro.com.

Reidsville

Southeast on U.S. Highway 280.

Gordonia-Alatamaha State Park and Golf Course (all ages) 🏌️🎣🏊

US 280; (912) 557-7744 or (800) 864-7275; www.gastateparks.org/info/gordonalt/. Open daily year-round, 7:00 a.m. to 10:00 p.m. Parking $3; camping $.

Fore! Chock-full of fun things to do, this 280-acre park is best known for offering golf for every level of ability—from miniature golf to a nine-hole golf course. If there is no budding Tiger Woods in your group, the park also offers plenty of waterborne activities. The backseat gang can take a dunk in the ol' swimming hole; little anglers can try their luck at fishing. Picnicking is an ideal solution for informal families on the go;

it's economical as well. The munchkins can play up a storm and release all their energy before you pack them back into the car and proceed on your excursion. Outdoorsy families can settle the tribe for a night of tent or trailer camping. For a budget-minded family on the road, this park can't be beat.

For More Information

Reidsville Chamber of Commerce,
120 West Brazell Street, Reidsville, GA 30453; (912) 557-6323.

Pooler

East on US 280.

Mighty 8th Air Force Museum (ages 6 to 12)

175 Bourne Avenue; (912) 748-8888; www.mightyeighth.com. Open daily year-round, 9:00 a.m. to 5:00 p.m. Closed Easter, Thanksgiving, Christmas, and New Year's Days. $$

They came from farms, small towns, and street corners of hundreds of U.S. cities. On average they were only nineteen, but they wanted to fight for liberty. The Mighty 8th was created in Savannah in 1942 and grew to be the greatest air armada ever committed to battle. This museum honors the sacrifice, bravery, resolve, and teamwork of the more than one million men and women who have served in the unit. Great for aircraft enthusiasts, the museum houses extensive Air Force memorabilia. Dynamic state-of-the-art displays of historic battles and missions tell the story of the Mighty 8th's role in military conflicts from the World War II air war over Europe and up through Desert Storm. Your little daredevils can even "fly" a simulated bombing mission and then eat lunch in a replica of a British pub.

A Georgia **History Lesson**

- Georgia was founded as a British colony in 1733 by James Oglethorpe and was the last of the original thirteen colonies.
- It was named for King George II of England.
- Savannah was the first city in the new colony.

A Christmas **Present**

What did Union general William Tecumseh Sherman give President Abraham Lincoln for Christmas in 1864? Savannah. The general captured the city in December 1864, just in time to deliver it to Lincoln as a Christmas present. Thankfully, Sherman spared the city from the destruction he wrought across much of Georgia.

Savannah

South on Interstate 95 and east on Interstate 16.

Savannah's a city made for walking. Without a doubt, each member of your family will surrender to this beautiful city's romantic past. One of founder Oglethorpe's most enduring legacies is the careful grid pattern he developed for the city—a design broken by twenty-four large parklike squares, which were originally used for markets. After more than 250 years, these attractive pocket preserves are shaded by gigantic, moss-draped live oaks and magnolias. Lushly landscaped with brilliant azaleas and oleander, the squares feature benches on which Mom and Dad can rest and admire the plantings, fountains, and monuments while the munchkins play hide-and-go-seek. On your travels around the city, make it a game for your detectives-in-training to discover in which square Forrest Gump waited for the bus with his box of chocolates while you look for landmarks and personalities from the book and movie *Midnight in the Garden of Good and Evil* or the television series *Savannah*.

A burst of construction in the late 1800s resulted in the opulent Italianate buildings you see today. Although many treasures were lost in the 1950s, citizens realized what they were sacrificing. An active preservation movement resulted in a 2.2-square-mile National Historic Landmark District downtown being designated by the National Trust for Historic Preservation. One of the largest such districts in the country, the area contains 1,800 historic structures, many of which have been restored to their former splendor. It's so easy to feel the past here that Savannah is a painless place to introduce the small fry to yesteryear. Any budding journalist working on a school paper will find plenty to write about here. Savannah sponsors frequent special events to keep things even more lively. And opportunities for sightseeing don't go down with the sun. Begin a visit to the Queen City with a stop at the Savannah Visitor Center, 301 Martin Luther King Jr. Boulevard. Many guided tours leave from here.

Fort Pulaski National Monument (ages 4 to 12) 🏛 👥

U.S. Highway 80 East; (912) 786-5787; www.nps.gov/fopu. Open daily 8:30 a.m. to 5:15 p.m. in winter and 8:30 a.m. to 6:30 p.m. June, July, and August. Note: the visitor center is open 9:00 a.m. to 5:00 p.m. and 9:00 a.m. to 6:00 p.m. respectively. Closed Christmas and Thanksgiving. $

Give your budding engineers a taste of the Civil War at this fortification. Ironically it was designed and built in part by Robert E. Lee when he was a young West Point graduate who went on to serve in the U.S. Army. Little did he know that he would be called upon to defend the fort when he became the commander of the Confederate forces. A state-of-the-art masterpiece of brick and masonry, the fort was thought to be impenetrable by the Confederacy, but it was no match for the Union's new rifled artillery; once it fell to the Union, it was used as a prison. Stroll through the fort and stop at the visitor center to peruse interpretive exhibits. If tiny folk start wiggling with boredom, move outside to explore the many nature trails. The kids will be mesmerized by the daily interpretive programs. For a peaceful way to drift away a lazy-daisy afternoon, bring a picnic; the grounds are an excellent place to savor an alfresco feast.

Juliette Gordon Low's Birthplace (ages 6 to 12) 🏫

10 East Oglethorpe Avenue; (912) 233-4501; www.girlscouts.org/who_we_are/birth place. Open Monday, Tuesday, and Thursday through Saturday 10:00 a.m. to 4:00 p.m., Sunday 11:00 a.m. to 4:00 p.m. There are numerous closings throughout the year including Wednesdays November through February, so it's best to call ahead. Adults and children ages six to sixteen $$. Discounts for seniors and Girl Scouts.

Any girl or adult who has ever been associated with the Girl Scout movement—or for that matter, any parent who has munched on the group's special cookies—will be intrigued by a visit to the childhood home of Juliette Gordon Low, founder of the Girl Scouts of America. The city's first designated National Historic Landmark, the gracious 1820 home, restored to its 1886 appearance and furnished with family pieces, gives an insight into her privileged life, but it's the stories about lively, young Juliette that are the most entertaining. The first Girl Scout was quite artistically inclined, and many of her works are scattered throughout the house.

It All Started **in Savannah**

Juliette Gordon Low founded the Girl Scouts of America in Savannah in 1912. Today it is the largest voluntary organization for girls in the world.

More **Georgia History**

Georgia's first Declaration of Independence celebration wasn't on July 4. It actually occurred in Savannah on August 10, 1776, because it took more than a month for a copy of the document to reach Georgia from Philadelphia. The declaration was taken to the Liberty Pole and read aloud, after which there was a torchlight procession.

Old Fort Jackson (ages 4 to 12) 🏛

1 Fort Jackson Road; (912) 232-3945; www.chsgeorgia.org/jackson/. Open daily 9:00 a.m. to 5:00 p.m. Closed Thanksgiving, Christmas, and New Year's Days. $; children younger than 6 free.

The small fry can get a bang out of the trip by checking out the largest black-powder cannon ever fired in the United States. The thirty-two-pounder is located at the oldest standing fort in Georgia. Situated on the south bank of the Savannah River, the stronghold saw action in the War of 1812 and the Civil War. Your offspring can get a glimpse into the history of Savannah and the coast by examining cannons, small arms, tools, and machinery, as well as artifacts from the sunken ironclad CSS *Georgia*. Between June 15 and August 15, the highlights of any visit to the fort are the weapons demonstrations and cannon firings at 11:00 a.m. and 2:00 p.m.

Ralph Mark Gilbert Civil Rights Museum (ages 6 to 12) 🅱

460 Martin Luther King Jr. Boulevard; (912) 231-8900; www.sip.armstrong.edu; then choose the entry for the museum. Open Monday through Saturday 9:00 a.m. to 5:00 p.m. $

We shall overcome! One of Savannah's newest attractions, this museum is dedicated to the story of Georgia's oldest African-American community from slavery to the present, with special emphasis on Savannah's struggle against segregation, which was led by Dr. Gilbert. Located in a restored historic building that was in its heyday the largest African-American bank in the country, the museum uses photographic and interactive exhibits, videos, and memorabilia to give your progeny an appreciation for what has been accomplished.

Amazing Savannah Facts

Eli Whitney invented the cotton gin in Savannah, leading to the dominance of King Cotton throughout the South.

Notables from Southeast Georgia

- **Johnny Mercer**—songwriter, Savannah
- **Flannery O'Connor**—author, Savannah
- **Burt Reynolds**—movie and television actor, Waycross

Riverfront (all ages)

Factor a stop here into your plans! The Savannah River, which brought the first settlers to establish the city on its bluffs, is the heart of the historic district. You'll want to spend some time at **Factor's Walk, Old River Street,** and **Riverfront Plaza**—all located along the river. Factor's Walk was the center of commerce when cotton was king. The buildings, many of which boast opulent iron balconies overlooking the river, not only housed the factors' (merchants') offices but also served as warehouses. Located on ballast-stone (carried in ships for weight) streets, these buildings, which are reached from Bay Street via iron pedestrian bridges, now house three inns and more than seventy-five restaurants, nightspots, boutiques, galleries, artists' studios, and museums. Shop 'til you drop can even apply to tiny shoppers—especially if they have some allowance burning holes in their pockets. If they don't have their own funds, they may empty your pockets begging for souvenirs to buy. Recently spruced up, the waterfront itself has been transformed into **Riverfront Plaza,** a 9-block brick-paved esplanade dotted with fountains, plantings, benches, and a play area with a pint-size tugboat to play on. Always a busy place, the plaza is the site of several annual festivals. Make sure to show the kids the **Olympic Cauldron Sculpture** (the sailing events for the 1996 Centennial Summer Olympic Games were held in Savannah), and by all means take them down to the far end of the plaza to see the life-size **Waving Girl Statue.** The walk will help use up some of their inexhaustible energy.

Who Was the **Waving Girl?**

Florence Martus, a young woman who was in love with a seaman who went off on a voyage and never came back. Did he die or did he just leave her? No one knows. But she hopefully greeted every ship that entered the port of Savannah from 1887 to 1931 anticipating his return. That's forty-four years. Ask your little mathematicians to imagine how many ships she must have greeted. Now there's a lesson in optimism.

Roundhouse Railroad Museum (all ages)
601 West Harris Street; (912) 651-6823; www.chsgeorgia.org/roundhouse/. Open daily year-round, 9:00 a.m. to 5:00 p.m. $

Move your caboose, and stay on track with a visit to one of the largest remaining pre–Civil War railroad repair and maintenance complexes in the nation. Among the thirteen original structures at Georgia's State Railroad Museum are the massive roundhouse and a 125-foot smokestack. Some of the exhibits that get the rapt attention of your young engineers are two of the oldest surviving steam engines in the country, a 1914 steam locomotive, antique repair machinery, and examples of antiquated rolling stock. Railroad fans will love all that steel and muscle. For contrast take a picture of the littlest kid in the family next to one of these lumbering giants.

Savannah History Museum (ages 4 to 12)
303 Martin Luther King Jr. Boulevard; (912) 651-6825; www.chsgeorgia.org/shm/. Open daily, Monday through Friday 8:30 a.m. to 5:00 p.m., Saturday and Sunday 9:00 a.m. to 5:00 p.m. Closed Thanksgiving, Christmas, and New Year's Days. $

When an infrequent bad-weather day puts a crimp in your outdoor plans, get a handle on local history by visiting this museum. Like searching through the city's attic, this repository permits you to delve into Savannah's 260-plus-year history. Of special interest is the Black Soldier's Exhibit, which highlights the 1st South Carolina Volunteer Infantry and the nearly 200,000 black men who fought in the War Between the States. Located in a restored passenger terminal, the museum offers a film with special effects about Savannah's past, but the kidlets will be fascinated by the 1890 steam locomotive, a cotton gin, and artifacts from Savannah's wars. You can stave off small hunger pangs at the snack bar or, for a more substantial meal, eat breakfast or lunch at the Whistle Stop Cafe located in a train car.

Savannah River Queen and the *Georgia Queen* (all ages)
Operated by the River Street Riverboat Company, 9 East River Street; (912) 232-6404 or (800) 786-6404; www.savannahriverboat.com. Call for a schedule of narrated sightseeing, lunch, brunch, dinner, and moonlight cruises. Rates range from $$$ to $$$$ for adults, $$ to $$$$ for children.

Climb on board. Those yearning to go down to the sea in ships can partially assuage their desires by making a voyage of discovery aboard one of these reproductions of old-fashioned paddle wheelers. For the ultimate in gracious Southern hospitality, this is a perfect way for the family to explore the Savannah River. Make sure to have a camera on hand to capture dramatic views of the city from the river—panoramic cameras and wide-angle lenses give the most pleasing results.

Amazing
Georgia Facts

Savannah has the second largest St. Patrick's Day celebration in the country—bigger even than that of Boston. The most popular unit in the miles-long parade is the spotted one. 101 Dalmatians? At least. Hundreds of local residents deck their handsome spotted dogs out in green collars, green bow ties, green hats, and other green costumes to march in the parade; cuddly, squirming dalmatian puppies in green finery are pulled in wagons.

Ships of the Sea Maritime Museum (all ages)

41 Martin Luther King Jr. Boulevard; (912) 232-1511; www.shipsofthesea.org. Open daily (except Monday) 10:00 a.m. to 5:00 p.m. Closed March 17 and Thanksgiving, Christmas, and New Year's Days. $

Avast me hearties! If the occasional inclement day threatens mutiny among your crew, a cruise over to this museum may get things back on an even keel. Seafarers can examine a large collection of models and maritime memorabilia representing 2,000 years of seagoing history. Espy fifty intricately constructed models ranging in size from a few inches to more than 8 feet in length—including miniatures of the *Titanic,* the SS *Savannah* (the first steamship to cross the Atlantic), and the NS *Savannah* (the first nuclear-powered merchant vessel). Don't get so caught up in the model exhibits, however, that you float by any of the other ship memorabilia.

For More Information

Savannah Convention and Visitors Bureau, 101 East Bay Street, Savannah, GA 31401; (912) 644-6401 or (877) SAVANNAH; www.savcvb.com.

Tybee Island

East on US 80.

Succumb to pier pressure on nostalgic Tybee (pronounced *tie–bee*) Island, where we take our annual multigenerational family reunion vacation. The island is reminiscent of the 1950s, when a trip to the beach was an inexpensive family vacation. So far the 5-mile beach hasn't been marred by high-rises—we fervently hope it will stay that way. Instead, Tybee Island is a laid-back town of Mom-and-Pop motels, rental cottages, and a few low-rise condominiums, as well as a new pavilion and fishing pier—in other words, a perfect place for good, clean, kid-oriented fun. The long expanse of white-sand beach invites sunbathing, water sports, surf fishing, sand castle building, and crabbing. Young beach bunnies will find plenty to do, and Mom and Dad or Grammy and Gramps can kick back and relax.

Tybee Turtle Tour (all ages)
(912) 786-5920; www.tybeearts.org. Free.

Don't be slow as a turtle when on the hunt for twenty huge fiberglass sea turtles scattered around the island. Who or what are these tortoises? As a quirky arts project to save the endangered loggerhead sea turtle, the Tybee Arts Association has commissioned artists to create whimsical creatures such as Myrtle Turtle, Mermaid Rodeo Bareback Rider, Hey-Diddle Turtle, In-Turtle-National Turtle, Tybeetron-Turtle Defender, and others. Two of our favorites are Terrapin Towers, which sports a sand castle on its back, and You Look Out for Me and I'll Look Out for You, which boasts a replica of the Tybee Lighthouse on its back. Get a map showing the locations of the turtles from the Tybee Visitor Center on US 80 and create your own scavenger hunt by driving, walking, bike riding, or skating to see how many your clan can find.

Capt. Mike's Dolphin Tours ⚠
Lazaretto Creek, P.O. Box 787, Tybee Island 31328; (912) 786-5848 or (800) 242-0166; www.tybeedolphins.com. Open daily 9:00 a.m. to 5:00 p.m. Tours offered at different times depending on the season; reservations a must. Adults $$$; children twelve and younger $$.

Climb aboard the SS *Dolphin Too, III,* or *IV,* small flat-roofed vessels reminiscent of the *African Queen,* for a magical cruise to see friendly bottle-nosed dolphins playing in their natural habitat, as well as to enjoy the scenery of the Old Cockspur Lighthouse, Fort Pulaski, the Tybee Lighthouse, and the north beach of Tybee Island. Sunset and fishing cruises are also offered.

Amazing
Georgia Facts

- The state has 100 miles of shoreline on the Atlantic Ocean; but with bays, offshore islands, and river mouths, the coastline actually measures 2,344 miles.

- Georgia has twelve barrier islands, several of which are known as the Golden Isles because the Spanish believed they would find gold there. Instead they found golden beaches. Their loss, our gain.

Tybee Island Lighthouse/Tybee Island Museum (ages 4 to 12)

30 Meddin Drive; (912) 786-5801; www.tybeelighthouse.org. Open year-round, 9:00 a.m. to 5:30 p.m. Closed Tuesday and St. Patrick's, Thanksgiving, Christmas, and New Year's Days. Adults $$, children $.

This one's a neck craner. One of the first public structures in Georgia and until recently an active aid to navigation, the 154-foot lighthouse is located at the north end of the beach. The lower 60-foot section was built in 1773, the top 94 feet in 1867. If only the walls could talk—what stories they would tell. Get your daily exercise, and wear out

A Thalimer **Adventure**

The multigenerational Thalimer clan, sometimes twenty-two strong, spends two weeks each June at a historic cottage on the south end of Tybee Island. This area, called the Back River where the ocean meets the bay and Lazaretto Creek, is prime dolphin country. In addition to sunning, swimming, shelling, reading, playing board games, biking, in-line skating, walking on the beach, sightseeing, and eating, one of our favorite pastimes is dolphin watching. From our beach and our screened-in porch, we watch the playful dolphins in singles, pairs, and schools as they cavort in front of us all day long. It's a bad day when we don't see any dolphins. Older daughter Elaine had the ultimate adventure in the summer of 2003. She spent a great deal of time kayaking, and the dolphins came right up and swam along with her. She was so close she was sprinkled by the spray from their blowholes and could almost touch them. She said they were sneezing on her.

your little lighthouse keepers, by climbing to the top. Once the intrepid adventurers arrive at their goal gasping for breath, they'll have more appreciation for the daily routine of the lightkeeper. Make sure to bring cameras; the panoramic vistas from the top of the lighthouse are well worth snapping for the vacation scrapbook or back-to-school show-and-tell. Your little explorers can investigate more about the lighthouse by perusing the exhibits in the small museum located in the adjacent keeper's cottage.

For More Information

Tybee Island Visitor Center, US 80 at Campbell Avenue, 802 First Street, Tybee Island, GA 31328; (912) 786-5444. Open daily in summer, weekends the rest of the year. If no one answers, call the Savannah Convention and Visitors Bureau (877-SAVANNAH).

Tybee Island Online, www.tybeeisland.com

Richmond Hill

South of Savannah on U.S. Highway 17.

Richmond Hill is known as the City Henry Ford Built. Say what? Henry Ford? Didn't he live in Detroit? Yes and no. In the 1920s Ford and his wife, Clara, discovered and fell in love with this rural coastal community when they were looking for a winter place to escape the pressures of his automobile enterprise. Ford purchased 85,000 acres and built a winter home, Richmond Hill Plantation, but he didn't stop there. His philanthropic nature led him to build 292 residential and commercial buildings, including schools, churches, a commissary, and medical facilities. Richmond Hill is also known for some of the best preserved earthwork fortifications built by the Confederacy and for the **Ogeechee River,** which is noted for its excellent fishing (particularly for shad) and its boating and camping opportunities.

Richmond Hill Historical Society Museum and Welcome Center
(ages 4 to 12) 🏛️
11460 Ford Avenue; (912) 756-3697; www.richmondhillga.com/museum/. Open Monday through Saturday 10:00 a.m. to 4:00 p.m. **Free,** donations accepted.

If bad weather produces thunderous pouting from the junior set, take a look at the past by visiting this museum, located in the Ford Kindergarten Building. This hidden treasure is worth seeking out for its displays of colonial, Revolutionary War, Civil War, and Henry Ford–era artifacts and memorabilia.

Did You **Know?**

- The idea for Rural Free Delivery (RFD) originated in Norwood, Georgia, and was introduced to the U.S. Congress by Senator Tom Watson.

- The sale of the familiar red Flanders Field Poppy, used as a memorial emblem for disabled American veterans, was begun by Monica Michael of Good Hope, an educator and patriot.

- Famous aviator Charles Lindbergh made his first solo flight at Souther Field outside Americus.

Fort McAllister Historic Park (all ages)

3894 Fort McAllister Road; (912) 727-2339; www.gastateparks.org/info/ftmcallister/ or www.fortmcallister.org. Museum open daily 8:00 a.m. to 5:00 p.m. Park open daily year-round, 7:00 a.m. to 10:00 p.m. Fort tour $; museum free; parking $3; saltwater fishing license required for fishing; canoe rental $ per hour; campsites $$$.

The past is always present at this park, where modern-day young folk can get a feel for a bygone era. A key earthwork fortification defending Savannah during the Civil War, the fortress fell to Sherman's troops in December 1864, sealing Savannah's doom. In fact, this is where his infamous March to the Sea ended and turned north. In addition to the preserved earthworks, Civil War artifacts bring that era to life. Shaded by giant live oaks along the beautiful salt marsh, the coastal park is just as well known for its recreational facilities. A boat dock and launching ramp keep boaters in hog heaven. Big and little anglers love to try their luck from boat or shore. Young and old environmentalists head for the nature trails. Camping families can settle in at tent, trailer, or pioneer campsites.

For More Information

Richmond Hill Convention and Visitors Bureau, US 17 and I-95, exit 87, Richmond Hill, GA 31324; (912) 756-2676 or (800) 807-4848; www.richmondhillga.org.

Midway

South on US 17.

Midway Museum (ages 4 to 12) 🏛 🔷

US 17; (912) 884-5837. Open Tuesday through Saturday 10:00 a.m. to 4:00 p.m., Sunday 2:00 to 4:00 p.m. Closed Monday and holidays. Adults and children ages four to twelve $.

Where can you get from the first of the twenty-first century to the early eighteenth century in just minutes? Right here in Midway. Take a peek into the past at the raised-style cottage patterned after those typically built on the coast in the 1700s. The museum contains artifacts, furniture, documents, and other memorabilia that represent the late eighteenth and early nineteenth centuries. Next door is the 1792 **Midway Church,** a classic example of colonial New England–style architecture, having never been modernized with a heating system or electricity. The small congregation, which had worshiped in several earlier structures, produced two signers of the Declaration of Independence, two Revolutionary War generals, and a U.S. senator. From the museum get a brochure for the self-guided tour of the Midway Cemetery.

Fort Morris Historic Site (ages 4 to 12) 🏛 🔷

Highway 38 (exit 76 off Interstate 95), 2559 Fort Morris Road; (912) 884-5999; www .gastateparks.org/info/ftmorris/. Open Thursday through Saturday 9:00 a.m. to 5:00 p.m. Closed Thanksgiving and Christmas. Adults and children ages six to eighteen $.

Here's a revolutionary idea! Mention "dead town" and you're sure to pique young ghouls' interest. At this historic site they can learn about the former town of Sunbury, how it died, and about Revolutionary War action in the area. Examine the Revolutionary War earthwork fortifications, and then tour the museum to see a cannon display, a diorama depicting the town of Sunbury, and information and artifacts concerning the Revolutionary War and the War of 1812.

Make a Game of It

Have your young Sherlock Holmeses play detective by challenging them to find the oldest tombstone in the colonial-era burial ground at the Midway Cemetery; then set them to looking for the crack in the wall that legend says has never been successfully mended because of the ghost of a murdered slave.

The World-Record **Largemouth Bass**

When George Washington Perry caught a whopping twenty-two-pound, four-ounce fish on Montgomery Lake in Telfair County in 1932, he thought he had snagged a log. Needless to say, the area is renowned for its good fishing, although anglers are still trying to top that record.

Hinesville

West on U.S. Highway 84.

Fort Stewart's Victory Museum (all ages) 🔘

Building T904, 2022 Frank Cochran Drive, Fort Stewart; (912) 767-7885; www.stewart.army.mil. Open Tuesday through Saturday 10:00 a.m. to 4:00 p.m. Closed Sunday, Monday, and federal holidays. **Free.**

The backseat gang is usually fascinated by things that have to do with the military. At this museum that focuses on the Third Infantry and Fort Stewart, your young troopers can linger to their hearts' content for close-up examination of weapons, uniforms, flags, equipment, vehicles, and historic photos from the Civil War to the present. Of particular interest are special collections relating to the Civil War's Merrill's Marauders, the Spanish-American War, and Desert Storm.

For More Information

Liberty County Chamber of Commerce Welcome Center, 500 East Oglethorpe Highway, Hinesville, GA 31313; (912) 368-4445; www.libertycounty.org.

McRae

West on US 280 at U.S. Highway 441.

Little Ocmulgee State Park (all ages) 🌊 🤸

US 441; (229) 868-7474 or (800) 864-7275, lodge reservations (877) 591-5572; www.ga stateparks.org/info/liocmulgee/. Open daily year-round, 7:00 a.m. to 10:00 p.m. Parking $3; campsites $, cottages $$–$$$, lodge $$; greens fee $$$; cart for eighteen holes $$$$; driving range $ per bucket; canoes $–$$$.

With the emergence of a new generation of young golfers, this sport is no longer considered an "old folks" game. A primary attraction at this state park is the eighteen-

New York and **Philadelphia South**

Liberty Square boasts a one-twelfth-size replica of the Statue of Liberty and a copy of the Liberty Bell that served as McRae's fire bell at the turn of the twentieth century.

hole championship **Wallace Adams Golf Course.** The golf facility also features a pro shop, cart rental, driving range, and a chipping/putting green. If the kids aren't aspiring regular golfers yet, let them get into the swing of things at miniature golf. The gang can camp here, but if your idea of outdoor fun doesn't include roughing it, stay in one- or two-bedroom cottages or in the thirty-room **Little Ocmulgee Lodge.** The lodge's **Fairway Grill** scores a hole-in-one with its kid-friendly menu. Loaded with things for active families to do, the park offers plenty of other ways for the backseat crowd to work off their excess energy: picnicking facilities, boat ramp and dock, waterskiing, canoe rental, fishing, swimming pool, tennis courts, and a nature trail. Although the beach area is open for day use by the general public, the swimming pool is for overnight guests only. What we love about this place is that once here, we have everything we need to stay put. Families desiring a secluded spot to get away from it all should check out this park.

For More Information

Telfair County Chamber of Commerce, 120 East Oak Street, McRae, GA 31055; (229) 868-6365; www.telfairco.com.

State Record **Flathead Catfish**

Caught in Wayne County's Altamaha River by Paul Duke of Hartwell on June 24, 1998, this finny giant weighed a whopping sixty-three and a half pounds.

Darien

East on Highway 251 at Highway 99.

Wrapped in history, Darien is Georgia's second oldest planned town. It was founded in 1736 by Gen. James Oglethorpe's Scottish Highlanders and later became a prosperous town favored by timber barons and sea captains. Today Darien is the home of a busy shrimping fleet and is known for caviar processing. One of the most anticipated events is the annual Blessing of the Fleet.

Fort King George Historic Site (all ages)

Fort King George Drive off US 17; (912) 437-4770; www.gastateparks.org/info/ftking george/. Open Tuesday through Saturday 9:00 a.m. to 5:00 p.m., Sunday 2:00 to 5:30 p.m. Closed Monday except federal holidays and Thanksgiving, Christmas, and New Year's Days. Adults and children ages six to eighteen $.

Budding historians can escape to the past at this reconstruction of an early-eighteenth-century fort and blockhouse. Without having to crack a book or lift a pencil, your school-agers can automatically advance their scholarship about early colonial and state history. In the interpretive museum you'll first see a short film about the site's history and then have an opportunity to examine artifacts from the Native American, Spanish missionary, and English settler eras. Popular living-history demonstrations given periodically allow the space-age set to see how things used to be done in a simpler time.

For More Information

McIntosh County Chamber of Commerce/Welcome Center, 105 Fort King George Drive, Darien, GA 31305; (912) 437- 6684 or (888) 849-5448; www.mcintosh county.com.

The Famous **54th**

During the Civil War, the Massachusetts infantry unit of African-American soldiers under the command of Col. Robert Gould Shaw saw some of its first action in Darien.

Sapelo Island

By ferry from Darien.

Expose the rug rats to nature and the almost-extinct African-American Gullah culture at one stop. A naturalist's and environmentalist's heaven, Sapelo Island—a place where time is endless and the people are very friendly—is accessed only by ferry from Meridian and Darien. Advance reservations are required. Call the Sapelo Visitor Center at (912) 437-3224 for more information or schedules. A tour of Sapelo Island, the fourth largest of Georgia's barrier islands and one of the most pristine, enables your clan to see a barrier island's natural ecosystem from the diversified indigenous wildlife of the forested uplands to the expanses of salt marsh, as well as the beach and dune system.

Sapelo Island National Estuarine Research Reserve (ages 4 to 12)

Visitor center 1 Landing Road, Meridian. Mailing address: P.O. Box 19, Sapelo Island, GA 31327; (912) 485-2251 for reservations; www.sapelonerr.org. Sapelo visitor center (912) 485-3224. Visitor center open Tuesday through Friday 7:30 a.m. to 5:30 p.m., Saturday 8:00 a.m. to 5:30 p.m., Sunday 1:30 to 5:00 p.m. Excursions available Wednesday and Saturday, September through May; Wednesday, Friday, and Saturday June to August; the last Tuesday of each month March through October. Tours depart on the Sapelo ferry from the mainland at 8:30 a.m. weekdays, 9:00 a.m. Saturday. Return to the mainland is 12:30 and 1:00 p.m. Adults and children ages six to eighteen $$.

An absorbing place for naturalists of all ages, the reserve protects miles of untouched beaches and the delicate salt marsh ecosystem. Access to the island is only by ferry from Meridian. Once on the island guided bus tours include wilderness areas as well as the Georgia Marine Research Institute, the exterior of the former mansion of tobacco magnate R. J. Reynolds, ruins of a nineteenth-century antebellum cotton and sugar plantation, the newly restored lighthouse, and Hog Hammock, a historic African-American community, which is one of the only places in the low country where remnants of the Gullah culture can be found. For those who can't make the trip to the island, the landside visitor center has exhibits about Sapelo including information about estuarine, barrier island, and shoreline ecosystems as well as facts about the island's rich cultural history; Hog Hammock community; the University of Georgia Marine Institute; Gray's Reef National Marine Sanctuary; and the National Estuarine Research Reserve System.

Spirit of Sapelo Mule-Drawn Wagon Tour (ages 4 to 12)

(912) 485-2170. Available daily 9:00 a.m. to 6:00 p.m. $$$

If the younger generation tends to be a little speed addicted, introduce them to the slow-paced mule. A fun-filled wagon tour meanders past the restored lighthouse, Hog Hammock, and Reynolds Mansion.

For More Information

Sapelo Island, Box 19, Sapelo Island, GA 31327; (912) 485-2251; www.sapeloisland reserve.org.

Brunswick

Gateway to the Golden Isles—south of Darien via US 17 at U.S. Highway 341.

Brunswick, gateway to the Golden Isles, boasts a major shrimping fleet. Quaint butterfly-netted boats returning with their day's catch are a common sight. Don't leave town without strolling along the docks to let the munchkins see the working fleet. Early morning or late afternoon are the best times. The fleet is a photographer's paradise, so equip amateur shutterbugs with one-use cameras so that they can be as creative as their imaginations allow. Tell the wide-eyed kiddies that the contents of the bulging nets they see being unloaded might just turn up on their dinner table tonight. Naturally, the local restaurants highlight rich coastal favorites such as Low-country Boil, cashew shrimp, and she-crab soup.

Earth Day Nature Trail (all ages) 🚶 🌿 ♿

1 Conservation Way, off US 17 at the Sidney Lanier Bridge; (912) 264-7218; www.dnr .state.ga.us/dnr/coastal. Open daily 8:00 a.m. to 4:30 p.m. Free.

Get your exercise and enjoy seeing wading birds in their natural habitat. If everyone keeps an eagle eye open, you might even catch a glimpse of an eagle or osprey in the osprey/eagle nesting platform. Wildlife observation decks and an observation tower provide plenty of opportunities to have nature lessons along the way. The trail was designed to be self-guided, and on weekdays you can get a brochure from the Coastal Resources Office (912-264-7218). If your children are Boy or Girl Scouts, they can earn an Earth Day Nature Trail Scout Patch by taking the Nature Trail Challenge. Have their scout leader make arrangements in advance so that you can pick up the activity booklet.

Amazing Georgia Facts

Brunswick Stew was first prepared right here in Brunswick, Georgia. A big black iron pot in which it was simmered is displayed at the St. Simons Causeway Welcome Center.

Mary Ross Waterfront Park (all ages) 🔞
Bay and Gloucester Streets; (no phone).

The quaint shrimp boats that make their homes along the docks here provide plenty of photographic opportunities. If you get there in the late afternoon, you might see the shrimpers offloading their treasures of the sea. The Brunswick Harbor Market at the park features the Liberty Ship Memorial Plaza, an outdoor musical playscape, and an amphitheater. This is also a great place to watch oceangoing freighters from around the world and to catch a spectacular sunset.

For More Information

Brunswick and the Golden Isles Visitors Bureau, 4 Glynn Avenue, Brunswick, GA 31520; (912) 265-0620 or (800) 933-2627; www.bgicvb.com.

Brunswick-Golden Isles Visitor Center, US 17 at F. J. Torras Causeway. Open daily 9:00 a.m. to 5:00 p.m. See a brief video about the area and the pot in which the first Brunswick stew was made.

St. Simons Island

Across the Torras Causeway from Brunswick.

St. Simons has a long and colorful history. Millions of adult readers have fallen under the island's spell by poring over the historical trilogy of novels by Eugenia Price: *Lighthouse, New Moon Rising,* and *Beloved Invader.* If you haven't read them, you should do so—before or after visiting the island. St. Simons was first inhabited by Guale Indians. French explorers landed in the sixteenth century, followed by Spanish Jesuit and later Franciscan missionaries who attempted unsuccessfully to convert

Factory That Never Was

"Are we there yet?" When the backseat gang asks that well-worn question, tell them that you're almost there when they see the huge chipped and broken redbrick chimney at exit 7 on I-95. In 1917 Glynn County was chosen as the site for a massive factory intended to produce vital war material for World War I explosives. On November 11, 1918, just thirty days from the scheduled completion of the factory, the war ended. All work halted immediately, never to be resumed. Most of the original buildings were immediately demolished, the rest fell down, and now the chimney is the sole survivor.

the Guale. In 1736 the English established the town of Frederica and built a fort on the banks of the river. Among the settlers were John and Charles Wesley, Anglican missionaries who sowed the seeds of Methodism here before they returned to England to found the Methodist Church. Tell the kidlets that if the British hadn't defeated the Spanish in 1742, Spanish might be the official language in Georgia today instead of English. The abundance of sturdy live oaks on the island resulted in a dynamic timber industry, and great antebellum plantations grew the world-famous Sea Island cotton. One way to get acquainted with the island is to take a trolley tour. The heart of town is the island's premier park, **Neptune Park** at St. Simons Village (912-265-0620), an active hub for fishing, crabbing, and miniature golf. Facilities include a theater where live performances are given in fall and spring, a large swimming pool, the town library, and a visitor center.

Fort Frederica National Monument (all ages) 🏛️ 🧭

6500 Frederica Road; (912) 638-3639; www.nps.gov/fofr. Grounds open daily year-round 8:30 a.m. to 5:00 p.m., Bloody Marsh unit open daily 8:30 a.m. to 4:00 p.m. Museum open daily year-round 9:00 a.m. to 5:00 p.m. Closed Christmas Day; films shown on the half hour. Parking $5 (good for seven days). Admission $ (also good for seven days); children younger than 15 free.

History, history everywhere—this site is an excellent place to satisfy your curiosity about the area's colorful past. Let the under-teenage set have their freedom to explore the ruins of the fort, the tabby powder magazine, and excavations of the village of Frederica—all built by General Oglethorpe in 1736. Meet up at the visitor center/museum to watch a film and examine artifacts and dioramas that give insight into the lives of Native Americans, explorers, and early settlers. Rent the forty-five-minute audio tape for a more in-depth tour.

Maritime Center at the Historic Coast Guard Station (ages 6 to 12) 🏛️ 🧭

4201 First Street, East Beach; call the Coastal Georgia Historical Society (912) 638-4666; www.saintsimonslighthouse.org. Open Monday through Saturday 10:00 a.m. to 5:00 p.m., Sunday 1:30 to 5:00 p.m. Adults $$, children $; discount and combination tickets with the St. Simons Lighthouse available.

Ollie, a fictitious Coast Guardsman, and his dog Scuttle greet visitors at the picturesque restored 1935 Coast Guard Station and lead them on an exploration of the region's natural assets and maritime and military history. Ollie's "letters home" introduce the galleries and tell what life was like for a Coast Guardsman who was stationed there. Among the galleries are ones devoted to the geology of the Georgia tidewater, the ocean beach, the salt marsh, the maritime forest, and the freshwater slough. Of special interest to youngsters are the exhibits about foragers of the deep—Atlantic right whales and loggerhead sea turtles. Several exhibits are hands-on, which helps keep the little ones occupied.

The Real **Neptune**

The Neptune after whom the St. Simons town park was named was not the mythical sea god but a loyal slave. Neptune followed his master to the Civil War and, when the owner was killed, brought his body home for burial. Neptune then returned to the war to serve the master's son. As a reward, he was given a plot of land where the park now stands.

St. Simons Island Lighthouse Museum (ages 4 to 12) 🏛️ 🕭

101 Twelfth Street; (912) 638-4666; www.saintsimonslighthouse.org. Open Monday through Saturday 10:00 a.m. to 5:00 p.m., Sunday 1:30 to 5:00 p.m. Closed Thanksgiving, Christmas Eve, Christmas, and New Year's Days. Adults $$, children $, five and younger free; combination ticket available to Maritime Center.

Don't be wimps; your energetic youngsters certainly won't. You can't visit this 1872 lighthouse without scrambling up the 129 steps to the top, where your chilluns can imagine the lightkeeper's daily chore of illuminating the beacon. Don't forget to take the camera, because you can get some wonderful pictures of St. Simons Village from the balcony around the light. Back on ground level, examine the displays about the history of lighthouses and St. Simons Island in the museum of coastal history located in the keeper's cottage. Don't leave your visit until too late in the day—you'll want to allow about forty-five minutes for full enjoyment.

Salt Marsh Nature Tour (all ages) 🔺

Provided by Hampton River Club, Hampton River; (912) 638-9354; www.marshtours .com. Call for a schedule. Advance reservations required; four people minimum/six people maximum. (You can join another tour if you have fewer than four people.) $$$$

During these relaxing tours, Mom and Dad can sit back while budding marine biologists are kept busy studying nature. Operated by Jeanne and Jim Pleasant, two-hour pontoon boat ride glides through tidal creeks and salt marsh while docents (accredited by the University of Georgia Marine Extension Service) point out the native animals, fish, birds, flora, and fauna—great opportunities for scrapbook photos. Optional tours that range from one to three hours include bird-watching and shelling excursions to Pelican Spit. Binoculars, water, and soft drinks are provided.

Amazing
Georgia Facts

Drive to Gascoigne Bluff, where timbers from strong live oaks were cut for the construction of the famous ship USS *Constitution*, fondly known as Old Ironsides.

Epworth-by-the-Sea (all ages) ⊖

100 Arthur J. Moore Drive; (912) 638-8688; www.epworthbythesea.org. Open year-round. Museum free; lodging $–$$$ per night for two people, $5 for each additional person older than twelve; younger than twelve free in the room with their parents; children twelve and younger eat for half price.

Even if your family isn't attending a retreat or conference at this Methodist haven located on the Frederica River, you can get inexpensive cafeteria-style meals and accommodations in the center's motels, apartments, and cabins. Extensive recreational facilities include tennis and basketball courts, ball fields, bicycle rentals, an outdoor swimming pool, and two fishing piers, as well as dolphin tours aboard the center's pontoon boat. Get a history lesson about coastal Georgia, St. Simons, and Methodism in early Georgia at the center's museum, the world's largest conference-owned United Methodist museum.

For More Information

St. Simons Visitors Center, 530-B Beachview Drive, St. Simons, GA 31522;

(912) 638-9014 or (800) 933-2627; www.bgivb.com.

Sea Island

Off the eastern shore of St. Simons Island.

Part of the Old Spanish Main, Sea Island—originally called Long Island—is among the most historic territories in America. In 1926 Howard E. Coffin, a founder of the Hudson Motor Car Company, bought Long Island and changed its name. Two years later he built the Cloister Hotel—a masterpiece of Mediterranean red-tile-roofed architecture surrounded by colorful gardens and lush foliage. One of the world's greatest resorts, it is Georgia's only five-star, five-diamond resort. Today Sea Island is an exclusive enclave that contains only the resort and residential neighborhoods, and is accessible only to overnight guests and residents.

The Cloister (all ages) 🚫⚠️🚫

100 First Street; (912) 638-5159 or (888) SEAISLAND (732-4752); www.cloister.com or www.seaisland.com. $$$$

Here's *the* vacation that will have the entire family packed and ready to go. The world-famous resort is a destination in itself. A variety of luxurious accommodations range from rooms and suites in the main inn to beachfront units and cottages, as well as the new lodge at the golf course. Much to the dismay of preservationists and those families who have visited the Cloister in the past, the historic main inn has been demolished and has been replaced by a brand-new one. Despite the loss of the famous structure, which had often been visited by presidents and royalty, the owners and management promise that everyone is pleased with the luxurious new inn and all its amenities.

Adding to the elegant retreat's extraordinary appeal are 5 miles of sparkling beaches, a beach club, three eighteen-hole golf courses, an eighteen-hole putting green, a nine-hole pitch-and-putt course, twenty-five tennis courts, a health spa, croquet courts, trap and skeet shooting, two pools, horseback riding, fishing, boating, and diving. *Golf* and *Tennis* magazines rate the facilities at the Cloister among the best places in the country to enjoy those two sports. A mustn't-miss activity for the entire clan is the jeep train safari around the island.

At the Cloister, American-plan dining includes three meals a day served with a variety of menus in a choice of settings such as the **Beach Club** and the **Golf Club.** In an increasingly casual world, the last bastion of elegant formality is the **Main Dining Room,** where coats and ties are required for men and young men older than twelve. There are few places left to expose your progeny to a gracious way of life before it disappears. Children in the same room with their parents stay free except for a meal charge based on age. In addition, there is no charge for golf greens fees and afternoon tennis for guests younger than nineteen.

Children's and Family Activities at The Cloister at Sea Island
(ages 3 to 12)

The Cloister at Sea Island, 1 First Street; (912) 638-3611/ext. 5111; www.seaisland .com. Year round, but programs and hours vary by season, so it's best to call ahead. Reservations required for each activity. Activities $-$$$$.

At the Cloister every day is play day, but some days are even more fantastic than others. Generations of families have made annual pilgrimages to The Cloister at Sea Island resort not only for its opulent accommodations, superb food, impeccable service, spa services, and extensive sports facilities, but also for its outstanding children's programs. In fact, the resort has been named the Best Resort for Families in the United States and Canada by *Conde Nast Traveler* and *Travel and Leisure.* It's heart-warming to see four generations re-creating a summer legacy for the newest little ones. Quite a few of the college-age counselors attended the camp themselves

as young guests. While the older generations are enjoying one of the resort's sporting activities or being pampered at the Sea Island Spa, the kiddies can cavort at their own planned activities for ages three through twelve. **Camp Cloister,** the resort's year-round program for ages three to eight, is world famous, but no matter what time of year you visit, there are almost endless activities for youngsters. Camp Cloister is offered mornings Monday through Saturday year-round with hours extended until 3:00 p.m. in the summer and on holidays for ages five to eight. Activities might include turtle walks, dunes discovery, fishing, sand sculpture, contests, tie-dye-on-the-beach, boat rides, a Jeep safari, and more. **Club Sea Island,** for ages nine to twelve, offers more advanced activities such as tennis and golf clinics and round robins Monday through Saturday 9:30 a.m. to 3:00 p.m. One of the most popular programs for young epicureans and their parents is the **Children's Dinner.** While Mom and Dad enjoy the resort's formal fine dining, children ages three to eleven can enjoy a semiformal dinner with each other. The kid-friendly menu and activities change nightly. Our grandchil-dren preferred eating dinner with friends they'd made during their camp experiences and joining us later for dessert. Other kid-oriented activities available year-round include bingo, cookie baking, bicycle rentals, and nature pro-grams, which range from reptile and raptor encounters to overnight campouts.

Little St. Simons Island

Accessible by private ferry from the northern end of St. Simons Island.

Lodge at Little St. Simons (ages 6 and up) 🐘 ⚠ 🏛
P.O. Box 21078, St. Simons 31522; (912) 638-7472 or (888) 733-5774; www.littlestsimons island.com. $$$$

A wonderful place to make "forever" memories for youngsters, parents, and even grandparents is Little St. Simons Island—in fact, this is an ideal place for a multigen-erational family reunion. Although restricted to children older than eight from Octo-ber through April (all ages the remainder of the year), the privately owned island is an outdoor adventure paradise where no one ever runs out of activities. Accessible only by a twice-daily private ferry, Little St. Simons has been owned for more than one hundred years by the Berolzheimer family, who open it to visitors several times a year. The 10,000-acre island caters to only thirty guests at a time in accommodations

Amazing
Georgia Facts

The stained-glass window in Faith Chapel on St. Simons Island is the only window personally created and installed by Louis Comfort Tiffany.

that range from a rustic turn-of-the-twentieth-century lodge to several more-modern cottages built in the 1980s. Truly a place to get away from it all, Little St. Simons has no radio, TV, or newspapers and only one phone—and that's for emergencies. But you won't miss or even think about them. (Why don't you throw caution to the winds and leave the cellular phone home, too?) In addition to enjoying the 7 miles of unspoiled beaches, activities include a swimming pool, hiking, horseback riding, fishing, canoeing, and kayaking. On-staff naturalists conduct turtle hunts and deer counts or introduce you to freely roaming deer, soaring eagles, alligators, armadillos, and myriad species of birds. This is one place where your offspring won't be torturing you to take them to amusement parks and other high-tech signs of civilization. At this extremely casual getaway, all you need to bring are your camera, your bathing suit, and a big appetite. Meals and activities are included in the price.

During the **Summer Fun for Families** program, the entire island is used as a natural classroom to encourage exploration through scavenger hunts, lessons in map and compass reading, role-playing in the Food Chain Game, safaris, fishing with seine and cast nets, fish printing (an arts and crafts activity), and much more. Meanwhile the oldsters can participate in any number of activities or do the ultimate—nothing.

A Thalimer **Adventure**

Although the Thalimer clan, with the exception of number-three-daughter Cathy, are all tenderfeet when it comes to horseback riding, we almost never miss an opportunity to do some touring mounted on a noble steed. On this particular visit to Little St. Simons, Grammy Carol was paired up with a horse named Elvis. During the ride, he was always lagging behind to nibble on succulent leaves and grasses, and no amount of prodding convinced him to hurry along. Despite the fervent hopes of the King's fans, we all came to the conclusion that Elvis is, in fact, dead.

Waycross

West of Brunswick on U.S. Highway 82.

Way to go! Waycross received its name because it held a strategic position where stagecoach roads and pioneer trails crossed. The city is one of the gateways to the **Okefenokee Swamp** (see also Fargo and Folkston), home of Pogo Possum, star of the *Pogo* comic strip created by Walt Kelly in the late 1940s to express environmental concerns and to poke fun at political matters. (Pogo has even been a presidential candidate.) When spending time in and around the swamp, don't forget insect repellent. The skeeters are super size and determined. They have absolutely no respect for your tender skin.

Laura S. Walker State Park (all ages)

5653 Laura Walker Road off Highway 177, Douglas; (912) 287-4900 or (800) 864-7275; www.gastateparks.org/info/lwalker. Open daily 7:00 a.m. to 10:00 p.m. Parking $3, admission free.

Here's a trivia question. How many state parks in Georgia are named for a woman? Answer: This is the only one. Laura Walker was a writer, teacher, civic leader, and naturalist who worked for the preservation of trees. A 120-acre lake is great for bass fishing and other watersports. Other amenities and activities include hiking trails, a swimming pool, fishing dock, canoe and fishing boat rentals, and a golf course. When a day of exhausting activity is over, you don't even have to leave the grounds; a campground beckons.

Obediah's Okefenok (all ages)

500 Obediah Trail off Swamp Road; (912) 287-0090; www.okefenokeeswamp.com. Open daily 10:00 a.m. to 5:00 p.m. Closed Christmas, New Year's Day, and Easter. Adults and children ages six to seventeen $; annual pass $$$$.

A fun-filled experience for all ages, this popular attraction, which provides a rare glimpse into a late-1800s swamper's lifestyle, honors the legendary Obediah Barber, who was known as the King of the Okefenokee. You don't have to be a kid to be enthralled by the yarns of this 6-foot, 6-inch swamper. Parents and kids love the spine-tingling legend of his encounter with a huge black bear—a confrontation in which Obediah emerged the victor. Your heirs can let their imaginations run free while scampering through this fun, working turn-of-the-twentieth-century homestead, which combines Obediah's historic log home with a dozen historic farm buildings and more than fifty exhibits of artifacts from the period, including a turpentine shed and a moonshine still. In addition, they'll love the exotic swamp animals and petting zoo. Boardwalks and trails offer plenty of vantage points for wildlife observation. Scheduled events and living-history demonstrations portray the life of a swamper as well as Native American culture. In other words, you could easily spend the whole day here.

Okefenokee Heritage Center (all ages) 🏛️ ⛾

1460 North Augusta Avenue; (912) 285-4260. Open Tuesday through Saturday 10:00 a.m. to 4:00 p.m. Adults and children ages five to eighteen $.

Swamp the kids with the area's history at this center, where they can learn more about the heritage and lives of the people who settled in the vicinity of the Okefenokee Swamp. Sure to excite a little squirt's imagination are a 1912 Baldwin steam locomotive, a tender, and additional railcars on which to clamber aboard. The collection of carriages and vintage cars is sure to appeal to youngsters of all ages, but there's even more: a 1900s print shop, the General Thomas Hilliard house, and an 1840s farmhouse with typical outbuildings. Other exhibits explore Native American, African-American, and other early settlements in the area; there's also an art gallery and changing exhibits.

Southern Forest World Museum (all ages) 🎡 ⛾

1440 North Augusta Avenue; (912) 285-4056. Open Monday through Saturday 10:00 a.m. to 5:00 p.m., Sunday 1:00 to 5:00 p.m. Closed Easter, Labor Day, Thanksgiving, Christmas Eve and Day, and New Year's Eve and Day. $ per person, children younger than five free.

It's as easy as falling off a log. Where else can the small fry walk inside a giant loblolly pine, see a mummified dog in a tree, or listen to a talking tree? Your little foresters can increase their knowledge of the timbering industry by visiting this educational exhibit center, where the story of forestry in the thirteen Southern states is told. Tree huggers can learn about forest industries, study naval stores operations of yesterday and today, and gain an understanding of the managed forest concept. In addition to trees they can climb, kids can see a collection of logging tools, climb the fire tower to observe the area, and explore the nature trails.

Southeast **Paul Bunyan**

In the early 1800s Obediah Barber was one of the first white settlers to live on the northern frontier of the Okefenokee Swamp. As a youngster he assisted state surveyors in determining the true boundary line between the state of Georgia and the territory of Florida. As an adult this frontiersman married three times, fathered twenty children, and made his living as a hunter, trapper, and cattle farmer. During the Civil War he provided beef to the Confederacy.

Okefenokee Swamp Park (all ages) (icons)

5700 Okefenokee Swamp Park Road off U.S. Highway 1 South; (912) 283-0583; www
.okeswamp.com. Open daily 9:00 a.m. to 5:30 p.m. Closed Thanksgiving and Christmas
Eve and Day. $$$; children two and younger free; canoe rentals $$$; boat tours $$$.

If you're feeling adventurous, a visit to this unusual park will intrigue your entire
brood. The highlight of any visit is a guided boat tour down the dark, reflective, lily-
decked waters of the mysterious swamp. Keep a sharp eye out for gators sunning
themselves on shore or lurking partially submerged near the water's surface. Back on
dry land, junior jaunters find plenty of other things to do. They can be kept totally
engrossed for hours at the nature center; wildlife observatory; Swamp Creation Cen-
ter with the Living Swamp display, an exhibit about the Wildes Family Massacre; and
at a swamp homestead.

The youngsters will come running when the whistle blows and the conductor
calls, "All aboard!" the park's newest attraction—*The Lady Suwannee,* **Okefeno-
kee Swamp Railroad.** The three-coach train pulled by a replica steam engine makes
a 1.5-mile trip around the park, with a thirty-minute stop at Pioneer Island. Another
park attraction is the **Pogo and Walt Kelly Museum.** Even those kiddies who never
knew that the cute, cuddly cartoon character was once proposed for president of the
United States will enjoy the exhibits. Although the late cartoonist wasn't from the
Okefenokee Swamp area, he based his longtime cartoon strip there, so what was a
more natural place for the museum to be located?

Allow at least four to five hours if you want to explore the entire park in depth.
Hunger pangs will surely strike during that long a visit; if you haven't brought your
own picnic, stop in between 10:00 a.m. and 2:00 p.m. at the Three Pigs BBQ Snack Bar
for some victuals.

Check for the schedule of periodic interpretive lectures and wildlife shows held
throughout the year. Canoe rentals are available for the active family, and roughing-it
types get a thrill from camping out on one of the platforms along the long-distance
canoe trails. Warning: Swimming is not permitted, and when canoeing or boating or
camping out on a platform, don't drag hands, feet, or fish you've caught in the

The Amazing **Okefenokee**

- The Okefenokee Swamp—covering 41,200 acres—is the largest fresh-
  water swamp in the United States.

- In the Okefenokee Swamp you can find 200 species of birds, 40
  species of mammals, 50 species of reptiles, 32 species of amphibians,
  and 32 species of fish.

More About the
Amazing Okefenokee Swamp

Native Americans called it the "land of the trembling earth." Today called "America's greatest natural botanical garden," the 950-square-mile depression is one of Mother Nature's most bizarre creations.

water—warm flesh is very attractive to gators. And these beasts haven't swallowed an alarm clock to warn you they're coming like the crocodile that stalked Captain Hook did.

For More Information

Waycross Tourism Bureau and Visitor Center, 315A Plant Avenue, Waycross 31501; (912) 283-3744; www.swampgeorgia.com.

Fargo

East on Highway 94.

Fargo is one of the gateways to the greatest family adventure you can imagine—the Okefenokee Swamp. A perfect place for a day trip, the swamp also offers challenging overnight canoeing-camping experiences.

Stephen C. Foster State Park (all ages)

17515 Highway 177; (912) 637-5274 or (800) 864-7275; www.gastateparks.org/info/ scfoster/. Open daily year-round, 7:00 a.m. to 7:00 p.m.; summer hours 6:30 a.m. to 8:30 p.m. Admission $; boat tours $$, children under three free; boat rentals, call for availability and rates; camping $; cottages $$$; museum free.

Way down upon the swampy river. Bring your little swamp rats to spend a day or more at this park, named for songwriter Stephen Foster. The preserve, one of the primary entrances to the Okefenokee National Wildlife Refuge, is a mecca for naturalists. Little environmentalists can check out the flora and fauna by taking a nature walk on an elevated boardwalk or get even closer to nature on guided boat tours. Active types can rent boats or canoes for fishing, wildlife observation, and exercise. In the Suwannee River Visitor Center an interpretive museum explains the natural history of the area through a film; mounted animals; live animal exhibits; and swamp, river, timber, and local history. When it's lullaby time, camp or rent a cottage.

Folkston

East on U.S. Highway 301.

Folkston Funnel Train Watching Platform (ages 3 to 12)
103 North First Street; (912) 496-2536; www.folkston.com.

Let's go play with trains. You're never too young or old to have a fascination with the huge behemoths. We remember when we were kids and we'd be stopped by a barrier on the highway while a train chugged slowly by. We'd get out of the car and count the cars and wave to the engineer and hope he'd toot the whistle at us. With the advent of interstate highways and bridges to keep the flow of traffic going, today's parents and kidlets don't have many opportunities to train watch. If you're in the area, Folkston is the place to go. The town is located on CSXT's double-track mainline to Florida, known as the CSXT Funnel. More than seventy trains per day, including eight Amtrak trains and intermodal and mixed freight trains, pass through each day, so the town has built a covered platform with seating, lighting, and even ceiling fans alongside the tracks to allow train buffs to watch and take pictures to their heart's content. Among the trains you might see are an Amtrak Auto Train or the Tropicana Juice Train. Visitors can even activate a scanner on the platform to listen to communications between the train engineers. During the Okefenokee Festival in October, the Orlando Society of Model Railroaders sets up an elaborate train layout nearby. Across the tracks, the historic depot has been renovated to house the chamber of commerce as well as some old train memorabilia. Anytime you're at the platform, your little railroaders can wave to the engineer and get a whistle-blown salute.

Okefenokee National Wildlife Refuge (all ages)
Highway 121/123; (912) 496-7836; www.fws.gov/okefenokee. Refuge open daily March through October one half hour before dawn to 7:30 p.m.; remainder of the year refuge open daily (except Christmas) one half hour before dawn to 5:30 p.m.; interpretive center open 9:00 a.m. to 5:00 p.m. Refreshment stand open daily. To find out more call (912) 496-7156. Admission $; boat rentals $$$$; canoes $$$$; guided tours adults $$$, children ages five to eleven $$; bicycles $$$ per day; campsites $; cabins $.

This is a truly fantastic place for families to spend a day or more. The orientation center shows films about the swamp, and exhibits portray the animal life from the 402,000-acre, 7,000-year-old primeval swamp. Drive or bicycle to the **Chesser Island Homestead,** a restored swamp dwelling and outbuildings that demonstrate to high-tech-addicted kiddies the self-sufficiency that was necessary for pioneer swamp families to survive. Among the hiking trails easy enough even for stubby little legs are the **Canal Diggers Trail,** the **Upland Discovery Trail,** and the **Deer Stand Trail.** In addition, the wildlife refuge features a 4,000-foot boardwalk and a 50-foot observation tower from which even the shortest tot can get spectacular views of the swamp.

At the same location the **Suwanee Canal Recreation Area and Okefenokee Adventures** (912-496-7156) or 866-THE-SWAMP offers guided boat tours, boat and canoe rentals, and a refreshment center.

For More Information

Okefenokee Chamber of Commerce,
202 West Main Street, Folkston, GA 31537;
(912) 496-2536; www.folkston.com.

Jekyll Island

East on Highway 520.

   A few million dollars here, a sixteen-room cottage there; after a while it all starts to add up. From 1886 to 1942 Jekyll Island was the private retreat of one hundred ultrawealthy families who came primarily in the winter to hunt. This was no rustic camp, however. The millionaires built a magnificent Victorian club/hotel and individual "cottages" that we'd consider mansions. For additional amusement they created a nine-hole golf course and both outdoor and indoor tennis courts for their private playground. During World War II the government requested that the island not be used, and afterward the rich and famous abandoned their exclusive haven for more exotic locations. Eventually purchased by the state of Georgia, the island's development is strictly regulated—ensuring that its charm is preserved. Today's Jekyll Island is a place where the small fry can easily alternate between the past and the present. Recreation is varied and family-oriented. Because growth has been strictly limited, the 10 miles of beaches are uncrowded and the streets are quiet. Jekyll Island offers hotel/motel properties in every price range and kid-friendly restaurants.

Amazing
Georgia Facts

The first transcontinental phone call in the United States was made from Jekyll Island to San Francisco.

Jekyll Island **Sports**

- **Biking/Jogging** (all ages). (912) 635-2648. Rentals $$$ per day, $$ half-day, $ hour. An extensive system of bicycle and jogging trails includes 20 miles of paved paths through the historic district and past woodlands, marshes, and along the beach. If you didn't bring your own cycles, rentals are available at the miniature golf course from 9:00 a.m. to 5:00 p.m., several hotels including the Jekyll Island Club, and the campground.

- **Boating/Fishing** (all ages). Your little anglers have numerous choices for casting their lines. One is to fish from the **Fishing Pier** (North Riverview Road; 912-635-3636 or 800-841-6586), located at the Clam Creek Picnic Area. If your thing is boating, the **Jekyll Harbor Resort Marina** (1 Harbor Road; 912-635-3137) has a complete facility with dry storage, dockage, charters, and rentals, as well as a cafe and a pool and spa for marina guests. The **Jekyll Island Historic Marina** (1 Pier Road off North Riverview Drive; 912-635-3152) provides dockage, deep-sea fishing charters, dinner or sunset/dolphin-watch sightseeing cruises, bait and tackle, personal watercraft and boat rentals, fishing equipment, and bike rentals.

- **Carriage Tours** (all ages). **Victoria's Carriages and Trail Rides,** 100 Stable Road; (912) 635-9500. Monday through Saturday 10:00 a.m. to 4:00 p.m. Since the kids are going back in time and experiencing life the way it used to be while exploring the historic district, why not have them experience some nonmotorized travel by taking a carriage ride? They'll be amazed at the slow pace of travel and what a feat it was to cover any distance. Carriage rides depart from the Jekyll Island History Center on Stable Road. You can even take your dog along—for free.

- **Golf** (ages 8 to 12). For more information about the courses or to set up tee times, contact the golf center on Capt. Wylly Road at (912) 635-2368. Daily greens fees on the eighteen-hole courses $$$$; juniors, twilight, and half cart $$$. Junior and senior duffers can whack balls off the tees at sixty-three holes of golf on Jekyll Island: nine holes at the historic **Oceanside Course** (constructed by the millionaires in 1898) and eighteen holes each at the **Oleander, Pine Lakes,** and **Indian**

Mounds courses. Jekyll Island is the home of the U.S. Kids Golf World championship and the Georgia State High School Championship.

- **Horseback Riding.** See Victoria's Carriages and Trail Rides. **Jekyll Island Welcome Center,** 901 Downing Musgrove Causeway, Jekyll Island, GA 31527; (912) 635-3636.

- **Tennis** (ages 6 to 12). **Jekyll Island Tennis Center,** 400 Capt. Wylly Road; (912) 635-3154. Open daily 9:00 a.m. to 6:00 p.m. Night play can be arranged by reservation. Tennis pros and novices in your family can improve their games or simply enjoy the thirteen fast-dry courts, seven of which are lighted, at the tennis center. Camps for every level of experience are offered in summer. Private lessons also are available.

Georgia Sea Turtle Information Center (ages 3 to 12)

Hopkins Road; (912) 635-4444. Open daily 10:00 a.m. to 7:00 p.m. Adults $$, children $, younger than three free; evening turtle walks, adults $$, children $; morning hatchling walks, adults $$, children $.

Get your budding naturalists interested in saving and appreciating sea turtles at this brand-new education and rehabilitation center—the only state-of-the-art emergency and rehabilitation sea turtle center in Georgia. Jekyll Island was chosen as the site because it has the most significant annual turtle nesting among all of Georgia's barrier islands. Exhibits describe the life cycle of these ancient and mysterious reptiles from egg to adulthood. Other displays explore Georgia's unique coastal ecosystem. Want to know more? The center offers turtle walks June 1 through August 1 when the turtles are nesting. These leave Monday through Saturday at 8:30 and at 9:30 p.m. Hatchling tours are offered at 7:00 a.m. on Wednesday, Saturday, and Sunday during the hatching season in August and September.

Jekyll Island Club National Landmark Historic District
(ages 4 to 12)

Stable Road; (912) 635-4036 or (877) 4JEKYLL; www.jekyllisland.com. Tours depart daily from the Jekyll Island Museum History Center, located in the Old Stables on Stable Road. Center open 10:00 a.m. to 4:00 p.m. except Christmas and New Year's Days. Adults $$, children ages six to eighteen $.

Let your little tax deductions see the extravagant lifestyle of a millionaire by touring the historic district. Traveling through the tree-shaded district by trolley, your brood can not only check out the insides of several of the restored mansion-size "cottages" but also admire the opulent period furnishings, decorative arts, and historical photographs of turn-of-the-twentieth-century life on the island.

Trolley tours of the historic district leave from the center. Assess your little ones' attention spans and stamina before choosing between the two tours offered. The shorter tour, which departs at 10:00 a.m. and 4:00 p.m. and lasts about forty-five minutes, is a trolley-only tour past the major sights in the district. The ninety-minute tour, which departs at 11:00 a.m. and 2:00 p.m., includes admission to two of the antique-filled "cottages." Ninety-minute walking tours of the district are offered on Tuesday and Thursday. These might be better for older children or, better yet, for Mom and Dad if the kiddies are enrolled in Club Juniors at the Jekyll Island Club Hotel (see next entry).

Jekyll Island Club/Club Juniors (ages 5 to 12)

Jekyll Island Club Hotel, 371 Riverview Drive; (912) 635-2600 or (800) 535-9547; www .jekyllclub.com. Monday through Saturday, Memorial Day through mid-August; full day $$$ per day for hotel guests, $$$$ per day for others; half-day $$ for hotel guests, $$$ per day for others.

For the small fry the fun starts at the resort hotel's children's program, which consists of a half-day or all-day schedule of exciting events such as bicycle safaris, beach fun, crabbing, arts and crafts, tennis, lawn sports, swimming, kite flying, and excursions to the Summer Waves water park, Tidelands Nature Center, and Jekyll Island's miniature golf course. Friday culminates with "That's Entertainment," a special series with visits from Okefenokee Joe and the Snakes, magicians, puppeteers, storytellers, and more. Nonguests of the hotel can also participate in Club Juniors for a higher fee.

Miniature Golf Course (ages 4 to 12)

North Beachview Drive; (912) 635-2648. Open daily, summer 9:00 a.m. to 10:00 p.m., fall through winter 9:00 a.m. to 5:00 p.m. $, four and younger free; ten-game pass $$$$.

Less serious golfers in your family might prefer to try their luck at these two lighted eighteen-hole courses, filled with animal likenesses and other challenging obstacles.

Sea Turtle Walks (all ages)

(912) 635-2284. June 1 through mid-August, from the visitor center Monday through Saturday evenings at 9:30 p.m. Reservations required.

A sighting of a sea turtle or a nest isn't guaranteed, but the whole family will enjoy the guided walk while they're searching. Eager participants meet at the center and watch an informative video before leaving on the 2-mile walk. You're bound to see other wildlife along the beach and dunes and learn lots of interesting facts.

Summer Waves Family Waterpark (ages 4 to 12) ⊗ ⊛

210 South Riverview Drive; (912) 635-2074; www.summerwaves.com. **Open some weekends prior to Memorial Day and after mid-August through Labor Day; Memorial Day to Labor Day, open Monday through Thursday; until 7:00 p.m. on Friday; until 8:00 p.m. Saturday; Sunday 11:00 a.m. to 7:00 p.m. General admission $$$, three and younger free, after 4:00 p.m. $.**

Get wet! On a hot summer day your water babies will enjoy a cool splash here. For all-day fun at one price, the eleven-acre water park features several spine-tingling water-slides, a wave pool, an endless river to drift down, a children's pool, and a McDonald's. What more could you ask for?

Tidelands Nature Center (all ages) ⊗ ⊛ ⊛ ⊛

100 Riverview Drive; (912) 635-5032; www.tidelands4h.org. **Open year-round, Monday through Friday 9:00 a.m. to 4:00 p.m., Saturday 10:00 a.m. to 2:00 p.m. Nature walks begin at 9:00 a.m. Monday and Wednesday year-round and Friday March through September. Admission to the center $; nature walks $ additional. Rentals $$; kayak tours $$$.**

Budding naturalists and environmentalists can get their hands on marine life at this University of Georgia 4–H marine science and environmental education program. Youngsters will enjoy the touch tanks and aquarium at the center as well as nature walks along the beach, the marsh, and the maritime forest. Either inside or outside, they're likely to spy fish, turtles, crabs, snakes, alligators, and other Georgia coastal critters. Three-hour guided kayak tours of Jekyll Creek and canoe and paddleboat rentals are offered seasonally.

For More Information

Jekyll Island Convention and Visitors Bureau, 381 Riverview Drive, Jekyll Island, GA 31527; (912) 635-4080 or (877) 4-JEKYLL; www.jekyllisland.com.

St. Marys

South on Highway 40.

St. Marys is a quaint river village with several historic attractions that make pleasant destinations on their own, but the small town is best known as the entry point for Cumberland Island National Seashore. If your intrepid explorers are catching the early-morning ferry to Cumberland Island, spend the night before in one of St. Marys's historic hotels.

A Thalimer **Adventure**

We had a rare experience when visiting Cumberland Island. A National Park Service ranger took us around in his truck so that we could see the entire island. It was hot, and he offered to stop by his house for a cool drink. Imagine our surprise when he pulled up in front of elegant Plum Orchard. Actually he lives in only a couple of simple rooms in the former servants' quarters, but he gave us a private tour of the mansion. What a treat.

Golf Cart Rentals

1926 Osborne Street; (912) 576-8170. Open weekdays 8:30 a.m. to 5:30 p.m., Saturday 9:00 a.m. to 1:00 p.m. $40 half day, $60 all day.

Can you imagine a town where traffic is so nonexistent that folks zip from one place to another by golf cart? Well, St. Marys is such a place. The citizens even have a decorated golf cart parade each year. Rentals are available so that you can join the unhurried lifestyle of the small hamlet and glide quietly from your hotel or bed and breakfast to a museum or other attraction. The rug rats will love it.

St. Marys Family Aquatic Center (all ages)

301 Herb Bauer Road; (912) 673-8118; www.ci.st-marys.ga.us/ac. Open late April (before Memorial Day weekends only) through early September (late August through September weekends only) generally Monday through Friday 11:00 a.m. to 6:00 p.m. with hours extended to 8:00 p.m. Thursday, Saturday 10:00 a.m. to 6:00 p.m., Sunday 1:00 to 6:00 p.m., but the days and hours are so variable, it's wise to call ahead or check the Web site. Adults $$, seniors and children $.

Marco Polo anyone? When it's hot and the kiddies are tired, go soak your head. This seven-acre family waterpark features plenty of thrills and spills to keep every age group occupied and happy. Splash Mountain is a zero-depth entry playground with sprinklers, water cannons, a two-story slide with plenty of twists and turns, and a huge bucket that dumps 300 gallons of water every five minutes, so watch out. For those who need even more thrills, Orange Crush is an enclosed twister slide. If Mom and Dad just want to relax, the Oasis area features an endless river down which they can drift. Other attractions include a lap pool, a play pool for small tykes, and a snack shack.

St. Marys Submarine Museum (ages 4 to 12) 🔊💬

102 St. Marys Street West; (912) 882-2782 (ASUB); www.stmaryssubmuseum.com.
Open Tuesday through Saturday 10:00 a.m. to 4:00 p.m., Sunday 1:00 to 5:00 p.m.
Closed Easter, Thanksgiving, and Christmas. $; children younger than six free.

Periscope up—literally. Look for the Type 8 submarine periscope sticking out of the
roof of the small white building on St. Marys's main street. St. Marys's newest attraction, the museum features World War II memorabilia including uniforms and medals,
an interactive computer kiosk, models, flags, insignia, awards, and a continuously
shown video about submarines. Major components of the USS *James K. Polk* are displayed as is a torpedo. The biggest hit, however, is the real, operational periscope
that lets everyone get a close-up view of southeast Georgia and northeast Florida.
Note: The museum is NOT on the grounds of the nearby submarine base.

For More Information

St. Marys Tourism Council, 406
Osborne Street, St. Marys, GA 31558;

(912) 882-4000 or (866) 868-2199;
www.stmaryswelcome.com.

Cumberland Island

At the turn of the twentieth century, the entire island was owned by the wealthy
Carnegie family, who built several mansions there. In 1971 they donated most of the
island to the United States for use as a national seashore.

Cumberland Island National Seashore (ages 4 to 12) 🔊💬

By ferry from St. Marys. Reservations for the ferry and campground are required. Call
(912) 882-4335 or (877) 860-6787 for more information or reservations; www.nps.gov/
cuis/. Mainland Visitor Information Center (912) 282-4336/ext. 254 open 8:00 a.m. to
4:30 p.m.; Mainland Museum open 1:00 to 4:00 p.m.; Ice House Museum on the island
open 8:00 a.m. to 4:00 p.m. Ferry departs at 9:00 a.m. and 11:45 a.m. March through
November; winter no departures on Tuesday or Wednesday. Adults $$$, children
younger than twelve $$.

Once you get there, wild horses couldn't drag you away. Accessible only via the passenger ferry *Cumberland Queen* from the downtown St. Marys waterfront, Cumberland Island is an almost untouched paradise where city kids can see wild horses,
deer, and armadillos. Adventurers can go backpacking or hiking through miles of
untouched maritime forest. Twenty miles of totally natural beach offer swimming,
saltwater surf fishing, and shelling.

Only 300 day-trippers and campers are allowed on this island Shangri-la each day,
and, other than the few used by the National Park Service, vehicles are not allowed

on the island. A visit here is a walking experience—or a biking experience if you bring your own. Among the sites you can see are a small museum in the **Ice House** at Dungeness Dock, with exhibits depicting the island's history, as well as the ruins of **Dungeness** and **Stafford Mansions.** Tours are offered to the **Plum Orchard Mansion** on the second and fourth Sunday of each month, departing by ferry from the Sea Camp Dock at 12:45 p.m. and returning at 4:15 p.m. There is an additional fee. *Note:* There are no stores on Cumberland Island; you must pack in *everything* you need and pack out your trash.

Interpretive programs are held by rangers daily on Cumberland Island at the dock upon the ferry's arrival as well as at 4:00 p.m. at the Sea Camp Ranger Station. Your intrepid explorers can become Junior Rangers and earn a badge and certificate while on the island. They simply pick up an activity booklet from the Mainland Visitor Information Center in St. Marys before boarding the ferry, or they can get one from the Sea Camp Ranger Station on the island. They simply complete the activities and turn the booklet into a ranger to get their badge and certificate. Families not lucky enough to make the trip to the island can still learn a lot about it at the Mainland Museum, where they can see Native American, African-American, and Carnegie-family artifacts and memorabilia brought over from the island.

Cumberland Island National Seashore Museum (ages 6 to 12)

129 Osborne Street, St. Marys; (912) 882-4336/ext. 229; www.nps.gov/cuis. Open daily 1:00 to 4:00 p.m. except Christmas. Free.

Get information about the ecology of Cumberland Island, ferry transportation, and what to see and do on the island from the visitor center, but to get historical information about the island, make a stop at this excellent small museum, which provides helpful background information for those about to embark on the ferry or for those who can't make the trip but would like to find out more about the history of the national seashore. Exhibits include artifacts from the Timicuan Indians, African Americans, and Carnegie family members who inhabited the island over hundreds of years. An additional exhibit called The Forgotten Battle, describes the last battle of the War of 1812, which occurred at nearby Peter Point.

Where to Eat in Southeast Georgia

Twin City

Canoochee Catfish, 2652 Canoochee-Garfield Road; (478) 237-7242. Cruise on over to this casual eatery for seafood, steaks, sandwiches, and salads. $–$$

Lew's Bar-B-Q, 407 South Railroad Avenue; (478) 763-3098. You can't fool a true barbecue aficionado. You'll get the real thing here: pit-cooked barbecue, ribs, and chicken. $

Other Things to
See&Do in Southeast Georgia

- **Georgia Southern University Museum,** Statesboro; (912) 681-5444; www.georgiasouthern.edu/

- **Ghost Talk-Ghost Walk,** Savannah; (912) 233-3896; www.savannah georgia.com/ghosttalk/

- **Savannah Light Tackle Fishing Company,** Savannah; (912) 238-5582

- **Skidaway Island State Park,** Savannah; (912) 598-2300 or (800) 864-7275; www.gastateparks.org/info/skidaway/

- **Telfair Academy of Arts and Sciences,** Savannah; (912) 790-8800; www.telfair.org

- **Marine Education Center & Aquarium,** Savannah; (912) 598-2496; information line (912) 598-FISH; www.uga.edu/aquarium

- **Wormsloe Historic Site,** Savannah; (912) 353-3023; www.gastate parks.org/info/wormsloe/

- **Bull River Cruises,** Tybee Island; (912) 898-1800 or (800) 311-4779; www.bullriver.com

- **Tybee Island Marine Science Center,** Tybee Island; (912) 786-5917; www.tybeemsc.org

- **Sea Kayak Georgia,** Tybee Island; (912) 786-8732 or (888) KAYAKGA; www.seakayakgeorgia.com

- **Hofwyl-Broadfield Plantation State Historic Site,** Brunswick; (912) 264-7333; www.gastateparks.org/info/hofwyl/

- **General Coffee State Park,** Douglas; (912) 384-7082 or (800) 864-7275; www.gastateparks.org/info/gencoffee/

- **Reed Bingham State Park,** Adel; (229) 896-3551; www.gastateparks .org/info/reedbing/

Savannah

Huey's, 115 East River Street; (912) 234-7385. How sweet it is. If you don't mind being covered in powdered sugar, drop into this taste of New Orleans for beignets (square, holeless doughnuts), po'boys, red beans and rice, and other Cajun favorites, as well as soups, salads, and sandwiches. $–$$

Mrs. Wilkes Dining Room, 107 Jones Street; (912) 232-5997; www.mrswilkes .com. A Savannah tradition, this restaurant serves a bountiful all-you-can-eat feast of Southern home cookin' served family style. Folks come from all over the world, so you'll have interesting table mates. Breakfast and lunch, Monday through Friday; no reservations, so get in line early. No credit cards, and you even take your own dishes to the kitchen. $

Pirates House, 20 East Broad Street; (912) 233-5757; www.thepirateshouse .com. Ahoy, me mateys! Your crew will be intrigued by eating in the rich, historic setting of an authentic 1733 tavern said to have tunnels used by pirates. With an emphasis on seafood, the restaurant serves dinner daily and lunch Monday through Saturday. Lunch $$, dinner and brunch $$$

Tybee Island

A-J's Dockside Restaurant, 1315 Chatham Avenue, (912) 786-9533. Now here's a dilemma. Do we tell you about our absolutely favorite casual restaurant on Tybee or do we keep it to ourselves so that it won't be any more crowded than it already is? When the Thalimer clan—sometimes more than twenty strong—stays out on the beach all day and early into the evening and then decides it's too late to fix dinner, we just stroll down the street to A-J's where we feast on a wide variety of seafood while sitting on the deck that juts out into the Back River. While we're chowing down, we watch the boat traffic zipping by and admire the most fantastic sunset on Tybee. $$-$$$

The Breakfast Club, 1500 Butler Avenue; (912) 786-5984. Offering simple, hearty fare for the budget-conscious traveler at breakfast (naturally), but also for lunch, this down-home casual eatery has been a fixture for years. The locals flock here to eat, so you know it's good. $

Crab Shack at Chimney Creek, 40-A Estelle Hammock Road; (912) 786-9857. Haul the kidlets in from the beach, dress 'em in something that can get messy, load 'em into the SUV, and head for this casual fish camp to fill 'em up with outstanding crab and other fish and shellfish. When the weather permits, eat out at the crude tables on the deck overlooking the creek and ask for lots of napkins—you'll all be dripping with butter and cooking juices. As you'd expect, everything is fresh, mostly caught that day. $–$$$

MacElwee's, 101 Lovell Avenue; (912) 786-8888; www.macelweesontybee.com. The oldest seafood restaurant near the beach, this restaurant is famous for its beer-batter and raw oyster specialties as well as for grilled and blackened seafood and hand-cut Black Angus rib-eye steaks. After a hearty repast, you can rid yourselves of some calories by taking a moonlight stroll on the beach. $$–$$$

Where to Stay in Southeast Georgia

Savannah

Savannah is blessed with a multitude of sleeping establishments. In addition to many large chain hotels in every price range, the city has wisely allowed the use of many of its historic warehouses and commercial buildings as intimate inns and of its aristocratic old homes as cozy bed-and-breakfasts—several of which welcome children.

Close to the action along Factor's Walk, River Street, and East Bay Street, several commercial buildings have been converted to inns and B&Bs. These are furnished with period reproductions and, with the exception of the Old Harbour and Planters Inns, have a restaurant. The town-house style of many of Savannah's historic homes permits the conversion of the garden level to a suite or apartment with a separate living/dining area and often with a full kitchen—making them perfect for families.

The Mulberry, 601 East Bay Street; (912) 238-1200; www.savannahhotel.com

East Bay Inn, 225 East Bay Street; (912) 238-1225 or (800) 500-1225; www.east bay.com

The Marshall House, 123 East Broughton Street; (912) 644-7896 or (800) 589-6304; www.marshallhouse.com

Old Harbour Inn, 508 East Factors Walk; (912) 234-4100 or (800) 553-6533; www .oldharbourinn.com

River Street Inn, 115 East River Street; (912) 234-6400 or (800) 253-4229; www .riverstreetinn.com

Planters Inn, 29 Abercorn Street; (912) 232-5678; www.plantersinnsavannah.com

The following outstanding B&Bs welcome children of any age:

17 Hundred 90 Inn, 307 East President Street; (912) 236-7122 or (800) 487-1790; www.17hundred90.com

Bed and Breakfast Inn, 117 and 119 West Gordon Street; (912) 238-0518

Eliza Thompson House, 5 West Jones Street; (912) 236-3620 or (800) 348-9378; www.elizathompsonhouse.com

Foley House, 14 West Hull Street; (912) 232-6622; www.foleyinn.com

Forsyth Park Inn, 102 West Hall Street; (912) 233-6800 or (866) 670-6800; www .forsythparkinn.com

Joan's on Jones, 17 West Jones Street; (912) 234-3863 or (888) 989-9806; www .joansonjones.home.comcast.net

Magnolia Place Inn, 503 Whitaker Street; (912) 236-7674 or (800) 238-7674

Mansion on Forsyth Park, 700 Drayton Street, (912) 238-5158; www.mansionon forsythpark.com. When you really want to splurge, this chic, ultra luxurious inn, located in a restored 1888 historic property, offers superb accommodations and culinary experiences as well as a spa, fitness center, cooking school, and art gallery. $$$$

Presidents' Quarters, 225 East President Street; (912) 233-1600 or (800) 233-1776; www.presidentsquarters.com.

Two fully equipped inns offer apartment accommodations, which are ideal for families:

Sea Cabins, 430 East River Street; (912) 790-8122

Suites on Lafayette, 201 East Charlton Street; (912) 233-7815; www.suiteson lafayette.com

Tybee Island

Hunter House Bed and Breakfast, 1701 Butler Avenue; (912) 786-7515; www.hunterhouseinn.com. Comfortable, though basic, accommodations for families with older children, in rooms and suites with kitchen facilities, are available 1 block off the beach. Hunter House is also well known for its second-floor restaurant and lounge, where the gang can enjoy fresh seafood and capture cooling sea breezes while gazing at the ocean. $$$–$$$$

Rivers End Campground, 915 Polk Street; (912) 786-5518 or (800) 786-1016. Located near the lighthouse and Fort Screven, the campground offers 130 sites with full hookups, as well as a pool and a camp store. $

Tybee Cottages, P.O. Box 1226, Tybee Island 31328; (912) 786-6746; www.tybee cottages.com. Daily and weekly rentals of one- and two-bedroom condos or beach houses with up to five bedrooms. $–$$$$

St. Simons Island

King and Prince Beach & Golf Resort, 201 Arnold Road at Downing Street; (912) 638-3631 or (800) 342-0212; www.kingandprince.com. The palatial historic beachfront resort offers hotel rooms, two- and three-bedroom villas, a restaurant, and tavern. Catering to families—many of whom have come here for generations—the resort's recreational facilities include clay tennis courts, one indoor and four outdoor swimming pools, and golf. $$$$

Sea Palms Golf and Tennis Resort, 5445 Frederica Road; (912) 638-3351 or (800) 841-6268; www.seapalms.com. You'll be on the go from the moment you arrive at this resort. In addition to superb golf and tennis, the resort offers bike rentals and a health club. $$$$

Jekyll Island

Jekyll Island Campground, 1197 Riverview Drive; (912) 635-3021 or (866) 658-3021. Those who want to sleep under the stars cooled by soft sea breezes may prefer to stay at this eighteen-acre site located 3 miles from the beach. With more than 200 developed and primitive campsites, the facility offers a camp store, laundry, and bike rentals. $

Jekyll Island Club Hotel, 371 Riverview Drive; (912) 635-2600 or (800) 535-9547; www.jekyllclub.com. Experience a small part of a millionaire's lifestyle by staying at the restored turn-of-the-twentieth-century, four-star, four-diamond National Historic Landmark hotel or one of the two restored millionaire's cottages, which combine Victorian opulence with all the modern amenities, including casual and fine dining, a croquet court, bicycle rentals, private beach club, heated swimming pool, and putting green. $$$$

St. Marys

Riverview Hotel, 100 St. Marys Street; (912) 882-3242; www.riverviewhotelst marys.com. The location of this bed-and-breakfast (once a historic hotel) couldn't be better—right across the street from the St. Marys River, town pier, boat landing for the Cumberland Island Ferry, and the offices of the National Park Service. Fully restored, the B&B has a restaurant, and the price includes breakfast. $$–$$$

Spencer House Inn, 200 Osborne Street; (912) 882-1872 or (888) 840-1872; www.spencerhouseinn.com. Built in 1872 as a hotel, this gracious Victorian structure retains the charm of yesteryear while offering B&B accommodations with all the modern conveniences. $$$$

Cumberland Island

Camping at Cumberland Island National Seashore. National Park Service, P.O. Box 806, St. Marys 31558; (912) 882-4336/ext. 254. Make reservations way ahead (up to a year in advance) for semideveloped (water and restrooms) and primitive campsites. This experience is for very hardy and dedicated campers—you must pack in absolutely everything you'll need, including a camp stove. You may have as much as a 10-mile walk one-way with your burdens to the campsite. $

Greyfield Inn, mailing address: 4 North Second Street, Fernandina Beach, FL 32035-0900; (904) 261-6408 or (866) 401-8581; www.greyfieldinn.com. If your idea of a good time doesn't include sleeping on the ground, families with offspring older than six can find luxurious accommodations in a former Carnegie residence located within easy walking distance of the beach. Three gourmet meals daily, use of bicycles, and ferry transportation (which is the only way to get here) are included. $$$$

Southwest Georgia

Georgia's "Other Coast," the southwestern corner of the state, lies along the Chattahoochee River and borders both Alabama and the Florida panhandle with several large lakes. In the nineteenth century parts of this region contained vast numbers of plantations and attracted wealthy Northerners who wintered in the mild climate to hunt deer and game birds. Today the state's best-kept secret still contains the largest concentration of working plantations in America and is being

Thalimers'
TopPicks in Southwest Georgia

1. Stopping to smell the roses at Callaway Gardens, Pine Mountain

2. Flying high with the circus at Callaway Summer Family Adventures, Pine Mountain

3. Going on a photographic expedition at the Pine Mountain Wild Animal Safari, Pine Mountain

4. Shooting the rapids on the Flint River, Thomaston

5. Connecting with communications history at the Georgia Rural Telephone Museum, Leslie

6. Time traveling back to 1850s Georgia at Westville Village, Lumpkin

7. Ogling rock formations at Providence Canyon, Lumpkin

8. Taking a walk on the wild side at the Chehaw Wild Animal Park, Albany

9. Exploring the grounds at Pebble Hill Plantation, Thomasville

10. Experiencing turn-of-the-twentieth-century life at the Agrirama: Georgia's Museum of Agriculture and Historic Village, Tifton

SOUTHWEST GEORGIA

rediscovered by tourists. The area is indelibly marked with the footprints of two twentieth-century giants: Franklin D. Roosevelt, who had a vacation retreat in Warm Springs; and Jimmy Carter, who still lives in Plains.

Largely rural southwest Georgia is recognized for peanut production, but you might be surprised to hear that it's the Pecan Capital of the World. The least populated area of the state, this off-the-beaten-track territory is primarily characterized by small towns, but it does boast several vibrant mini-cities such as Albany, Columbus, Tifton, and Thomasville. But don't think this means the area is short on attractions. Rolling hills, emerald forests, diamond-dazzling lakes, fantastic fishing, exciting whitewater rapids, Georgia's Grand Canyon, and lots of wide-open spaces attract those bent on outdoorsy pursuits. A world-class garden and resort, two living-history villages, several covered bridges, ancient Indian mounds, and modern, state-of-the-art attractions draw families searching for laid-back fun. Your tribe's exploration of southwestern Georgia will be well rewarded.

Pine Mountain

West on Highway 116.

Callaway Gardens (all ages) 🍁

Highway 18/354; (800) CALLAWAY or (800) 225-5292; www.callawaygardens.com. The hours the gardens are open vary with the season, but a good rule of thumb is daylight to dusk. Adults $$$, children six through twelve $$; children five and under free.

Georgia's Garden of Eden, this lush garden is not only a celebration for the eye but also a feast for the soul. A place where precious memories can be made, the gardens and resort were voted the "best day trip from Atlanta" by readers of *Atlanta Magazine*. The fabulous 2,500-acre gardens showcase gorgeous floral arrays, deep woodlands, and crystal-clear lakes that serve as a backdrop for both educational and recreational pursuits. Among the eye-popping attractions in the gardens proper are one of the largest collections of azaleas in the country; 450 species of holly; the **John A. Sibley Horticultural Center,** a five-acre indoor/outdoor greenhouse; **Mr. Cason's Vegetable Garden,** the Southern set for the PBS series *The Victory Garden*; the new **Virginia Hand Callaway Discovery Center** at the newly constructed entrance to

Amazing Georgia Facts

The rare orange plumleaf or prunifolia azalea grows only within a 100-mile radius of Callaway Gardens.

the gardens; the 40-acre **Callaway Brothers Azalea Bowl,** the world's largest azalea garden ablaze with the world's greatest collection of azaleas; the **Ida Cason Callaway Memorial Chapel;** and the **Cecil B. Day Butterfly Center,** where more than 1,000 "jewels of the air" from three continents dazzle would-be butterfly catchers. Only you don't catch them with a net but with your camera. Challenge the kidlets to keep their eyes peeled for different species, and tell them that if they stand very still, a brilliant-hued butterfly may light on them; then snap a memorable shot. Sure to be a favorite with all ages, the free-flight Birds of Prey show allows raptors to demonstrate their natural behaviors in a controlled situation. The yearly activity calendar is loaded with special events such as the Summer Family Adventures, Harvest Festival, the Steeplechase at Callaway, and Fantasy in Lights. Although your clan can explore the gardens by car, it's ever so much more fun on foot or by bicycle.

Callaway Summer Family Adventure Program (ages 3 to 16 years)

Resort at Callaway, U.S. Highway 27; (800) CALLAWAY; www.callawaygardens.com. $$$$ per child per day.

Guaranteed to create lifelong memories, this glorified summer camp consists of week-long sessions of all-day, everyday activities for all ages. Central to the program is the Florida State University Flying High Circus. In addition to the pure entertainment provided by the performers, the FSU students also serve as counselors for the special, structured activities for kidlets ages seven through teenage. The child care center has a wide range of activities for tykes three through six. Once the small fry reach seven, they're eligible to join the circus, where they'll learn simple magic tricks and circus acts such as juggling, tightrope walking, tumbling, and swinging on the trapeze (don't worry—all kinds of safety precautions are taken). Undoubtedly working with the circus will be a never-forgotten highlight of this adventure. Munchkins who come back year after year progress in the difficulty of circus tricks they can perform and may actually develop into adept performers. Tell the truth now. Didn't you at some time in your life want to run away with the circus? Well, your little squirts are no different. It may be too late for you, but this is an opportunity to make those dreams come true for them. Best yet, while the small fry frolic at their own pursuits, Mom and Dad can indulge in the resort's many options or relax and do nothing. Together time is worked into the

Amazing
Georgia Facts

The Day Butterfly Center is the nation's largest glass-enclosed free-flight butterfly conservatory.

schedule, though, with stage shows, theme dinners, movies, beach volleyball, camp-fires, scavenger hunts, bike hikes, trail walks, beach bingo, storytelling, nature Olympics, and bird-watching basics. Families are normally accommodated in the cottages or villas, where they have access to a separate swimming pool and laundry facilities. Whew! After all this, you might need a vacation from your vacation.

Fantasy in Lights (all ages)

Resort at Callaway, US 27; (800) CALLAWAY; www.callawaygardens.com. Friday before Thanksgiving to late December. Tickets must be purchased in advance. Adults $$$, children $$$.

Visions of sugarplums dance in the kiddies' heads at Callaway's Christmas extravaganza. The largest Christmas lights show in the Southeast, the 5-mile ride-through sound-and-light tour meanders through dozens of fanciful, lighted scenes. Tiny tots, mesmerized by the eight million white and colored lights, think they really are in a winter wonderland of gigantic toy soldiers, poinsettias, snowflakes, toys, icicles, and more, but don't be fooled into thinking this lights-and-music spectacle is an event just for tykes—it captivates all ages. After the ride through, the kiddies can personally deliver their Christmas wish list to Santa and shop for trinkets inexpensive enough for their tiny pocketbooks. Sounds of caroling, aromas of tangy spices, and flavors of hot cider and hot chocolate complete the festive ambience.

Birds of a Feather

- **What birds participate in the Birds of Prey show at Callaway Gardens?** An eagle, a falcon, hawks, owls, and a buzzard.

- **Won't they fly away?** No, they've either been rehabilitated from injuries or never developed the skills they need to survive in the wild.

- **Are the shows the same?** No, three to five birds appear in each show, so no two shows are ever alike.

- **Where is the show held?** At the lakeside Discovery Amphitheater near the Virginia Hand Callaway Discovery Center, where the birds swoop directly over your head or inside the center in inclement weather.

- **When are the shows?** March through December there are three or four shows a day, at 10:30 a.m. and 12:30 and 2:00 p.m.; on weekends a fourth show is added at 3:30 p.m.; in winter there is one afternoon show, at 2:00 p.m.

Resort at Callaway (all ages) ⬛ 🎭 🎡
US 27; (800) CALLAWAY; www.callawaygardens.com.

Resort at Callaway knows how to take care of kids, so the rug rats will be busy from the moment you get to this fantastic family playground where no one ever runs out of activities. For a spectacular all-round vacation not soon forgotten, the resort abounds with recreational amenities for any generation: thirty-six holes of championship golf, a tennis complex, fishing lakes, hiking trails, a fitness trail, boat and bike rentals, and a 10-mile bike trail. You can take fly-casting lessons from a pro at the fly-fishing center and then cast a line from the banks of the lake or take out a boat. In fact, the resort is a perfect place for even the littlest fisherfolk to learn. Cool dunks in Robin Lake or at the various pools are refreshing on hot, humid summer days, and the large man-made beach is perfect for building sand castles. Kiddies find a tremendous number of facilities geared just for them: pedal boat rentals, miniature golf, and a miniature train that carries little passengers through heavy woods and around the lake. Despite all these diversions, the highlight of the summer season is the residency of the Florida State University Flying High Circus, which gives seven totally different performances each week.

Danger! Calorie alert! Cuisine at Callaway Gardens is legendary. In fact, many of the fruits and vegetables used at the restaurants or in the prepared food items sold at the resort's various outlets come from the complex's own gardens. Overlooking the golf course and lake within the gardens, the **Gardens** restaurant offers a variety of healthful luncheon choices. Among the fabled dining outlets on the resort side are the **Plantation Room** at the inn; the **Country Kitchen** at the Callaway Gardens Country Store; **Champions** at the golf course; and the **Flower Mill,** a sandwich shop and ice-cream parlor at the cottages. Ice cream goes down oh so smoothly on a hot summer day, but be sure to wrap plenty of napkins around the kids' cones to catch the inevitable drips. In addition, concession stands at the beach stave off imminent starvation.

When it's sleepy time, comfortable accommodations are offered in a hotel, spacious two-bedroom cottages, and luxurious two-, three-, or four-bedroom villas as well as in a new Lodge and Spa (see Where to Stay). Perfect for family getaways, each cottage or villa features a fully equipped kitchen, a living/dining area with a fireplace, a deck, and a screened-in porch.

Steeplechase at Callaway (ages 4 to 12)

Resort at Callaway, US 27; (706) 324-6252; www.callawaygardens.com. November. $$$$

Equestrian-minded clans will find this horsey event a real treat, but it's fun and festive for nonequestrians as well. A 2.6-mile turf oval located on a beautiful 200-acre rolling course surrounded by hardwoods and pines sets the scene for the handsome hunt meet. Here's a perfect chance to watch spirited horses maneuver around abrupt curves, up and down steep grades, and over exciting jumps. Occasional spills by both horses and riders add to the thrills and excitement. Even the youngest among race fans can cheer on their favorite. Food is an integral part of the day's activities whether you're feasting on an elegant repast in one of the sumptuous private tents, enjoying an informal tailgate picnic, or indulging in the Taste of the Chase—a sampling of dishes from different restaurants. Pre-race activities, including a decorated buggy parade, junior pony races, and Jack Russell terrier races, bring joy and delight to young ones. If you want to make a weekend of it, the resort offers a weekend package that includes admission to the races, accommodations, and other events.

Franklin D. Roosevelt State Park (all ages)

2970 Highway 190 East; (706) 663-4858; www.gastateparks.org/info/fdr/. Open daily year-round, 7:00 a.m. to 10:00 p.m. Parking $3; camping $.

Hikers and nature lovers seeking a quiet getaway couldn't do better than to spend considerable time investigating all the amenities of this outdoor nirvana. Named for the president who spent so much time in the area, the 9,000-acre park incorporates FDR's favorite scenic driving route and picnic spot, but it's best known for fishing and hiking. The more vigorous in your flock can explore 37 miles of trails, and fishing enthusiasts can keep their poles busy. The park also boasts a swimming pool and trading post. When it comes time to bed down, overnight facilities include cabins, RV sites, and pioneer camping.

Pine Mountain Trail (ages 4 to 16)

Free.

Avid hikers can step out of the frenetic modern world and into the serenity of nature by tramping along all or part of the 23 miles of blazed trail that runs from the Callaway Country Store on US 27 in Pine Mountain to the WJSP–TV tower on Highway 85 West in Warm Springs. Running along a ridge, the trail affords sweeping views of the valley below as you pass through tranquil woods, gurgling streams, tumbling waterfalls, rock outcroppings, and lush foliage. This halcyon natural environment is abundant with indigenous animals. There are very few steep grades to trouble little hikers, so there shouldn't be too much struggling or complaining. Diehards who want to cover significant sections of the trail can find camping facilities available at nine sites. Get a trail map from the FDR State Park office (706-663-4858).

The Wonders of Southwest Georgia

- **Providence Canyon**—Known as Georgia's Little Grand Canyon, it features deep ravines and unusual rock formations.

- **Radium Springs**—The state's largest natural spring, it has a constant year-round temperature of 68 degrees Fahrenheit.

- **Warm Springs**—This mineral spring is reputed to have restorative qualities.

Wild Animal Safari (all ages)

1300 Oak Grove Road; (706) 663-8744 or (800) 367-2751; www.animalsafari.com. Open daily at 10:00 a.m. The park closes at 5:30 p.m. January and February and the day after Labor Day to December 31. It is open until 6:30 p.m. in March and April and until 7:30 p.m. May through Labor Day. Closed Christmas. $$$; children two and younger free.

Buy your wild bunch some one-use cameras and set off on a photographic safari to this 500-acre wildlife preserve, where you can bag 200 or more species of wild animals from every continent. Encourage your sharp-eyed explorers to identify zebras, camels, giraffes, and other exotic beasts that rove almost freely along the 3.5-mile paved road. During some seasons, the park operates a safari bus; at other times you drive though in your own car or rent one from the park. Call for a bus schedule.

Intrepid little adventurers won't have to worry about there not being enough to do—the park also has a serpentarium, an aviary, and a monkey house. An authentic farm with a petting zoo provides dozens of critters to stroke and snuggle. In this petter's paradise, little city slickers can actually milk a cow and bottle-feed a calf.

For More Information

Pine Mountain Tourism Association, 101 East Broad Street, Pine Mountain, GA 31822; (706) 663-4000 or (800) 441-3502; www.pinemountain.org.

Can You **Believe It?**

Despite his immense family wealth, the only house Franklin D. Roosevelt ever actually purchased was the Little White House in Warm Springs.

Warm Springs

West to Highway 85 West and US 27 Alternate.

Franklin D. Roosevelt began coming to the rehabilitation facility in Warm Springs in 1924 to obtain treatments from the healing waters to relieve the pain of his polio. In 1932, the same year he became president, Roosevelt built himself a small house nearby. Whenever FDR was in residence, the town became a beehive of activity, filled with the press, Secret Service agents, Hollywood stars, and visiting dignitaries—both American and foreign. When the president died at the Little White House in 1945, the town folded up and slept like Rip van Winkle—almost completely forgotten—for more than forty years. Today, however, Warm Springs is revitalized as a tourist town that sports sixty-five quaint shops and restaurants. The charming village makes an excellent base from which to explore the area.

Little White House Historic Site (ages 6 to 12)

401 Little White Road at the intersection of Highway 85 Alternate and US 27 Alternate; (706) 655-5870; www.fdr-littlewhitehouse.org. Open daily 9:00 a.m. to 4:45 p.m. Closed Thanksgiving, Christmas, and New Year's Days. Adults and children ages six to eighteen $.

Your personal politics and voting preferences aside, take your party to visit the former president's getaway home. (First, you may have to educate the kids a little about who FDR was.) Then tour his simple, white frame, three-bedroom cottage, which remains as it did the day he died on April 12, 1945. To keep the rug rats from whining with boredom, make sure to point out the leash still hanging on a peg by the back door. It belonged to Roosevelt's famous little Scotty, Fala. Then turn the kiddies loose to run up the flag-lined stone path lined with stones representative of a rock indigenous to each state. Challenge the junior set to find the flag and stone from Georgia or that of any other state in which you've lived. At the museum there's a film, and your offspring can examine the memorabilia from Roosevelt's life and presidency. You'll see the famous unfinished portrait for which the president was sitting when he became ill as well as FDR's 1938 Ford convertible with hand controls.

For More Information

Warm Springs Area Tourism Association, 30 Broad Street, Warm Springs, GA 31830; (706) 655-3322; www.warm springsga.com.

Official Georgia

- **Bird:** brown thrasher
- **Butterfly:** tiger swallowtail
- **Crop:** peanuts
- **Game bird:** bobwhite quail
- **Insect:** honeybee
- **Wildflower:** azalea

Thomaston

East on Highway 74.

Flint River Outdoor Center (ages 6 to 12)

Highway 36; (706) 647-2633; www.flintriverwatchers.com. Memorial Day to Labor Day, open Monday to Wednesday 9:00 a.m. to 9:00 p.m.; Thursday to Saturday 9:00 a.m. to 10:00 p.m.; Sunday 9:00 a.m. to 6:00 p.m.; the rest of the year by appointment. Reservations required for guided trips. Four-person raft rentals $$$$, when the river level permits.

Want to get the adrenaline flowing? Wet and wild thrills, chills, heart-pounding excitement, and high adventure await on the Flint River's Class I, II, and III rapids. Organized and unguided trips are available for excursions of one half to four days. Other services provided by the center include canoe and raft rentals, camping, and concessions. And don't worry about being caught downstream without a paddle. A shuttle service returns wet, happy daredevils to the center. On more placid sections of the river, lazybones can simply drift along on inner tubes or rafts.

For More Information

Thomaston-Upson County Chamber of Commerce, 213 East Gordon Street, Thomaston, GA 30286; (706) 647-9686; www.thomastonchamber.com.

The Rock

North on Highway 36.

Corn Maze (ages 2 to 12)
The Rock Ranch, 5020 Barnesville Highway; (706) 647-6374; www.therockranch.com/ Maze.htm. September and October; call for hours. $$; younger than five free.

If anyone's ever told you to get lost, you can go ahead and do it and still have fun at this amazing sixteen-acre corn maze. In 2003 the pattern honored the centennial anniversary of Crayola crayons. There's a new spectacular design each year. No matter what the pattern, the maze takes guests on a one- to two-hour journey through twists and turns, with correct answers to questions helping participants find their way. If your navigational skills aren't the greatest and you get corn-fused, don't worry. Employees stationed in observation towers can provide a helping hand. Friday and Saturday nights offer a special challenge, doing the maze in the dark (BYOF—bring your own flashlight). October 31 and November 1 are Spooktacular. If family members aren't exhausted from threading their way through the maze, there are many other activities including duck racing, horseshoes, various ball games, corn cannons, hayrides, and a hay jump. Even the littlest ones can get into the act with small hay, rope, and tricycle mazes as well as the Kid's Korner Play Area. When The Rock Ranch isn't operating its maze, there are lots of other things to do, such as Conestoga Campouts, or you can spend the night at The Rock Ranch Guest House.

Columbus

Southwest on Highway 36.

Although Columbus is known as the birthplace of Coca-Cola and several other soft drinks, the city is also a sports mecca. Golden Park was the center of world attention during the 1996 Olympic Women's Fast Pitch Softball competitions. Today Columbus is the home of the Cottonmouths, a professional ice hockey team; Georgia Pride, a women's professional fast-pitch softball team; and Columbus Catfish, a minor-league farm team of the Los Angeles Dodgers. Check to see if any games are being played while you're in town.

Trivial **Pursuit**

The National Civil War Naval Museum at Port Columbus is the only one in the country.

Coca-Cola Space Science Center (ages 4 to 12) 🌐

701 Front Avenue; (706) 649-1470; www.ccssc.org. Open Tuesday through Thursday 10:00 a.m. to 4:00 p.m., Friday 10:00 a.m. to 8:00 p.m., Saturday 10:30 a.m. to 8:00 p.m. Entrance free; shows $$.

A visit to this spaced-out center, one of thirty-one Challenger centers in the nation, will take your little space voyagers to the moon and stars. Small astronauts can experience a simulated space flight and bring the universe to their doorstep in the observatory. Star-struck youngsters gawk at the spectacular laser programs in the planetarium. Catch a falling star and put it in your pocket? Stop in at the Star Gazers Gift Shop for a souvenir. Primarily for classes and groups.

Columbus Museum (ages 4 to 12) 🌐

1251 Wynnton Road; (706) 748-2562; www.columbusmuseum.com. Open Tuesday through Saturday 10:00 a.m. to 5:00 p.m., Thursday open until 9:00 p.m., Sunday 1:00 to 5:00 p.m. Free.

Whet the chilluns' appetite for art by visiting the second largest museum in Georgia, where the outstanding art collection is sure to please any adult or budding Monet or Picasso. The kidlets, however, may be more interested in the Chattahoochee Legacy, a regional history gallery that uses a film of the same name as well as life-size period settings to spin tales of the Chattahoochee River Valley region. Intriguing hands-on activities in the children's gallery are designed to arouse curiosity and excite imaginations.

Hollywood Connections (ages 4 to 12) 🎳 🍿

1683 Whittlesey Road; (706) 571-3456. Open Sunday through Thursday 11:30 a.m. to 9:00 p.m., Friday and Saturday 11:30 a.m. to midnight. $

When tiny tots start whining about seeing one more museum, switch gears. Kick back and enjoy the ultimate in family entertainment: a ten-plex theater with stadium seating in some of its auditoriums, Xanadu Skate Center, Fun Zone amusements and rides, Mind Games Arcade, Ultrazone Laser Tag arena, Caddyshack miniature golf, and Lieutenants Restaurant—a good place to stave off hunger pangs.

Famous Products
Developed in Columbus

- Coca-Cola

- Royal Crown Cola

- Nehi

What Is a **Scramble Dog?**

Years ago the cooks at the lunch counter at the Dinglewood Pharmacy in Columbus created a new taste sensation called the Scramble Dog—and it's been served in Columbus and the nearby area ever since. The special hot dog on a bun is heaped with onions, cheese, chili sauce—and oyster crackers, if you can believe it!

National Civil War Naval Museum at Port Columbus (ages 6 to 12)

1002 Victory Drive; (706) 327-9798; www.portcolumbus.org. Open daily 9:00 a.m. to 5:00 p.m. Closed Christmas Day. $; donations accepted.

Put the kidlets' imaginations to the test at this unusual museum. There's little left of the hulls of the Confederate ironclad *Jackson* and the gunboat *Chattahoochee*, but sketches will let curious kidsters see what the boats looked like more than 125 years ago. The CSS *Jackson* is the largest surviving scratch-made ironclad ship in the world. A steel ghost skeleton has been constructed over the hull to give an idea of its size. The hull can be viewed from above and below. Other relics from the Confederate navy are exhibited at the one-of-a-kind museum including a partial replica of the USS *Hartford*, Union Admiral David Farragut's flagship; a full-size sectional reconstruction of the USS *Monitor*; as well as the country's only full-size ironclad Civil War combat simulator. Both Union and Confederate uniforms are displayed as well as rare Civil War flags. Get your little sailors into the mood by watching the video about the Union attack.

National Infantry Museum (ages 4 to 12)

Building #396 Baltzell Avenue; (706) 545-2958; www.benningmwr.com/museum.cfm. Open Monday through Friday 10:00 a.m. to 4:30 p.m., weekends 12:30 to 4:30 p.m.; closed Thanksgiving, Christmas, and New Year's Days. Free.

Things military, especially big things like tanks, always fascinate the small fry. Engross your progeny in tracing the evolution of the U.S. infantry from the French and Indian War to the present at Fort Benning's special museum. Junior jaunters and even the oldsters are mind-boggled by the largest and most complete collection of military and small arms in the United States, as well as military documents signed by each of America's presidents, silver presentation pieces, military band instruments, and a tribute to Gen. Omar Bradley. Even the most pseudo-sophisticated preteen will be fascinated by the artifacts from each of America's military involvements from colonial America to the military actions in Somalia and particularly by the captured enemy paraphernalia.

Did **You Know?**

Fort Benning is the largest infantry training center in the world. The facility's National Infantry Museum has an example of every gun ever used by the U.S. Army. Who knows when those pieces of trivia might come in handy?

Riverfront/Riverwalk (all ages) 👫

Columbus has a secret that you might miss if you're not careful: the striking path and park along the bluffs and banks of the Chattahoochee River, stretching 12 miles from downtown to the National Infantry Museum. A perfect place to walk, jog, in-line skate, or simply gaze at the cataract that marks the end of navigability on the Chattahoochee, the brick-paved promenade is embellished with ironwork, historical markers, and sculptures. While the kiddies race up and down the path, Mom and Dad can find a bench on which to share some quiet time or a cuddle while they people-watch and survey the river.

Springer Opera House Children's Theater Series (ages vary) 🎵

Springer Opera House, 103 Tenth Street; (706) 324-5714; www.springeroperahouse .org. Children's plays are offered three times a year; adult performance season September through May. Prices and times vary.

If there are any budding thespians or theater lovers in your cast, check ahead when you're in Columbus to see if there are any performances of the Children's Theater Series. Plays such as *Winnie the Pooh, The Little Baby Snoogle-Fleejer,* and *Sarah Plain and Tall* are sure to entertain. Children's performances are primarily matinees, but there are some evening performances if you want to save the daylight hours for sightseeing and outdoor adventures. Many of the regular season's Broadway musicals, comedies, and dramas are suitable for family audiences as well. The lavishly restored opulent 131-year-old theater is the State Theater of Georgia. Many of today's youngsters, who are used to sterile shoebox cineplexes, have never seen anything like this. If you can't be there for a show, tours of the theater are available by appointment. Call (706) 324-5714.

For More Information

Columbus Convention and Visitors Bureau, 900 Front Avenue, Columbus, GA 31901; (800) 999-1613; www.visitcolumbus ga.com.

Buena Vista

Southeast on Highway 26.

St. EOM's Pasaquan (ages 4 to 12) 🏛

Eddie Martin Road off County Road 78 off Highway 137; call P. J. Rogers (229) 649-9444, or e-mail him at pjrogers@sowega.net; www.pasaquan.com. Open only for guided tours by appointment. Admission $, children younger than twelve free.

If you gave your young artists paintbrushes and unlimited paint in brilliant primary colors and then told them they could paint your walls, floors, cabinets, furniture and everything else in sight, this riotous work of art is what they might create. The back-seat gang won't know where to look first as they feast their eyes on bizarre and brilliantly painted walls, pagodas, totems, and other outdoor sculptures at the four-acre complex created by the late folk artist Eddie Owens Martin, who dubbed himself St. EOM. The small fry will get a giggle out of the smiling humans and happy-looking snakes that figure so prominently. This is a perfect place for shutterbugs in training.

For More Information

Buena Vista–Marion County Chamber of Commerce, 113 Broad Street, Buena Vista, GA 31803; (800) 647-2842 or (229) 649-2842.

Andersonville

Southeast on GA 26 to Highway 228.

Andersonville National Historic Site (ages 6 to 12) 🏛 ♿

496 Cemetery Road; (229) 924-0343; www.nps.gov/ande. Open daily year-round, 8:00 a.m. to 5:00 p.m.; 8:00 a.m. to 7:00 p.m. on Memorial Day. Free.

Take a trip back in time to see a haunting place where the past is always present. Touring a historic prison camp—when you know for sure you can get out whenever you want to—gives ghoulish kids a spine-tingling thrill. At this infamous Civil War prison camp, pampered young people can see how horrific life was for captured Union soldiers. Almost 13,000 Northern soldiers died and were buried here—the highest percentage of deaths at any prison camp, North or South. During living-history presentations, reenactors relate the gory details about the inhuman conditions under which the prisoners lived and demonstrate some of the cruel tactics used to keep them subdued. Sometimes willing youngsters are pressed into service as "prisoners." Eventually they'll be released with a big sigh of relief. At the visitor center view a film about the ordeal of being a prisoner and exhibits about Andersonville and other Civil

War prisons. In addition, this is the only park in the national system to serve as a memorial to all American prisoners of war throughout this country's history. The **National Prisoner of War Museum** traces American wars from the Revolution to Vietnam. A particularly touching time to visit the site is on Memorial Day, when the National Cemetery is awash in a sea of fluttering American flags placed on each grave. The latest addition to the museum is a re-creation of a room from the Hanoi Hilton (the infamous Vietnam War Prison). A brochure and audiotape are available for a self-guided tour of the site.

For More Information

Andersonville Welcome Center, 114 Church Street, Andersonville, GA 31711; (229) 924-2558.

Americus

South on Highway 48.

Global Village and Discovery Center (ages 6 to 12)

Habitat for Humanity, 721 West Church Street; (800) 422-4828 or (229) 924-6935/ext. 2811; www.habitat.org/gvdc/. Open Monday through Saturday 9:00 a.m. to 2:00 p.m., Sunday closed. Closed Thanksgiving, Christmas, and New Year's Days. $

A visit to Habitat for Humanity's Global Village is guaranteed to be an eye-opener for your progeny. After a brief stop at the visitor welcome center to learn about the history of Habitat for Humanity, you'll start on a journey through the Living in Poverty Area, where you'll experience the living conditions of disadvantaged people who live in cardboard boxes or shanties. Then you'll enter the Village Area, with examples of Habitat houses from fifteen countries. These homes show how simple local materials can provide adequate housing for poor people and substantially raise their standard of living. Hosts and guides describe the lives and customs of families who would live in these houses. In the Experience Area, families can learn how to make bricks and tiles. The Marketplace contains a photo gallery, exhibits, a theater, a store, and an exploration center.

Plains

West on US 280.

Jimmy Carter National Historic Site (ages 6 to 12) 🏛️ 🚂

300 North Bond Street; (229) 824-4104; www.nps.gov/jica/. Visitor center open daily 9:00 a.m. to 5:00 p.m. except Thanksgiving, Christmas, and New Year's Days. Boyhood farm open 10:00 a.m. to 4:00 p.m. Free.

Today's youngsters may not really understand who Jimmy Carter is, but they're bound to be impressed by visiting the boyhood home and other sites significant to a living U.S. president. They can't help but contrast the opulent lifestyle of the White House to the former president's humble beginnings at the farm in Archery. Visitors should first stop at **Plains High School,** which serves as the visitor center. There they can watch a video and wander through the exhibit rooms. The old **Plains Depot,** on Main Street at M. L. Hudson Street, served as Carter's 1976 campaign headquarters and is open for tours.

The highlight of the historic site is the **Carter Boyhood Home** at Archery, 5 miles away. You can get there by car or aboard the SAM Shortline Railroad. In fact, you could walk there—Carter often did as a boy (and remember that's 10 miles round-trip). The farm is restored to its 1930s appearance. In various rooms of the house, you can press a button and listen to President Carter's voice reminiscing about his life there. At the national historic site, children ages seven to twelve may participate in the Junior Ranger Program, earning a special badge and certificate.

Leslie

South on Highway 195.

Georgia Rural Telephone Museum (ages 4 to 12) 🚂

135 Bailey Avenue; (229) 874-4786; www.sowega.net/~museum/. Open Monday through Friday 9:00 a.m. to 3:30 p.m. Free.

It seems that everyone has a cell phone stuck to his or her ear these days—even the kids, but the first telephones didn't resemble today's instruments in the slightest. Young communicators can trace the entire evolution of the telephone at this outstanding museum located in the tiny town of Leslie. Tommy C. Smith amassed this astounding collection as his personal hobby. Today it is one of the largest collections of antique telephones and telephone memorabilia in the world. Beginning in 1876, the museum takes a trip through the history of telecommunications. Not just limited to telephone equipment, the museum also has a re-creation of a Creek Indian village, murals by Georgia artists, a variety of antique clocks and furnishings, and vehicles dating from the early 1800s. Particularly enchanting to children is Bubba the Bear, who speaks to children via telephone. During our visit we were especially amused at children's fascination with trying out that strangest of all instruments—the dial telephone.

Cordele

East on Highway 30.

Georgia Veterans Memorial State Park and Golf Course (all ages)
Ⓐ Ⓖ Ⓢ

2459 U.S. Highway 280; park (229) 276-2371, golf course (229) 276-2377; www.gastate parks.org/info/georgiavet. Both open daily year-round; the park: 7:00 a.m. to 10:00 p.m., the museum: 8:15 a.m. to 4:15 p.m., golf course: first tee time 8:00 a.m., play until dark. Parking $3; camping $; hotel $$$$; golf $$$$.

When the backseat bunch is feeling really boisterous from being cooped up in the car too long, pack your favorite picnic and swing on over to this popular park for a day's play. A museum memorializing Georgia's veterans is only one of the attractions; youngsters and oldsters will find plenty of outdoorsy things to do. In addition to an eighteen-hole golf course, there's a swimming pool, beach, boat ramp and dock, waterskiing, and picnicking. After a day of whooping it up, everyone should sleep like lambs in the new ultramodern Retreat at Lake Blackshear—a lodge and villas—or one of the cottages; or camp at one of the tent, trailer, or pioneer sites.

Southwest Georgia Excursion Train—SAM Shoreline (ages 2 to 12)
Ⓜ

P.O. Box 845, Cordele 31010; (229) 276-2715, (800) 864-7275, or (877) 427-2457; www .samshortline.com. Generally operates Thursday, Saturday, and Monday; call or check the Web site for prices of coach and first-class tickets and exact departure times from each town.

Riding the rails aboard 1949-vintage railcars is a great way to see this section of Georgia. The Southwest Georgia Excursion Train (better known as the **SAM Shortline** because the route was once part of the Savannah, Americus, and Montgomery line) operates between Cordele and Archery, with stops at Georgia Veterans State Park, Leslie, Americus, and Plains. With excursion names such as the Peanut Express, the Americus Adventurer, and the Archery Express, the trains make different stops, so be sure to check the route. You can get off at any of the stops to see the sights or have a meal and get back on a return train or spend the night at a historic hotel or bed-and-breakfast and return another day.

For More Information

Cordele-Crisp County Tourism Committee, 302 East Sixteenth Avenue, Cordele, GA 31015; (229) 273-1668; www.cordele-crisp-chamber.com.

Lumpkin

Northwest to Highway 27 at US 27.

Bedingfield Inn (ages 6 to 12)

Courthouse Square; (229) 838-6419; www.bedingfieldinn.org/home. Open Wednesday through Saturday 1:00 to 4:00 p.m. Closed Sunday and Monday. $

Transport your spoiled modern-day travelers back to stagecoach days and see what wayfarers faced at overnight stops by visiting this circa 1836 inn, now a museum. Depending on the price they paid, overnight guests could get a private room, but more than likely they'd share a bed with several other strangers in the common room or sleep on the floor. Can you imagine? Don't leave without picking up a brochure for the **Stagecoach Trail,** a driving tour past twenty-three pre-1850 homes. This little spin will take only a few minutes by car, so the rug rats shouldn't get too cranky about this history lesson. While you are there see if they can give you a tour of Dr. Hatchet's Drug Store across the street.

Westville Village (ages 4 to 12)

Martin Luther King Boulevard; (229) 838-6310 or (888) 733-1850; www.westville.org. Open Tuesday through Saturday 10:00 a.m. to 5:00 p.m. Closed Thanksgiving, Christmas Eve and Christmas Day, and New Year's Day. Adults $$, kindergarten through eleventh grade $.

Instead of visiting another place, why not visit another era. At Westville, where you'll experience living history at its best, the junior set will think they've really taken a time machine back to an 1850s Georgia town. The funny thing is, Westville never existed. Entirely assembled of mid-1800s buildings that have been relocated to this spot from all over Georgia, a mid-nineteenth-century hamlet has been created. A variety of homes range from log cabins to elegant town houses. Then there are all the things that made a successful village: churches, a school, stores, a cobbler shop, a cotton gin, and numerous farm buildings. Westville is not, however, a ghost town. Farm animals ramble in some of the farmyards, and you'll meet costumed Westville "residents" as they go about their daily duties—cooking, gardening, basket weaving, and making pottery, rakes, and shoes. If you're lucky, you'll get there just as someone takes some fresh gingerbread out of the oven and offers you a slice. Just follow your nose. Encourage your wannabe paparazzi to get lots of shots of all these reenactors for some show-and-tell or for a school paper or project when they get home. Among the special events held at Westville each year, the two most significant are the autumn Fair of 1850 and the Christmas festivities. During the fall fair demonstrators show fascinated kiddies how to grind sugar cane and make syrup as well as how the cotton gin operates.

Providence Canyon State Conservation Park (ages 4 to 12) 🏞️🚗

Highway 39-C; (229) 838–6202; www.gastateparks.org/info/providence/. Open September 15 through April 14, 7:00 a.m. to 6:00 p.m. and April 15 through September 14, 7:00 a.m. to 9:00 p.m.; museum open daily 8:00 a.m. to 5:00 p.m. Parking $3; free on Wednesday. Backpacking $ per person per night.

Travel down old country roads to one of Georgia's Seven Natural Wonders and take a gander at the results of an ecological phenomenon. The youngsters can hardly believe that little more than one hundred years of erosion from bad farming practices have created the spectacular 150-foot-deep gorge known as Georgia's Little Grand Canyon. Even more stunning than the depth and the kaleidoscopic, varicolored canyon walls are the phantasmagorical formations resembling aboveground stalagmites that punctuate the chasm.

Without expending much physical effort, you can get several striking views of the formations and canyon walls from rim overlooks. There's little you can do at first but stand in awe. Then get your best would-be photojournalist to whip out the panoramic camera for some wide-angle views, because the walls present an ever-changing painting as different qualities of light strike them. The more energetic among you can hike down into the canyon by way of several hiking trails—one 3 miles long, the other 7 miles. Providence Canyon is also noted for having the largest concentration of wildflowers in the state and a large collection of orange plumleaf or prunifolia azaleas, which grow only within a 100-mile area. In addition, the park offers an interpretive center with a video about how the canyon was formed. Overnight backpacking is allowed on the 7-mile trail.

Omaha

Northeast on Highway 39.

Florence Marina State Park (all ages) ⛺🎣🏊

Highway 39-C; park (229) 838-6870, museum (229) 838-4706; www.gastateparks.org/info/flormarin/. Open daily year-round, 7:00 a.m. to 10:00 p.m., museum 8:00 a.m. to 5:00 p.m. Parking $3; boat rental $ per hour; swimming pool $; camping $; cottages $$–$$$.

Water figures prominently in outdoor activities at Lake Walter F. George, where you can create a memorable voyage of discovery for your crew. This park has everything you need and a little more: in addition to boating facilities for those who BYOB (boat, that is), rental fishing boats, and a swimming pool, it boasts tennis courts and the **Kirbo Interpretive Center,** which houses nature exhibits and artifacts from the former pioneer town of Florence, as well as relics from local Native American history that stretches back to the Paleo-Indian period. After all this activity, when the sun goes down and it's sleepy time down South, your choice of accommodations runs from campsites to cottages.

Fort Gaines

South on Highway 39.

George T. Bagby State Park and Lodge (all ages) ⊗ ⊖ ⊜

230 Bagby Parkway; (229) 768-2571; golf course (229) 768-3714; www.gastateparks .org/info/georgetb/. Open daily year-round 7:00 a.m. to 10:00 p.m. Parking $3; golf $$$$ with cart; johnboats $$$ per person for four hours, canoes $ per person per hour; hotel $$–$$$$; cottages $$$.

Outdoor enthusiasts should head straight for this excellent park on Lake Walter F. George. There won't be a spare moment unless you make a point of scheduling some downtime. Kids and parents get into the action by fishing, playing tennis, swimming at the beach or pool, hiking, or playing golf on an eighteen-hole course. The park provides boat facilities and canoe and fishing boat rentals. Even the smallest tykes can learn to skip stones or play in the water until they turn into prunes. When the sandman comes, you can curl up in a cottage or the sixty-room lodge. There's no need to go hungry either—the lodge's restaurant serves up simple, good eats along with a lakeside view.

Frontier Village (all ages) 🏛

www.fortgaines.com. Open daylight hours daily. Free. For more information, call the City of Fort Gaines (229) 768-2443.

Chart a trail to this re-created village located on a scenic bluff overlooking the Chattahoochee River. Established in 1814 to protect settlers from Indian attacks, the original also served as a Confederate fort in 1863, when the Confederacy tried to keep the Union from getting up the Chattahoochee River to the vital town of Columbus. The one-third-actual-size replica of the fort is just the right size for young pioneers. A hand-carved 18-foot-tall oak totem of an Indian brave's head is the only memorial to the Creek Indians ever erected in the old Creek Nation. The **Outpost Replica** is a reconstruction of an 1816–1830 fort used to protect settlers from attacks by Creek and Seminole Indians.

"If the Good Lord's Willin' and the Creek Don't Rise."

How many times have you used this old phrase to mean "if all goes well"? Did you think it had something to do with flooding? Actually it has nothing to do with high water at all; rather it refers to the possibility of uprisings by Creek Indians who inhabited southwest Georgia.

For More Information

Clay County Library and Visitors Bureau, P.O. Box 275, Fort Gaines, GA 39851; (229) 768-2248; www.fortgaines .com.

Blakely

South on Highway 39.

Kolomoki Mounds State Park (all ages) ⊜ ⊜ ⊜

205 Indian Mounds Road off US 27; (229) 724-2150; www.gastateparks.org/info/ kolomoki. Open daily year-round: park 7:00 a.m. to 10:00 p.m.; interpretive center daily 8:00 a.m. to 5:00 p.m. Parking $3; museum $ adults and children ages six to eighteen; swimming $; boat rentals $; miniature golf $; camping $.

Here's a rare experience for your tribe: access into a partially excavated Native American mound with actual artifacts and replicas of skeletons in place where the originals were found. The focal point of the park is a collection of seven large mounds from the Mississippian culture that flourished here more than 1,000 years ago. Among the mounds is the oldest temple mound in Georgia and one of the largest east of the Mississippi. A visit to the interpretive center allows amateur archaeologists to examine artifacts unearthed from the site. But that's not all. If you have some more time built in to your agenda, the park offers numerous recreational facilities and camping.

Albany

East on Highway 62 at U.S. Highway 19.

Chehaw Wild Animal Park (all ages)

105 Chehaw Park Road; (229) 430-5275; www.parksatchehaw.org. Open daily 9:00 a.m. to 5:00 p.m.; weekends Memorial Day to Labor Day, the park remains open until 7:00 p.m. on Friday, Saturday, and Sunday evenings. Admission $ (admission to the park and zoo are separate; you can buy individual tickets or purchase a combo pass); parking $3; camping $.

Take a walk on the wild side at this zoo located within the grounds of the **Parks at Chehaw.** Throughout the tree-shaded one-hundred-acre wildlife preserve, trails and elevated walkways allow explorers to see native Georgian wildlife as well as elk, ostrich, llama, deer, zebra, elephant, buffalo, and other exotic visitors to Georgia in natural settings. In addition, the petting zoo, Ben's Barnyard and Children's Farm, provides budding animal trainers with an opportunity to get up close and personal with some of the gentler critters. The park's naturalists present numerous wildlife programs in

Georgia Trivia

The Chehaw Wild Animal Park was designed by Georgia native Jim Fowler of *Wild Kingdom* fame.

the amphitheater Saturday at 2:00 and 3:00 p.m. and Sunday at 2:30 and 3:30 p.m. Spring through fall Wednesday and Sunday at 3:00 p.m., your herd will watch wide-eyed as gigantic alligators are fed at the Muckalee Swampland Station. The newest attraction is Eyes in the Sky Free-Ranging Lemurs. Other attractions include a twenty-minute ride on the Wiregrass Express, the park's miniature train (additional cost).

Chehaw Park itself is a 700-acre recreational park that knows how to entertain its guests for hours on end. Jogging, bicycle, and nature trails, as well as play areas and campgrounds, will engage your wild bunch. As if all this excitement isn't enough, the park has an official bicycle motorcross (BMX) track (229-894-5822). Anyone can watch the thrills and spills. Practice times vary, so call ahead. Local races are run every week on Tuesday and Saturday, with the exception of weekends of state and national races. You must be a member of the National Bicycle League to ride.

Always inviting, always exciting, the park is the home of the **Chehaw National Indian Festival,** held the third Saturday in May. A major cultural event in the Southeast, this colorful festival features traditional Native American dancers, skills demonstrations, crafts, and storytelling.

Flint RiverQuarium and Imagination Theater (all ages)

101 Pine Avenue; (229) 639-2650; www.flintriverquarium.com. Open Monday through Friday 9:00 a.m. to 5:00 p.m., Saturday 10:00 a.m. to 6:00 p.m., Sunday 1:00 to 5:00 p.m. RiverQuarium $$, theater $$, combo $$$.

Dive into fun at this small aquarium which tells the story of the Apalachicola, Chattahoochee, and Flint River basins. Special attention is given to the mysterious blue-hole springs that help create the Flint and southwest Georgia's unique underwater inhabitants. An open-air 175,000-gallon freshwater tank is filled with fish, turtles, and alligators native to the area. Other exhibits showcase reptiles, amphibians, regional plants, and rivers of the world. The adjacent Adventure Center houses a three-story-tall IMAX theater where adventure and 3-D films are shown.

RiverFront Park and Turtle Grove Play Area (all ages)

Front Street, (contact Albany Tomorrow, 229-430-3910). Open daily all hours. Free.

Giant fiberglass turtles painted by local artists in all manner of designs and scenes create a natural magnet for the small fry as well as irresistible photo ops for Mom and Dad. The park, which is adjacent to the Flint RiverQuarium and along the banks of the Flint

River, features six interest areas including a Dino Dig, Tot Lot, Critters Area, Big Kids Area, mosaic area, and music area. Numerous porch-type swings provide places to relax or read a book. The park is also popular for picnicking and is a prime spot from which to watch the Fourth of July fireworks.

Thronateeska Heritage Museum of History and Science (all ages)

Heritage Plaza, 100 Roosevelt Avenue; (229) 432-6955; www.heritagecenter.org; info@ heritagecenter.org. Museum open Thursday through Saturday noon to 4:00 p.m.; the science center gives programs at 2:45 p.m. during the school year; planetarium shows on Friday at 2:45 p.m., Saturday at 12:30, 1:30, and 2:30 p.m. $.

On a gloomy day, perk up dejected spirits with a visit to this complex, which has something educational and entertaining for everyone in your flock. Located in and around a historic railroad depot, the museum offers a chance to get acquainted with Albany's history. Interactive exhibits help eager young historians discover riverboat days and learn about the great floods of 1925 and 1994, but the biggest hits with the little squirts are bound to be the giant mounted grizzly bear and the collection of Native American artifacts. Outside you can survey an old train as well as a model train exhibit housed in a baggage car. Located in an old Railway Express building adjacent to the depot, the complex also includes the **Science Discovery Center,** where children can participate in such hands-on activities as forecasting the weather or capturing lightning, and the **Wetherbee Planetarium,** the only planetarium in southwest Georgia. The discovery center is primarily for classes and groups.

For More Information

Albany Convention and Visitors Bureau, 225 West Broad Avenue, Albany, GA 31701; (229) 434-8700 or (800) 475-8700; www.albanyga.com.

When in Georgia, **Pronounce It Right!**

If you stop to ask directions and get some blank stares, you're probably not pronouncing something the way locals do. Albany, for example, is pronounced *All-BEN-nie;* Houston is pronounced *HOUSE-ton;* La Fayette is pronounced *La FAY-ette,* and Vienna is pronounced *VI-enna.*

Ashburn

From Albany, travel east on U.S. Highway 82 and Highway 112.

The small town is perfect for day trips, mystery tours, or just a stop along the way. It's the home of the Crime and Punishment Museum, the Last Meal Cafe, the World's Largest Peanut, and the famous Fire Ant Festival.

Crime and Punishment Museum/Last Meal Cafe (ages 3 to 12)

214 East College Avenue; (229) 567-9696 or (800) 471-9696; www.jailmuseum.com. Museum open Tuesday through Saturday 10:00 a.m. to 5:00 p.m.; cafe open the same days 11:00 a.m. to 1:00 p.m. $$

Your little ghouls will relish the tales about infamous criminals, murders, hangings, ghosts, and a couple love stories at this museum, which occupies the historic 1906 Turner County Jail. The National Register of Historic Places structure once served as the living quarters of the jailer downstairs and a jail upstairs and was known at the time as Castle Turner because the Romanesque architecture was so impressive and the jailer kept the landscaping so well done. In fact, a visitor to town thought the building was a hotel. Boy was he shocked when he found out it was a jail. Visitors can see the old cells, the "death" cell, hanging hook, and the trapdoor where two men were hung for murder and among the artifacts is a replica of Old Sparky—an electric chair. See Where to Eat in Southwest Georgia for a description of the Last Meal Cafe.

World's Largest Peanut (all ages)

The Ashburn monument is the largest of its kind in the United States. It reminds residents and visitors about the heritage of rural South Georgia and its number one crop—peanuts.

Fitzgerald

East on Highway 107.

Fitzgerald was founded by Civil War soldiers who had fought on both sides of the conflict as a means of effecting reconciliation and the town continues to be known as "Where North and South Reunited." The streets are named for northern and southern generals, trees, and flowers. The sidewalks of the historic district are paved with gray and blue bricks. Today Fitzgerald is also known for gaudy wild Burmese chickens, which may be seen wandering just about anywhere.

Blue and Gray Museum (ages 6 to 12) 🎭💡

116 North Johnston Street; (229) 426-5069 or (229) 426-5033 or (800) 386-4642; www.fitzgeraldga.com. Open Tuesday through Saturday 10:00 a.m. to 4:00 p.m. $

Begin by educating the kidlets about the Civil War and the tremendous reconciliation that was necessary to form Fitzgerald by watching the film *Marching as One*. Then let the youngsters peruse the artifacts which include a key from the infamous Andersonville Prison, a Civil War war drum and a Southern Cross of Honor, as well as uniforms, weapons, and medals from all America's wars.

Fitzgerald Fire Museum (ages 3 to 12) 🎭💡

315 East Pine Street; (229) 426-5030. Open daily 10:00 a.m. to 4:00 p.m. $

Wannabe firemen and ladies will be fascinated by this collection of antique equipment including horse-drawn engines and the first gas-powered engine the department acquired in 1915. Perhaps even more fun, the rug rats can slide down a shiny brass fireman's pole and admire the most up-to-date, state-of-the-art equipment next door at the active fire station.

Tifton

South on U.S. Highway 319.

Agrirama: Georgia's Museum of Agriculture and Historic Village (ages 4 to 12) 🏛💡

Interstate 75 and Eighth Street; (229) 386-3344 or (800) 767-1875; www.agrirama.com. Open Tuesday through Saturday 9:00 a.m. to 5:00 p.m. Closed New Year's Day, Thanksgiving Day, and the three days prior to and including Christmas Day. Adults $$, children ages four to eighteen $; family day-pass for parents and children younger than eighteen $$$$.

Leave the modern world far behind and get a feel for life in turn-of-the-twentieth-century Georgia. Depicting the period from 1870 to 1890, the rural village has been created by relocating thirty-five restored nineteenth-century buildings from around Georgia, including several farmsteads; townhomes; a church; a school; commercial buildings such as a newspaper office, a feed and seed store, and an apothecary shop; a railroad depot; and an industrial complex that includes a cooper's shop, blacksmith's shop, and a turpentine still. Costumed guides set newspaper type and carry out other chores from the late 1800s. At the working sawmill fascinated kids can watch tree trunks being sliced, diced, and chewed up. They can find out how grain becomes meal or flour at the gristmill. Then chug around the complex in wooden open-air cars pulled by a steam locomotive. Be sure to stop in at the old-fashioned drugstore soda fountain for lemonade or a soft drink. If your flock has also visited the

1850s town of Westville in Lumpkin (also featured in this section), the youngsters can compare how much life had progressed in twenty to forty years. The state's agricultural treasures are exhibited in the **Museum of Agriculture Center**—28,000 square feet of space dedicated to Georgia's farming history. Among the special events that take place at the Agrirama, the **County Fair of 1896** in September, the November **cane-grinding parties,** and the **1890s Victorian Christmas Celebration** draw many visitors. The Agrirama's RV park features forty-two full-service hookup sites.

For More Information

Tifton County Tourism Association, 115 West Second Street, Tifton, GA 31793; (229) 386-0216; www.tiftontourism.com.

Valdosta

South on I-75.

Wild Adventures Theme Park (all ages) 🐾 🐘

3766 Old Clyattville Road; (229) 219-7080 or (800) 808-0872; www.wild-adventure.com. Open year-round, but days and hours vary by season. Generally open daily March through Labor Day, Friday through Monday the remainder of the year, but call ahead to check. Parking $7, RV $9. Adults and children three to nine $$$$, two and younger free. Second day free pass for regular-priced tickets. Reduced-price twilight passes after 5:00 p.m. available on some nights when the park is open until 10:00 p.m.

If your pack yearns for fast-paced, in-your-face rides and face-to-face encounters with exotic wild animals, make a safari to Wild Adventures Theme Park. Rivaling gigantic national theme parks, Wild Adventures is a family-owned regional park with fifty-six rides, including five water rides and nine coasters as well as a variety of rides for toddlers. Not just an amusement park, Wild Adventures also is home to 500 wild animals in natural habitats scattered throughout the park and offers a full schedule of concerts and other entertainment. Adventure Quest is a park within a park, with an eighteen-hole adventure golf course, an arcade, and a go-kart track. See playful primates, exotic birds, and other amazing reptiles and mammals as you visit such habitats as the Australian Outback, a swamp, an African jungle, and more. Nine to twelve entertainment shows a day may include acrobats, musical song and dance reviews, or headliners in country, pop, rock, Christian, R&B, and other musical forms. The newest attraction is Wild Adventures on Ice—an ice-skating show.

For More Information

Valdosta-Lowndes County Chamber of Commerce, 416 North Ashley Street, Valdosta, GA 31601; (229) 247-8100; www.valdostachamber.com.

Thomasville

West on U.S. Highway 64.

In the waning years of the nineteenth century, Thomasville enjoyed a golden age as wealthy Northerners discovered that the area made an attractive place to spend the winter. The privileged classes were particularly drawn by the abundance of wild game for hunting. These visitors built magnificent vacation homes and developed a rich cultural life there as well. Although the extension of the railroads into Florida and the general vagaries of the rich and famous eventually decreed that Thomasville lost out to more trendy destinations, the city still has much to offer.

Birdsong Nature Center (all ages)

2106 Meridian Road; (229) 377-4408; www.freenet.tlh.fl.us/birdsong. Open Wednesday through Saturday 9:00 a.m. to 5:00 p.m., Sunday 1:00 to 5:00 p.m. $

All the little birdies go tweet, tweet, tweet at this haven for wildlife, originally Birdsong Plantation. The Bird Window allows children to observe birds up close; at the Listening Place, if the kids are quiet and listen carefully, they'll hear a symphony of bird calls, frogs, alligators, and other sounds of nature. A sanctuary of habitat and wildlife diversity, the center features a butterfly garden and nature trails.

Pebble Hill Plantation (house ages 6 to 12; grounds all ages)

US 319 South; (229) 226-2344; www.pebblehill.com. Grounds open Tuesday through Saturday 10:00 a.m. to 5:00 p.m., Sunday 1:00 to 5:00 p.m. Closed in September. Guided tours of the house are conducted intermittently during those hours; you'll rarely have to wait more than a half hour. House and grounds tours are purchased separately. Grounds: $; house tour: adults $$, children $.

For most of us the good old days were never this good. Invite your youngsters to make believe that they've been transported back to the opulent times enjoyed by Thomasville's turn-of-the-twentieth-century winter visitors by exploring this extraordinary estate. The mansion is filled with antique furnishings, sporting art, and an extensive collection of Native American artifacts. Please note that children younger than six are not admitted to the house. That's not to say, however, that little squirts will be left out or disappointed. The extensive grounds are a destination in themselves. Tour

The **Rose City**

There are more roses in Thomasville than people.

the magnificent stables and other outbuildings, which include the kennels, school, infirmary, and other structures important to running a plantation. Youngsters particularly enjoy the garage filled with vintage cars and carriages and are delighted with a child-size replica of Noah's Ark that was once used as a playhouse/jungle gym.

Thomas County Museum of History (ages 4 to 12) 🖐️

725 North Dawson Street; (229) 226-7664; www.rose.net/~history. Open Monday through Saturday 10:00 a.m. to noon and 2:00 to 5:00 p.m. Adults and children six and older $.

You and the junior set can travel back to yesterday by examining memorabilia from the great hotel era of the late 1800s, artifacts from the area's many plantations, and exhibits on the Civil War and antebellum Thomas County, a turn-of-the-twentieth-century bowling alley, and several antique automobiles. Also on the grounds are an 1860s log house and kitchen, an 1870s middle-class cottage, and the 1892 Metcalf Courthouse.

For More Information

Thomasville and Thomas County Historic Plantations Convention and Visitors Bureau, 401 South Broad Street, Thomasville, GA 31792; (229) 228-7977 or (866) 577-3600; www.thomasvillega.com.

Shades **of Scarlett**

Thomasville is located in the center of the biggest concentration of still-operating plantations in America.

Cairo

West on U.S. Highway 84.

Cairo Antique Auto Museum (ages 4 to 12)

US 84; (229) 377-3911. Open the first Saturday of the month 10:00 a.m. to 4:00 p.m. $

Oh, how we wish we could get Wayne and Rosa Ann Hadden to open this gem of a museum more often. Mint-condition vehicles represent every decade since 1900. In addition, there are antique bicycles and motorcycles, thousands of Matchbox cars, and other collectibles. Among the treasures are four Studebaker Presidents from 1928, two from 1929, and another from 1930. Now we do have to admit that the Haddens are rather busy with their Mr. Chick Restaurant, located in front of the museum. You might want to drop in there for some great Southern home cooking as well as seafood, subs, sandwiches, and pizza. Cairo is the home of the **Southern Antique Car Rally**, held the second weekend in May. In addition to more than 120 antique cars, the festival includes a gaslight parade and other activities.

Bainbridge

West on US 84.

Lake Seminole (all ages)

(229) 662-2001; www.sam.usace.army.mil/op/rec/seminole/. Boat launching $; camping $.

For anglers in the family, spend a day or more at this water world, located at the confluence of the Chattahoochee and Flint Rivers. The 37,500-acre lake, renowned for its superb freshwater fishing, is considered to be one of the best bass fishing lakes in the country. Fisherfolk can try their luck for lunker, largemouth, hybrid, striped, Florida, and white bass. Why, we've heard that the finny creatures jump right into your boat. Twenty public-access points around the lake provide endless opportunities for camping, picnicking, and water sports.

For More Information

Bainbridge-Decatur County Chamber of Commerce, 100 Boat Basin Circle, Bainbridge, GA 39817; (229) 246-4774 or (800) 243-4774; www.bainbridgega chamber.com.

A Thalimer **Adventure**

In Georgia barbecue isn't simply a way to fix ribs—it's a family tradition, a way of life. The ultimate test of your secret recipe is to compete in the "Big Pig Jig," a barbecue cook-off in Vienna. We judged this annual competition for several years and came early so that we could see the entertainment competition, talk to the team members as they set up their booths (some are quite fancy), and see if we could get any good hints for our efforts at home. The event starts on Friday night with the entertainment competitions, then the fires are laid and the pigs are dressed. Saturday morning we reported for judging duty while the kids scouted out the teams, watched more entertainment, and checked out the festival rides. Because we were still only neophyte judges, we were only allowed to participate in the first-round tasting. Only certified judges do final judging. You've never been treated as royally as you are as a judge, so sign up—they're always looking for volunteers. As soon as we finished with our "duties," it was time to share a cold beer and big plate of the best barbecue in the world.

Where to Eat in Southwest Georgia

Warm Springs

Bulloch House, US 27A/U.S. Highway 41; (706) 655-9068. Located in a charming 1892 Victorian house, the restaurant serves "country with class." $$

Columbus

Dinglewood Pharmacy, 1939 Wynnton Road; (706) 322-0616. For generations local folks have been flocking to this popular old soda-fountain-style eatery for Scramble Dogs. $

Ashburn

Last Meal Cafe, 214 East College Avenue; (229) 567-9696 or (800) 471-9696; www.jailmuseum.com. Open the Tuesday through Saturday 11:00 a.m. to 1:00 p.m. It was a time-honored tradition that condemned prisoners could request any meal of their choice for the last meal before their execution. At the Last Meal Cafe in the Crime and Punishment Museum, present-day youngsters can get a "meal to die for," including Southern favorites and desserts, without having to pay the ultimate penalty (see the description of the museum under Ashburn). $$

Where to Stay in Southwest Georgia

Pine Mountain

Lodge and Spa at Callaway Gardens, GA 18/354; (800) CALLAWAY; www.callaway gardens.com. Reminiscent of the great national park lodges, the addition of the lodge adds 150 rooms to the Callaway Gardens Resort. These feature a nature-inspired design and are luxuriously appointed with all the modern comforts and amenities—all with a scenic view. Guests enjoy a pool with a waterfall and all the amenities of the resort. While the kiddies are otherwise occupied with activities, Mom and Dad might enjoy a visit to the Spa Prunifolia for a variety of relaxing treatments. $$$$

Warm Springs

Hotel Warm Springs, 47 Broad Street; (800) 366-7616. The town's historic 1907 hotel, restored to its 1941 appearance, operates as a bed-and-breakfast where spacious, high-ceilinged guest rooms are filled with Roosevelt memorabilia, collectibles, and antiques. Nightly rate includes a full Southern breakfast. $$–$$$$

Andersonville

Andersonville RV Park, Church Street. The park is run by the town, so call the welcome center at (229) 924-2558. This shady campground in the historic village is within walking distance of the welcome center and shops and is just a short drive to the historic cemetery. $

A Place Away Cottage, 110 Oglethorpe Street; (229) 924-1044 or (229) 924-2558. Revel in the rustic country charm of yesterday while enjoying today's modern conveniences at this tin-roofed former sharecropper's cottage, now a bed-and-breakfast. $$

Fort Gaines

Cotton Hill Park, off GA 39; (229) 768-3061. A good place for camping families to stay while exploring Fort Gaines, the park provides RV and tent sites on Lake Walter F. George, as well as playgrounds, fish-cleaning stations, a boat ramp, and hiking trails. $

Bainbridge

Jack Wingate's Bass Island Campground, 139 Wingate Road off Highway 97 Spur; (229) 246-0658. Anglers of all ages will find Wingate's a fisherperson's paradise. There's nothing like some early success to serve as an inspiration for little fisherfolk, so start them off on a fishing career when they're young and enthusiastic. On June 5 a catfish pond is stocked just for kids, and even tiny tots can dig for worms. An all-round resort, Wingate's boasts a campground and motel rooms in Lunker Lodge. Feel hungry enough to eat a whale? Folks come from miles around to chow down on the catfish and Georgia barbecue in the casual restaurant. Lodging $; meals $–$$

Other Things to
See&Do in Southwest Georgia

- **Mt. Zion Albany Civil Rights Movement Museum,** Albany; (229) 432-1698; www.albanycivilrights.org

- **Native American and Early Pioneer Museum,** Colquitt; (229) 758-2400

- **Georgia Cotton Museum,** Vienna; (229) 268-2045

- **Old South Farm Museum and Learning Center,** Woodland; (706) 674-2894

Fairs and Festivals in Georgia

Some of the festivals and others are described in detail in individual chapters.

January

- **Augusta Futurity Cutting Horse Competition,** Augusta; (706) 823-3417; www.augustafuturity.com
- **King Week,** Atlanta (many activities throughout the city); contact the King Center (404) 526-8900; www.thekingcenter.org

February

- **Annual Groundhog Day Celebration,** Yellow River Game Ranch, Lilburn; (770) 972-6643; www.yellowrivergameranch.com/ghday.htm

March

- **Blessing of the Fleet,** Darien; (912) 437-6684; www.blessingofthefleet.com
- **Cherry Blossom Festival,** Macon; (478) 751-7429 or (800) 768-3401; www.cherryblossom.com
- **Festival of Camellias,** Massee Lane Gardens, Fort Valley; (478) 967-2358; www.camellias-acs.com/calendar
- **Forsythia Festival,** Forsyth; (478) 994-3247 or (888) 642-4628; www.forsythiafestival.com
- **Georgia National Rodeo,** Perry; (478) 988-3247 or (800) 987-3247; www.gnfa.com
- **St. Patrick's Celebration,** Savannah; (912) 234-4804; www.savannahsaintpatricksday.com

- **St. Patrick's Festival,** Dublin; (478) 272-5546; www.saintpatricksfestival.com
- **Savannah Irish Festival,** Savannah; (912) 232-3448; www.savannahirish.org
- **Spring Farm Days and Dixieland Master Cup Stock Dog Trials,** Hickory Flat; (770) 345-5591 or call (770) 704-5713 for recorded information; www.cagles dairy.com/stockdogtrials.htm

April

- **Baxley Tree Fest,** Baxley; (912) 367-7731; www.baxley.org
- **The Cotton Pickin' Country Fair,** Gay; (706) 538-6814; www.cpfair.org
- **Georgia Renaissance Festival,** Fairburn; (770) 964-8575; www.garenfest.com
- **Hawkinsville Harness Horse Festival and Spring Pig Ribbin' Cook Off,** Hawkinsville; (478) 783-1717; www.hawkinsvillechamber.org/festival.htm
- **Kudzu Cook-Off and Festival,** Dalton; (800) 733-2280; www.georgiahighcountry .org/events.html
- **Magical Easter Eggstravaganza,** Cleveland; (706) 865-5356
- **Mossy Creek Barnyard Festival,** Perry; (478) 922-8265; www.homestead.com/ mossycreekbf/
- **National Mayhaw Festival,** Colquitt; (229) 758-2400; www.colgwitt-georgia.com
- **Riverfest Weekend/Salisbury Fair,** Columbus; (706) 324-7417; www.columbus riverfest.com
- **Sheep to Shawl Day,** Atlanta; (404) 814-4000; www.atlantahistorycenter.com
- **A Taste of Toccoa,** Toccoa; (706) 282-3269; www.mainstreettoccoa.com
- **Vidalia Onion Festival,** Vidalia; (912) 538-8687; www.vidaliaonionfestival.com

May

- **Georgia Renaissance Festival,** Fairburn; (770) 964-8575; www.garenfest.com
- **Mayfest on the Rivers,** Rome; (706) 295-5576 or (800) 444-1834; www.rome georgia.org/festivals.asp
- **Ocmulgee Wild Hog Festival of Abbeville,** Abbeville; (229) 467-2144; www.hogfestival.com

June

- **Annual Putnam County Dairy Festival,** Eatonton; (706) 485-7701; www .pceatonton.org/dairy

- **Georgia's Peach Festival,** Fort Valley; (478) 825-4002 or (877) 322-4371; www .gapeachfestival.com
- **Georgia Renaissance Festival,** Fairburn; (770) 964-8575; www.garenfest.com
- **Watermelon Days Festival,** Cordele; (229) 273-1668; www.cordele-crisp-chamber.com/festival.html

July

- **Fantastic 4th Celebration,** Stone Mountain; (770) 498-5690 or (800) 401-2407; www.stonemountainpark.com
- **Homespun Festival,** Rockmart; (770) 684-8760; www.polkofgeorgia.org/home/ homespun

August

- **Hamp Brown Bottom Festival,** Milledgeville; (478) 452-4687 or (800) 653-1804; www.milledgevillecvb.com

September

- **Barnesville Buggy Days,** Barnesville; (770) 358-5884; www.barnesville.org/ buggy.html
- **Flatlanders Fall Frolic,** Lakeland; (229) 482-9755; www.georgia-festivals.com
- **Georgia State Fair,** Macon; (478) 746-7184; www.georgiastatefair.org
- **Oktoberfest,** Helen; (800) 858-8027; www.helenga.org/oktoberfest.html
- **Plains Peanut Festival,** Plains; (229) 824-5373; www.plainsgeorgia.com/ peanut_festival.html
- **Powers' Crossroads Country Fair and Art Festival,** Newnan; (770) 253-2011; www.newnan.com/cowetafestivals/powers
- **Riverfest Arts and Crafts Festival,** Canton; (770) 345-0400; www.riverfest.org
- **Sky High Hot Air Balloon Festival,** Callaway Gardens, Pine Mountain; (800) CALLAWAY; www.callawaygardens.com
- **Yellow Daisy Festival,** Stone Mountain; (770) 498-5690 or (800) 401-2407; www.stonemountainpark.com

October

- **Andersonville Historic Fair,** Andersonville; (229) 924-2558; www.andersonville georgia.com/

- **Big Pig Jig,** Vienna; (229) 268-8275 or (229) 268-8615; www.doolychamber.com or www.bigpigjig.com
- **Chiaha Harvest Fair,** Rome; (706) 235-4542; www.chiaha.org
- **The Cotton Pickin' Country Fair,** Gay; (706) 538-6814; www.cpfair.org
- **Georgia Apple Festival,** Ellijay; (706) 636-4500 or (706) 635-7400; www.georgia applefestival.org
- **Georgia Marble Festival,** Tate; (706) 692-5600; www.pickenschamber.com/ marblefest.html
- **Georgia National Fair,** Perry; (478) 987-3247 or (800) YUR-FAIR (in Georgia only); www.gnfa.com
- **Heritage Holidays Festival,** Rome; (800) 444-1834 or (706) 232-3780; www .romegeorgia.org/calendar.asp
- **Kaolin Festival,** Sandersville; (478) 552-3288; www.washingtoncounty-ga.com/ kaolinfestival.htm
- **Mossy Creek Barnyard Festival,** Perry; (478) 922-8265; www.homestead .com/mossycreekbf/
- **Mule Day Southern Heritage Festival,** Washington; (706) 678-2013; www .washingtonwilkes.org
- **Okefenokee Festival,** Folkston; (912) 496-2536; www.folkston.com
- **Oktoberfest,** Helen; (800) 858-8027; www.helenga.org
- **Oliver Hardy Festival,** Harlem; (706) 556-0401; www.harlemga.org/ohfest.htm
- **Praters Mill Country Fair,** Varnell; (706) 694-6455; www.pratersmill.org
- **Sorghum Festival,** Blairsville; (706) 745-5789 or (877) 745-5789; www.blairsville chamber.com
- **Stone Mountain Highland Games and Scottish Festival,** Stone Mountain; (770) 498-5690 or (800) 401-2407; www.smhg.org
- **Sunbelt Agricultural Exposition,** Moultrie; (229) 985-1968; www.sunbelt expo.com
- **A Tour of Southern Ghosts,** Stone Mountain Park, Stone Mountain; (770) 469-1105; www.artstation.org

November

- **Plantation Wildlife Arts Festival,** Thomasville; (229) 226-0588; www.pwaf.org
- **Rock City's Enchanted Garden of Lights,** Lookout Mountain; (706) 820-2531 or (800) 854-0675; www.seerockcity.com

- **Stone Mountain Indian Festival,** Stone Mountain; (770) 498-5690 or (800) 401-2407; www.stonemountainpark.com
- **Toccoa Harvest Festival,** Toccoa; (706) 282-3269 or (706) 282-3232; www.mainstreettoccoa.com
- **Winter Alpine Lights,** Helen; (800) 858-8027; www.helenga.org

December

- **Rock City's Enchanted Garden of Lights,** Lookout Mountain; (706) 820-2531 or (800) 854-0675; www.seerockcity.com
- **A Southern Christmas at Stone Mountain Park,** Stone Mountain; (770) 498-5690 or (800) 401-2407; www.stonemountainpark.com
- **Underground Atlanta New Year's Eve Peach Drop,** Atlanta; (404) 523-2311; www.underground-atlanta.com
- **Winter Alpine Lights,** Helen; (800) 858-8027; www.helenga.org

Index

About the Authors

Carol and Dan Thalimer have been writing about travel for the last twenty years. In addition to the hundreds of articles they've written for newspapers and magazines nationwide, they've contributed to numerous travel guides and have compiled several travel guides of their own, including *Quick Escapes: Atlanta, Romantic Days and Nights in Atlanta, Recommended Country Inns: The South,* and *Recommended Bed & Breakfasts: The South,* all published by The Globe Pequot Press. Their other travel guides include *Georgia Outdoor Activity Guide, Georgia B&Bs, Country Roads of Georgia, Country Roads of Alabama, Country Roads of South Carolina, Deep South Travel Smart, Romantic Tennessee, An Explorer's Guide: Georgia* and *Great Destinations: Atlanta.*